BIG Questions about THE HUMAN BODY!

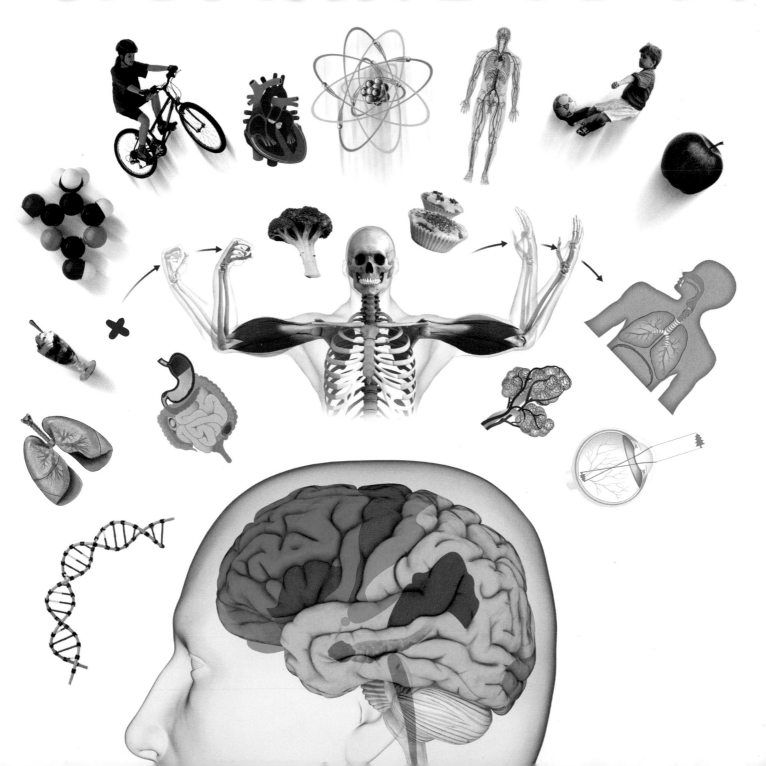

EDITORIAL TEAM
Bharti Bedi, Sreshtha Bhattacharya, Alexander Cox, Agnibesh Das, Leon Gray,
Elizabeth Haldane, Joe Harris, Wendy Horobin, Rob Houston, Lorrie Mack,
Antara Moitra, Ben Morgan, Tejaswita Payal, Sheryl Sadana, Zahavit Shalev,
Penny Smith, Fleur Star, Anneka Wahlhaus, Susan Watt, Lee Wilson,
Jessamy Wood, Chris Woodford

DESIGN TEAM
Ranjita Bhattacharji, Kshitiz Dobhal, Rachael Grady, Spencer Holbrook,
Karen Hood, Hedi Hunter, Laura Roberts-Jensen, Sonia Whillock-Moore,
Claire Patané, Nidhi Rastogi, Lauren Rosier, Sadie Thomas

PRODUCTION TEAM
Harish Aggarwal, Siu Yin Chan, Sean Daly, Sachin Gupta, Claire Pearson,
Gillian Reid, Vivienne Yong

US editors Margaret Parrish, Allison Singer
Picture researcher Liz Moore
Jacket designer Dhirendra Singh
Managing editors Linda Esposito, Kingshuk Ghoshal
Managing art editors Philip Letsu, Govind Mittal, Clare Shedden
Publishers Bridget Giles, Sue Leonard, Mary Ling, Andrew Macintyre
Art directors Jane Bull, Rachael Foster, Karen Self, Martin Wilson
Design director Stuart Jackman
Associate publishing director Liz Wheeler
Publishing director Jonathan Metcalf

Special sales and custom publishing manager Michelle Baxter

Consultants Dr. Sarah-Jayne Blakemore (*What Goes on in My Head?*),
Dr. Emma Ross (*Body Science*)

Content previously published as *What Makes Me Me?* (2004, 2015),
What Goes on in My Head? (2010, 2016), and *Body Science* (2009)

This edition published in 2019 in the United States by
DK Publishing, 1450 Broadway, 8th Floor, New York, NY 10018

A catalog record for this book is available from the Library of Congress.
ISBN: 978-1-4654-8775-9

DK books are available at special discounts when purchased in bulk for sales
promotions, premiums, fund-raising, or educational use. For details, contact:
DK Publishing Special Markets, 1450 Broadway, 8th Floor, New York, NY 10018
SpecialSales@dk.com

Printed in China

A WORLD OF IDEAS:
SEE ALL THERE IS TO KNOW

www.dk.com

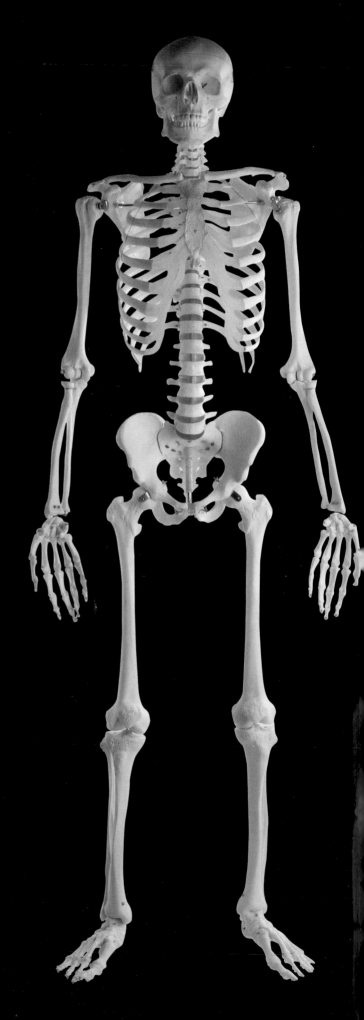

CONTENTS

YOUR BODY

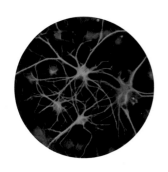

YOUR BRAIN

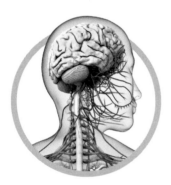

BODY SCIENCE

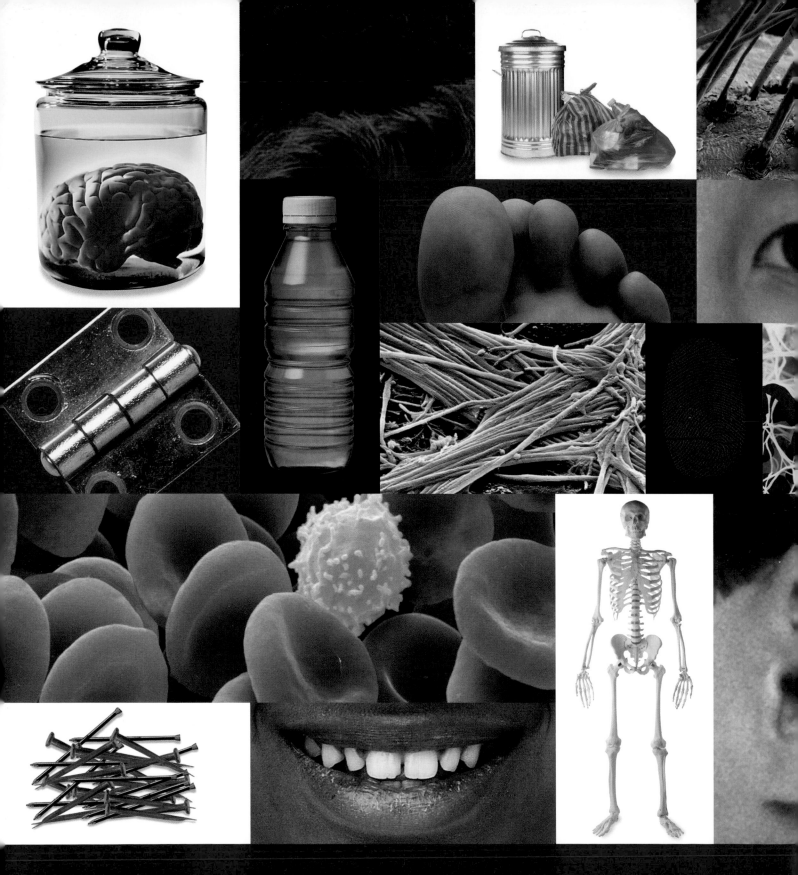

"Your body is a fantastically complicated machine made of 5 billion billion billion atoms.

People have been trying to figure out how the body works for at least 4,000 years, and there are still lots of mysteries—like how our brains work and why we hiccup.

But one thing we know for sure is what we're made of: just water, carbon, and a handful of simple chemical elements that you can find anywhere. In fact, you could dig up all the atoms you need to make a human body in your back yard garden."

The INGREDIENTS

Imagine trying to build a human body from scratch, using the simplest ingredients possible. You could do it with only 13 chemicals, called **elements**. There's nothing special about the elements in the human body. We're made from exactly the same stuff as all other living things, from **fleas** to **whales**.

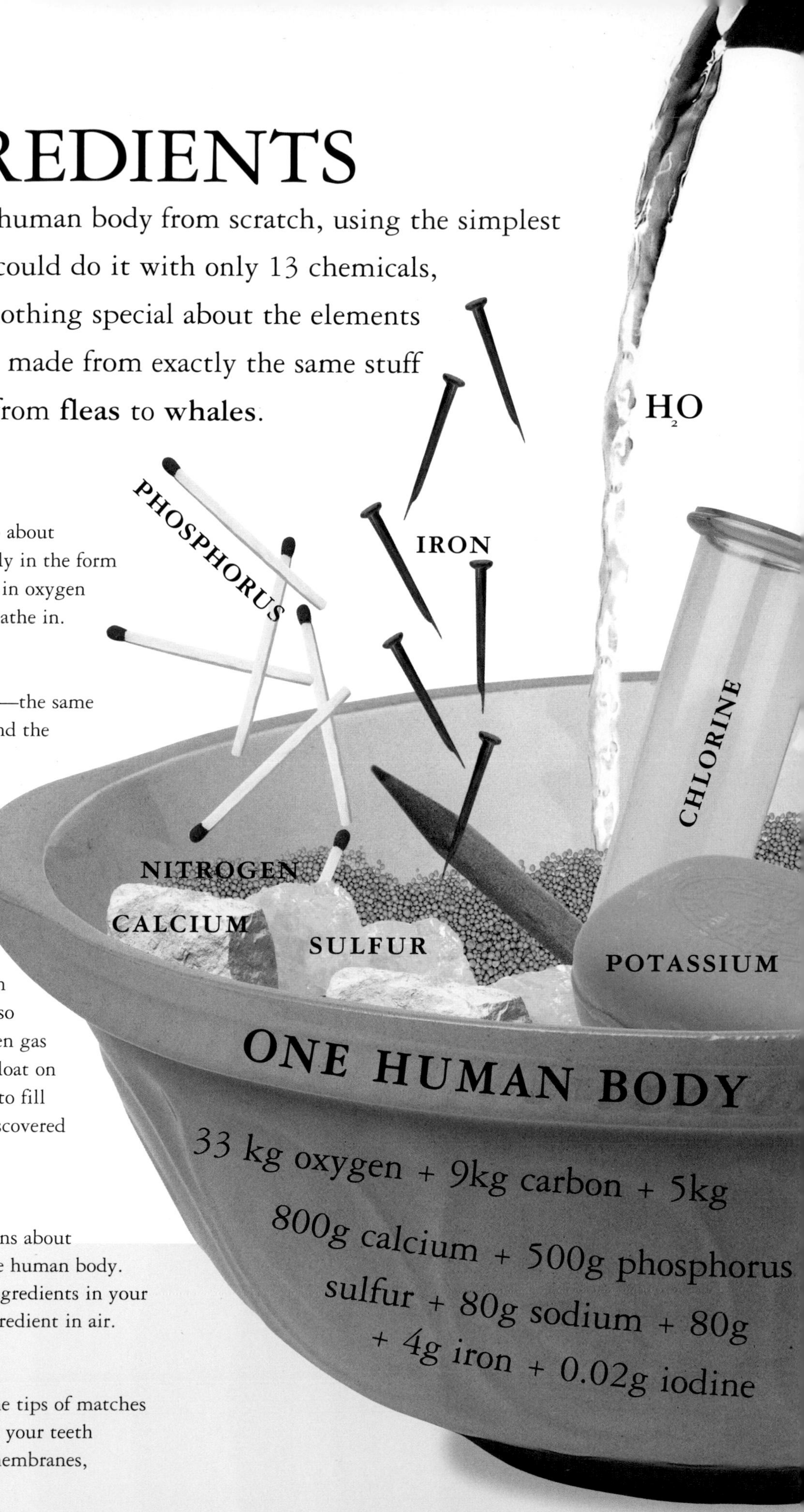

1 ### 65% Oxygen
The element oxygen makes up about two-thirds of your body, mostly in the form of water (H_2O). You also take in oxygen from the air each time you breathe in.

2 ### 18% Carbon
Nearly a fifth of you is carbon—the same element that coal, diamond, and the lead of pencils are made from. Carbon atoms link together in long chains, forming the backbone of all the most complex molecules inside you.

3 ### 10% Hydrogen
Hydrogen is the most common element in the universe and also has the tiniest atoms. Hydrogen gas can **pass through walls** and float on air, which is why people used to fill balloons with it (until they discovered how easily it explodes).

4 ### 3% Nitrogen
A bag of plant fertilizer contains about as much nitrogen as an average human body. Nitrogen is one of the main ingredients in your muscles. It's also the main ingredient in air.

5 ### 1% Phosphorus
This element is what makes the tips of matches burst into flame. It also makes your teeth and bones strong, forms cell membranes, and helps carry energy.

PHOSPHORUS

IRON

H_2O

CHLORINE

NITROGEN

CALCIUM

SULFUR

POTASSIUM

ONE HUMAN BODY

33 kg oxygen + 9kg carbon + 5kg 800g calcium + 500g phosphorus sulfur + 80g sodium + 80g + 4g iron + 0.02g iodine

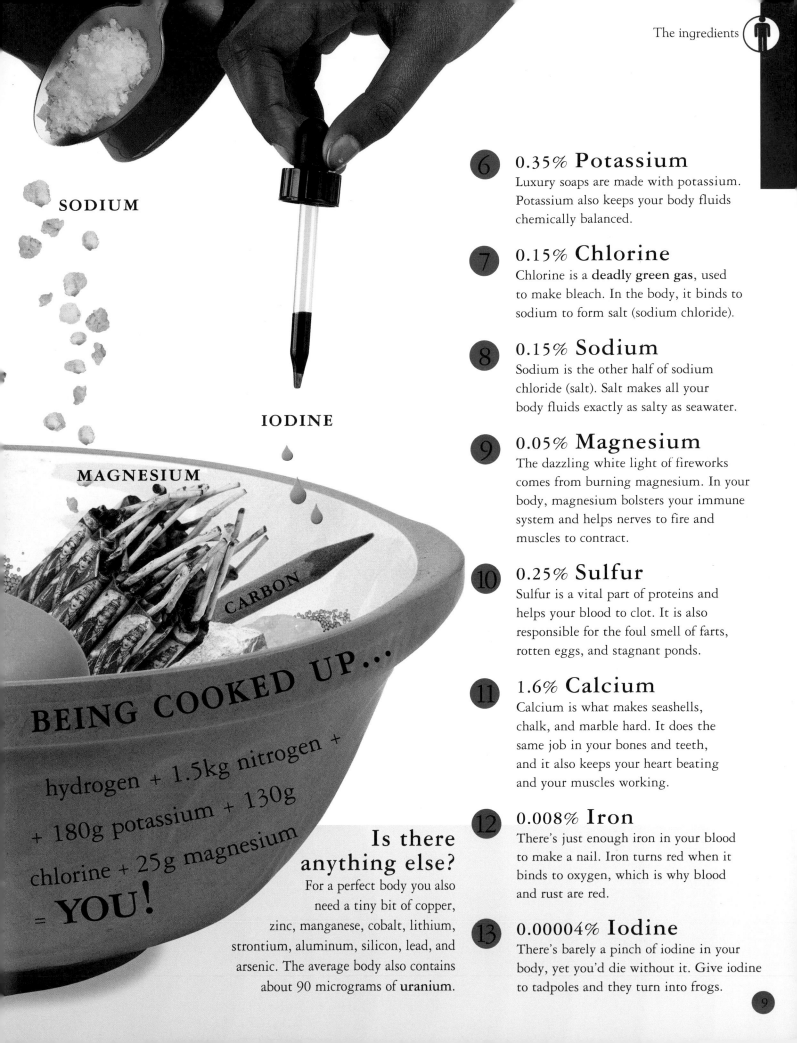

SODIUM

IODINE

MAGNESIUM

CARBON

BEING COOKED UP...

hydrogen + 1.5kg nitrogen + + 180g potassium + 130g chlorine + 25g magnesium = **YOU!**

Is there anything else?

For a perfect body you also need a tiny bit of copper, zinc, manganese, cobalt, lithium, strontium, aluminum, silicon, lead, and arsenic. The average body also contains about 90 micrograms of **uranium**.

6 0.35% **Potassium**
Luxury soaps are made with potassium. Potassium also keeps your body fluids chemically balanced.

7 0.15% **Chlorine**
Chlorine is a **deadly green gas**, used to make bleach. In the body, it binds to sodium to form salt (sodium chloride).

8 0.15% **Sodium**
Sodium is the other half of sodium chloride (salt). Salt makes all your body fluids exactly as salty as seawater.

9 0.05% **Magnesium**
The dazzling white light of fireworks comes from burning magnesium. In your body, magnesium bolsters your immune system and helps nerves to fire and muscles to contract.

10 0.25% **Sulfur**
Sulfur is a vital part of proteins and helps your blood to clot. It is also responsible for the foul smell of farts, rotten eggs, and stagnant ponds.

11 1.6% **Calcium**
Calcium is what makes seashells, chalk, and marble hard. It does the same job in your bones and teeth, and it also keeps your heart beating and your muscles working.

12 0.008% **Iron**
There's just enough iron in your blood to make a nail. Iron turns red when it binds to oxygen, which is why blood and rust are red.

13 0.00004% **Iodine**
There's barely a pinch of iodine in your body, yet you'd die without it. Give iodine to tadpoles and they turn into frogs.

CELLS

You'd never build a human body simply by mixing chemical elements—that would be like expecting a storm in a junkyard to put together a jumbo jet. Instead, you need to start with the right building blocks. The tiniest building blocks are microscopic units called **cells**, but you'd need to collect up to **100 trillion** of these and arrange them in an impossibly complicated jigsaw puzzle. Here are just a few.

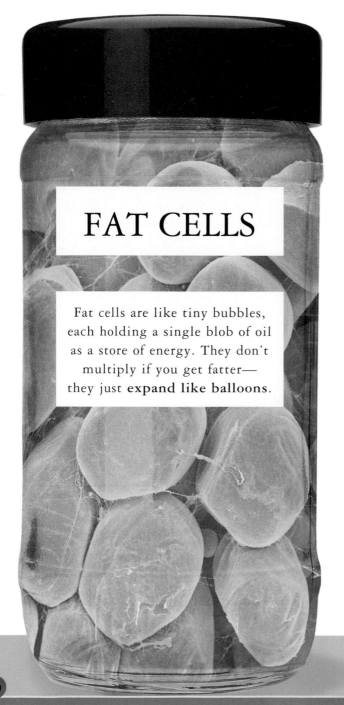

FAT CELLS

Fat cells are like tiny bubbles, each holding a single blob of oil as a store of energy. They don't multiply if you get fatter— they just **expand like balloons**.

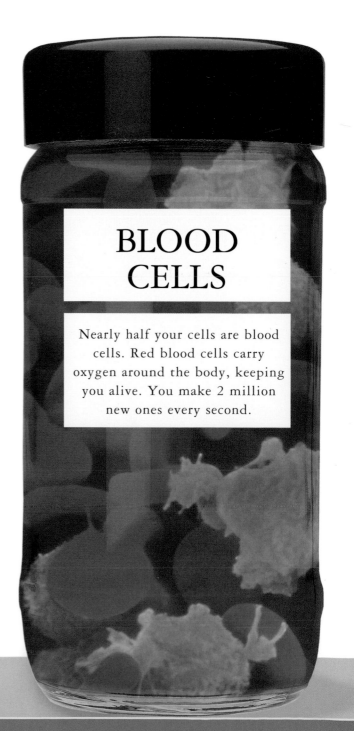

BLOOD CELLS

Nearly half your cells are blood cells. Red blood cells carry oxygen around the body, keeping you alive. You make 2 million new ones every second.

Eye cells

The cells in the back of your eyes detect light and so give you the sense of vision.

Goblet cell

The slimy liquid (**mucus**) in your nose and intestines comes from goblet cells.

Sperm cells

When a sperm cell from a man joins a woman's egg cell, they form a new baby.

Skin cells

Flaky skin cells protect your fragile insides from the world outside.

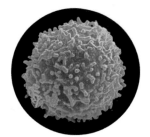

White blood cell

This cell is a kind of roving soldier. It searches for germs and **kills them**.

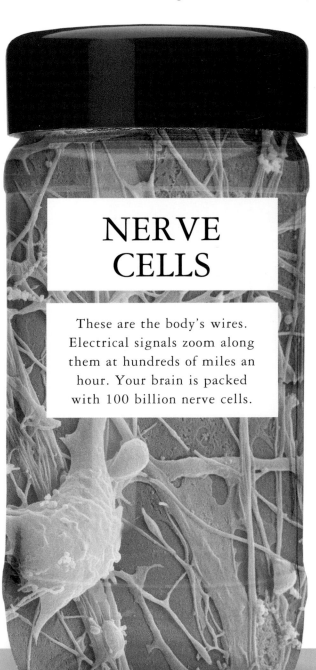

NERVE CELLS

These are the body's wires. Electrical signals zoom along them at hundreds of miles an hour. Your brain is packed with 100 billion nerve cells.

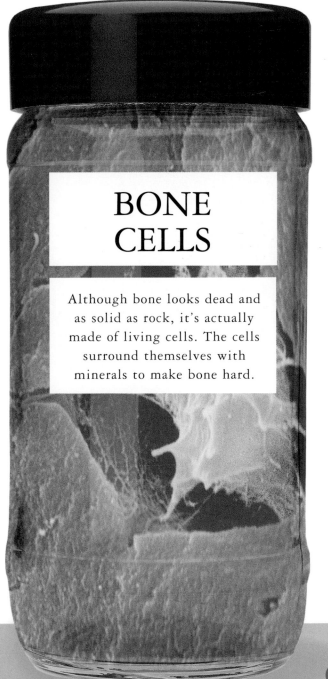

BONE CELLS

Although bone looks dead and as solid as rock, it's actually made of living cells. The cells surround themselves with minerals to make bone hard.

BODY PARTS

It would take **forever** to build a body from 100 trillion separate cells, but you could speed things up by starting with larger building blocks. Cells normally group together with cells of a similar type to make **tissues**, such as fat, nerves,

9 bottles of **blood**, 2 square yards (2 square meters) of **skin**, 5 million **hairs**, 1 bucket

Blood	Skin	Hair	Fat

Blood is a liquid tissue that carries vital supplies around the body. It's made of trillions of red cells suspended in a watery mix of salt, sugar, and other chemicals.

The largest organ is the skin, which protects the insides from damage. Its outer surface is continually wearing away.

Hairs cover the body except for the eyes, lips, palms, and soles of the feet.

The body stores spare energy as fat under the skin and around organs.

1 **heart**, 2 **lungs**, 2 **kidneys** plumbed into 1 **bladder**, 1 **stomach**, 9 yards (9 meters)

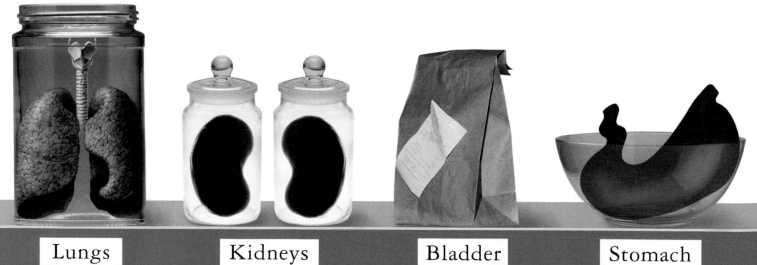

Lungs	Kidneys	Bladder	Stomach

Lungs suck in life-giving **oxygen** from the air and pass it to the blood.

The body is continually making waste chemicals. The kidneys filter out the waste and turn it into urine.

Urine from the kidneys drains into a stretchy bag called the bladder. When it fills up, it triggers the urge to urinate.

The stomach is a J-shaped chamber that churns food around and begins to break it down with acid.

or muscle. When two or more different tissues join together to make a body part with a specific job—such as the heart, stomach, or brain—we call it an **organ**. So what tissues and organs would you need to build a body?

of **fat**, 206 **bones** tied to 640 **muscles**, 62,000 miles (100,000 km) of **blood vessels**,

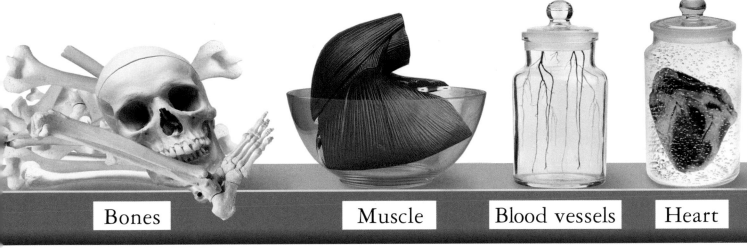

Bones

Bones make up the skeleton, which holds everything in place and makes movement possible, thanks to its amazingly flexible joints.

Muscle

Muscles pull on bones and move the body. Muscles also make up the walls of inner organs like the heart.

Blood vessels

Blood flows through tubes called blood vessels (arteries, veins, and capillaries).

Heart

This is the pump that drives blood around the body. It never stops (until you die).

of **intestines**, 1 **liver**, 32 **teeth**, 1 **brain**, and a set of **sense organs**.

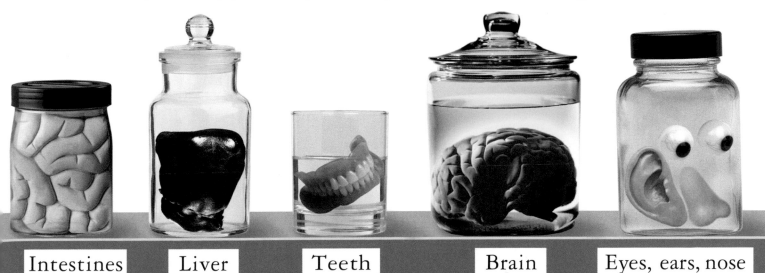

Intestines

These tangled tubes digest food into simple chemicals that the blood can absorb.

Liver

The liver is kind of chemical factory that processes chemicals in the blood.

Teeth

Teeth chop up food and mash it into a paste that is easy to swallow.

Brain

This is the body's control center and the smartest part, where thoughts, memories, and feelings happen.

Eyes, ears, nose

The eyes, ears, and nose are the most important sense organs.

13

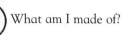
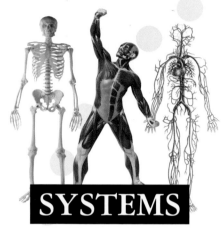

SYSTEMS

YOU

ELEMENTS

PUTTING EVERYTHING TOGETHER

ORGANS

CELLS

Once you've amassed a full set of **body parts**, you can start putting them together. Just as elements make cells and cells make organs, organs fit together in **systems**, each doing a particular job. The first system to build is the skeleton, which creates a frame for everything else. Then you simply add all the other organs, connect them together, wrap the whole works in a layer of skin, and switch on the sense organs.

SKELETON

The skeleton is an inner framework of bones that holds the body in place. Without a skeleton, you'd collapse on the floor like jelly. About 25 percent of your body weight is bone, and half your 206 bones are in your hands and feet. The bones are held together by an ingenious system of **joints** and hinges that let the whole body move.

Bones feel pain and bleed when cut

What's in a bone?

Bones aren't as solid and heavy as they look. Their insides are riddled with **hollow spaces** to keep them light and to carry blood vessels and nerves.

How do they heal?

Bone is a **living tissue**—it can grow or heal itself just as skin can. When you break a bone, new bone tissue quickly forms and plugs the gap. If you exercise, your bones get denser and stronger.

What are joints?

Joints lock bones together but also allow them to move to some extent. The joints in your fingers, elbows, and knees work like **hinges**, restricting movement mostly to one direction only.

How do hips work?

Hips and shoulders are **ball-and-socket** joints. This clever design lets your arms and legs swing freely in any direction. As with all mobile joints, a capsule of fluid surrounds the joint and keeps it working smoothly.

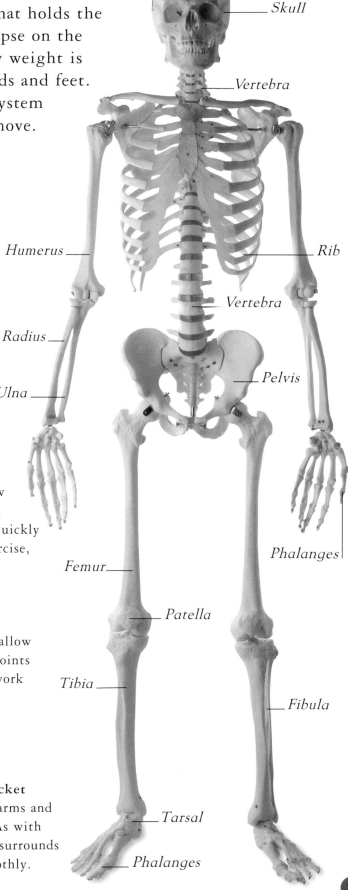

Skull

Vertebra

Humerus

Rib

Vertebra

Radius

Pelvis

Ulna

Phalanges

Femur

Patella

Tibia

Fibula

Tarsal

Phalanges

MUSCLES

Muscles are what make you move. Your biggest muscles wrap around bones and are tied in place with tough, stringy cords called **tendons**. When muscles contract, they pull on the bones and move your skeleton. You have conscious control of about 640 muscles, but there are hundreds more that you can't move voluntarily.

About 40% of your body weight is muscle

Fake smile

The **60 muscles** in your face are only partly voluntary. A fake smile uses a different set of muscles from those in a genuine, involuntary smile.

Blinking fast

Your fastest muscles are in your eyelids. They make you blink about 20 times a minute to keep your eyes moist. If you didn't blink, your eyes would dry out and you'd **go blind**.

My finger's stuck!

Put your hand in this position and lift each finger one by one. Your ring finger is stuck because it's tied to the same tendon as the middle finger.

Tongue-twister

The most flexible part of your body is your tongue. It is made of at least **14 muscles** wrapped in a complicated bundle that can twist and turn in any direction.

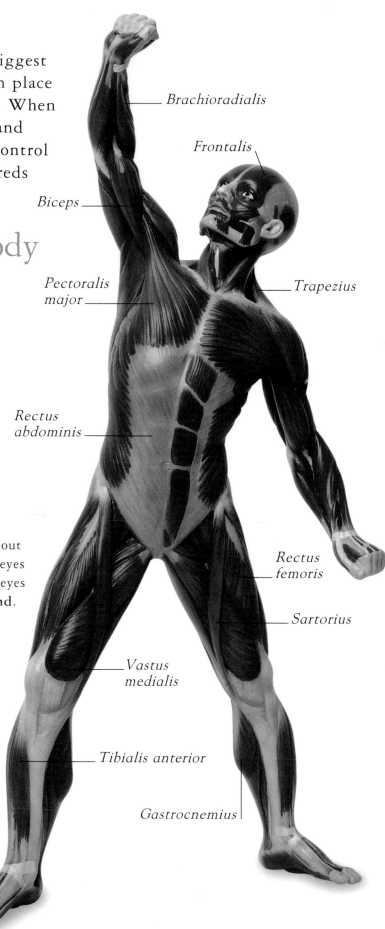

Brachioradialis

Frontalis

Biceps

Pectoralis major

Trapezius

Rectus abdominis

Rectus femoris

Sartorius

Vastus medialis

Tibialis anterior

Gastrocnemius

CIRCULATORY SYSTEM

Blood is the body's transportation system. Pumped by the heart, it shoots around the body through tubes called blood vessels, delivering all the **oxygen**, food, and chemicals that cells need. It also carries cells to fight germs, and it takes away waste materials and spreads heat. You can lose about a third of your blood and still survive, but if you lose half, you die.

Your heart beats about 100,000 times a day

Red blood cells
A single drop of blood contains about 5 million red blood cells. They are full of the iron-rich chemical **hemoglobin**, which picks up oxygen in the lungs and then releases it around the body.

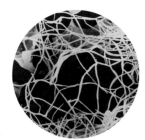

Blood clot
When you cut yourself, chemicals in the blood react with air and form a tangle of sticky fibers that trap blood cells like fish in a net. The clot dries to become a scab.

Heart
The heart is a hollow ball of muscle as big as a fist, but much stronger. When it beats, it squirts about a cupful of blood around your body. **Arteries** take blood away from the heart and **veins** bring it back.

Check your pulse
Your pulse is blood stopping and starting with each beat of your heart. Your heart normally beats about 70 times a minute, but it can go up to 200 if you're excited.

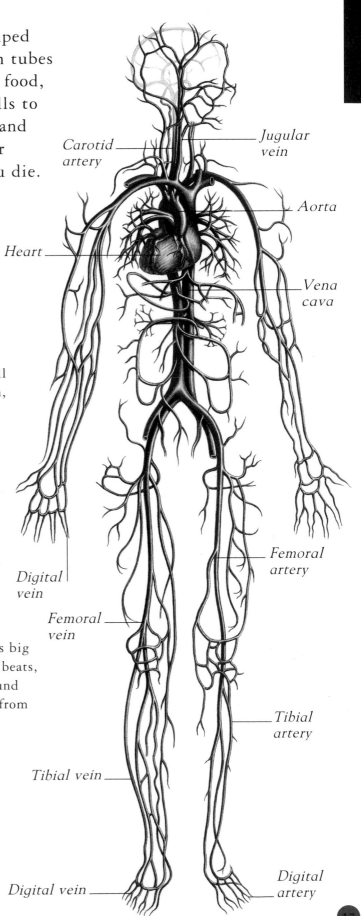

Carotid artery

Jugular vein

Aorta

Heart

Vena cava

Femoral artery

Digital vein

Femoral vein

Tibial artery

Tibial vein

Digital vein

Digital artery

NERVOUS SYSTEM

This system allows your body to react to the world with **lightning speed**. It works like a network of electric wires and cables, but it carries information instead of power. Its control center is the brain, which takes in signals from the sense organs, processes the information, and sends out new **signals** that tell the body how to react.

Signals zoom along nerves at 250 mph (400 kph)

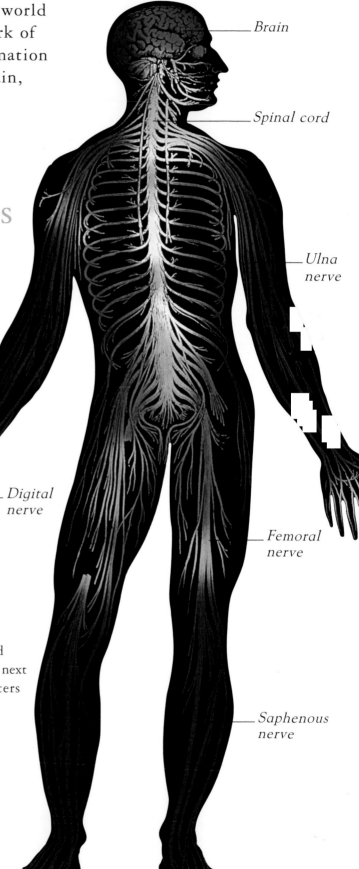

Brain

Spinal cord

Ulna nerve

Digital nerve

Femoral nerve

Saphenous nerve

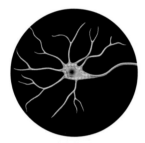

What's a neuron?
The nervous system is made of cells called neurons, which have spindly fibers that carry electrical signals. Some neurons have fibers several feet long.

Nerve
Nerves are the body's major cables and contain hundreds of neuron fibers. The fibers run to every nook and cranny of the body.

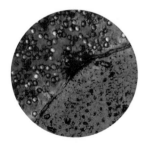

Bridging the gap
When an electrical signal reaches the end of a neuron, a tiny gap called a **synapse** stops it from jumping to the next cell. Chemicals called neurotransmitters cross the gap and trigger the next cell, passing the signal on.

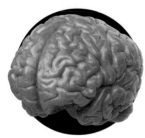

Control center
Your brain is about the size of a coconut and has a wrinkled surface like a walnut. It connects to the rest of the nervous system via a tube of neurons called the **spinal cord**.

DIGESTIVE SYSTEM

Everything you eat passes through your digestive system—a long, complicated tube that runs through your body and takes up most of the space in your belly. The digestive organs produce powerful chemicals called **enzymes**. These attack the large molecules in food and break them into tiny fragments that your body can **absorb**.

A meal takes 18–30 hours to pass through you

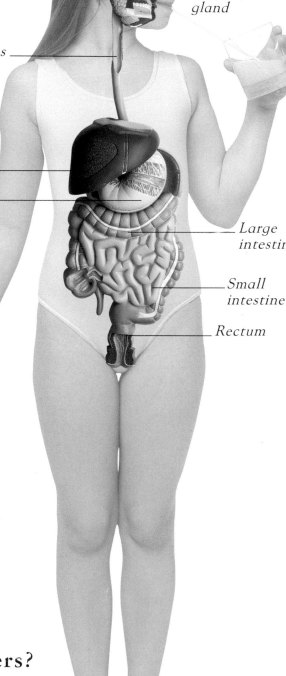

Salivary gland

Esophagus

Liver

Stomach

Large intestine

Small intestine

Rectum

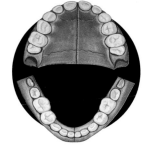

Teeth

These are the hardest parts of your body. They break up food and mix it with **saliva**—a liquid containing digestive enzymes. Most people have a set of 32 teeth by age 21.

In your stomach

Your stomach stretches to store food and churns it around with acid and enzymes until the food turns into a thick, creamy liquid. A meal spends up to 4 hours in your stomach.

Small intestine

The small intestine is a long, tangled tube that produces many different enzymes to digest food. The digested food is then absorbed through tiny fingers, or **villi**, that line the inner wall. Food spends up to 6 hours in your small intestine.

What happens to leftovers?

Undigested leftovers end up in your large intestine. This broad tube absorbs water from the leftovers and then expels the waste from your body. Harmless bacteria flourish here and help you absorb vitamins.

RESPIRATORY SYSTEM

All your body's cells need a supply of the life-giving gas **oxygen**, which comes from the air. Your respiratory system takes in oxygen and passes it to your blood. The main organs in this system are your **lungs**, which suck in air whenever you breathe. They work like giant sponges, except that they take in air instead of water.

You breathe in and out 23,000 times a day

 Voice box

Windpipe

Lung

Heart

In and out

Air travels to your lungs through a tube in your neck called the windpipe, or **trachea**. The windpipe splits into smaller and smaller branches, forming a maze of airways throughout the lungs.

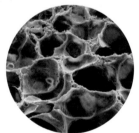

Air pockets

The airways end in tiny pockets called **alveoli**. Blood flows around these, picking up oxygen and getting rid of the waste gas carbon dioxide. Your lungs have about 600 million alveoli—if you laid them out flat, they'd cover a tennis court.

Keeping clean

Air contains dirt and germs, which your lungs must get rid of. Coughing and sneezing help clear the worst of it. Your airways also secrete a layer of sticky **mucus** to trap dirt. The mucus is carried up to the back of your throat and swallowed.

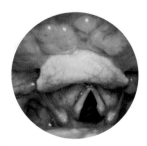

Making noise

Your voice comes from a chamber called the voice box at the top of your windpipe. As you breathe out, air passes between two small flaps of tissue. When these are drawn together, they **vibrate** and create sound. The tighter they are, the higher the pitch.

SKIN AND HAIR

About 22 square feet (2 square meters) of skin protects your body from dirt, germs, cold, and injury. This tough, waterproof layer is your biggest sense organ—it's packed with nerves that sense touch, pain, and heat. Your skin's outermost layer is continually wearing away, so it **replaces itself completely** about once a month.

The entire surface of your body is dead

Get a grip
The swirling ridges of skin on the tips of your fingers are there to help you grip things. Along the ridges are tiny pores that secrete sweat and oil to improve your grip.

Shed your skin
The surface of your skin consists of tough, dried-out flakes of dead tissue. These are continually rubbing off—you shed about **10 billion** a day. Most of the dust in your home is old skin flakes.

Hair today
Thick hair covers the top of your head to keep your brain warm, and the rest of your body is covered by fine hairs. (You have as many hairs as a chimpanzee.) Each hair has a **tiny muscle** that can make it stand up when you're cold.

Sweat and smells
You make at least half a pint of sweat a day. Your skin produces two types of sweat: eccrine sweat, which cools you down; and apocrine sweat, which gives you **B.O.** Your apocrine sweat glands become more active when you reach your teens.

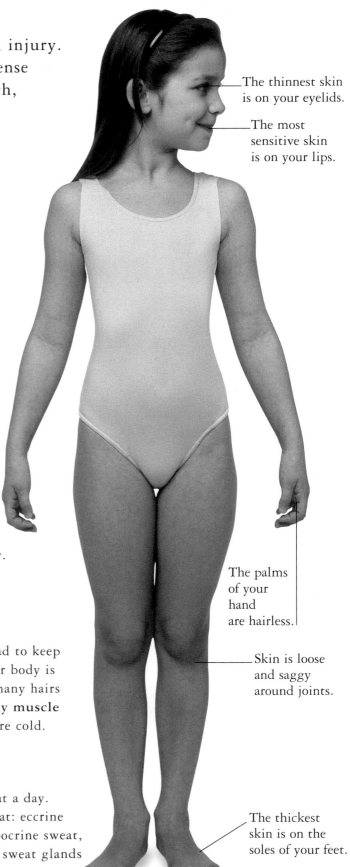

The thinnest skin is on your eyelids.

The most sensitive skin is on your lips.

The palms of your hand are hairless.

Skin is loose and saggy around joints.

The thickest skin is on the soles of your feet.

VISION

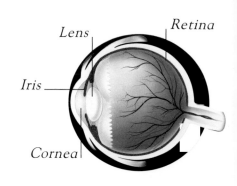

Lens · Retina · Iris · Cornea

HEARING

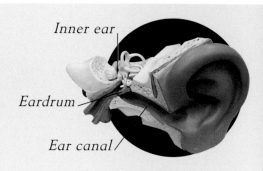

Inner ear · Eardrum · Ear canal

SMELL

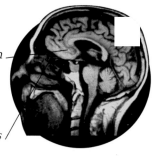

Smell center in brain · Smell receptors

TASTE

Bitter · Sour · Sour · Salty · Salty · Sweet

TOUCH

The five senses

VISION is our top sense. We can see more colors and better detail than most animals can, but our vision is terrible in darkness. Each eye is a 1-inch-wide (2.5-cm-wide) ball of transparent **jelly** that works like a camera. Light enters a hole called the pupil and is focused by a lens onto the **retina**—a sheet of light-sensitive cells in the back of the eye. These cells detect the color and strength of the light and send signals to the brain, which builds an image.

HEARING is the ability to sense invisible **vibrations** in air—sound. The odd shape of the outer ears funnels sound and helps tell where it comes from. The sound passes along a thin canal to the middle ear, where a miniature drum and a set of tiny levers transmit the vibrations from the air to liquid in the inner ear. Nerve cells in the inner ear then send signals to the brain.

SMELL is the ability to sense odor molecules floating in air. This sense is more important than you might think. The flavor of food actually depends more on smell than taste. The average person can recognize 4,000 different smells, and a well-trained nose can recognize 10,000. The smell molecules are detected by a patch of neurons high up in each nostril. When an odor molecule binds to a matching neuron, it triggers a signal.

TASTE is your ability to detect simple chemicals inside your mouth. When you chew food, these chemicals dissolve in your saliva and trigger taste buds, mainly on your tongue. The best-known tastes are sweet, salty, bitter, and sour, which are located on different parts of the tongue. Taste buds can also detect a chemical called **glutamate**, which makes food taste meaty and savory.

TOUCH receptors cover your entire body. Different types of receptors sense different types of touch, such as light pressure, heavy pressure, hair movements, and vibration. Touch is all about movement—we **actively explore** objects with our fingers, lips, and tongue. With touch alone, we can identify even the different coins in a pocket without looking at them.

DO I HAVE A SIXTH SENSE?

The human body has far more than five senses. Here are just a few of the things your special senses can detect:

Gravity
Deep in your inner ear are tiny gravity sensors called **otoliths**. These tell your brain which way is up or down, helping you balance.

Motion
Your inner ear also contains motion sensors that can sense movement in any direction. If you spin around and around, they stop working and make you dizzy.

Heat
Heat sensors all over your skin can feel warmth or cold, even at a distance. Your lips and tongue are the most heat-sensitive parts of your body. They can tell whether a drink is too hot without touching it.

Pain
Pain is a special sense triggered by damage to your body. Pain has a purpose because it makes you leave the damaged area alone. Itching and tickling are both a mixture of touch and pain.

Muscles
Your muscles contain **stretch sensors** that tell your brain what each part of your body is doing. This makes you aware of the whole body. Without it, you wouldn't be able to stand still, move around, or pick things up.

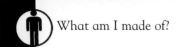

Are you allergic to...?

| GRASS POLLEN | HOUSEHOLD DUST | DUSTMITE FAECES | CAT HAIR | PEANUTS | WHEAT PROTEIN | COCKROACH DUNG |

FAQ

Why do I cough and sneeze?

If germs get through your nose or mouth, your body will try to get rid of them. Coughs and sneezes blow germs out of your lungs and airways. Vomiting and diarrhea get rid of germs that have gotten into your stomach or intestines.

Why do cuts swell up?

If germs get under your skin, white blood cells soon find them. They release the chemical histamine, which makes blood rush to the area. The blood-filled zone becomes **inflamed**—red, swollen, hot, and unusually sensitive to pain. Inflamed skin is not necessarily damaged—it just means your immune system is doing its job.

What do antibodies do?

Antibodies are molecules that identify and stick to germs. There are millions of differently shaped antibodies floating around in your body fluids. When one meets a germ whose surface molecules match its shape, it locks onto it and tells your white blood cells to **attack** the germ.

Immune SYSTEM

Every time you sneeze, cough, vomit, or get a scratch, a bite, a cut, a swelling, a rash, a zit, a cold, an upset stomach, a runny nose, diarrhea, or a raging temperature, you are seeing your **immune system** at work.

Your immune system never stops hunting for **germs** and doing everything it can to isolate them, destroy them, or expel them from your body. Pain is part of the immune reaction, too—it tells you to **keep your hands off!**

Your *immune system* is one of the

INSECT STINGS	MOLD SPORES	SHELLFISH	POISON IVY	PENICILLIN	LATEX	LAUNDRY DETERGENT

Why am I allergic?

Your immune system has to deal with thousands of different invaders, from viruses to flesh-eating maggots. With such a tough job to do, it's bound to **make mistakes**. Sometimes it attacks harmless substances (allergens) as though they were germs, and this is what causes **allergies** and **asthma**. You're more likely to develop allergies if you grow up in a very clean home, where your immune system does not get much practice attacking real germs.

The symptoms of an allergy depend on where the allergen makes contact with your body.

AIRWAYS

Sneezing, coughing, and breathing difficulties can happen when you breathe in allergens like dust or pollen.

DIGESTIVE TRACT

If you swallow allergens, your digestive system reacts as though germs have gotten into it and tries to expel the food. This may cause stomach cramps, vomiting, or diarrhea.

MOUTH

Food allergies can make your mouth tingle and your lips and tongue swell up.

SKIN

A rash or blisters may break out on your skin if you touch something that causes an allergy. Some allergic rashes are just like the itchy lumps produced by stinging nettles.

FAQ

Why don't I self-destruct?

Your immune system would attack your own cells if they did not have a kind of molecular name tag. The tag is made up of a set of proteins called the major histocompatibility complex (MHC), and it's **utterly unique** to you.

What's sex got to do with it?

Germs breed very quickly and keep changing. Some of the new forms manage to sneak past the human immune system by mimicking our MHC proteins. One of the reasons we reproduce sexually is to outsmart these germs. Sexual reproduction gives everyone different MHC proteins, scrambling the cellular combination locks that protect us.

Can you smell true love?

Some scientists think that we instinctively choose partners who will give our children varied MHC proteins—and hence a strong immune system. We seem to do this by **smell**. Overall, people tend to prefer the body odor of a partner whose MHC genes are very different from their own.

most individual things about YOU

Your body: What makes me UNIQUE?

"Though we're all built to the same plan, we're also completely different from each other. There are hundreds of things that make you different from everyone else, from your taste in music and your sense of humor to the sound of your voice and the shape of your face.

So how did you become unique?

Part of the answer lies in your genes. Your parents would have to have another

1,000,000,000,000,000

babies to stand a chance of having another child with the same genes as you. And part of the answer lies in the experiences that shape your personality as you grow up."

UNIQUE TO YOU

Imagine someone stole your I.D., had plastic surgery to look just like you, and then **pretended to be you**. Could they get away with it? Fortunately, there are lots of ways of proving you're the real you, and

FINGERPRINTS IRIS IMMUNE SYSTEM

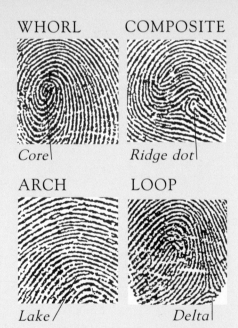

WHORL   COMPOSITE

Core   Ridge dot

ARCH   LOOP

Lake   Delta

The patterns on your fingertips are utterly unique. Even **identical twins** have different fingerprints, though their footprints and handprints are very similar. Fingerprints stay the same for life, and if you injure the skin, the same prints grow back. Your left and right prints might look like mirror images, but if you look carefully, you'll see they're all unique.

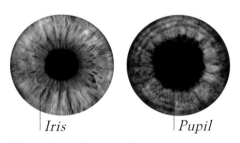

Iris   Pupil

The colored part of your eye is your iris, and it's as unique as a fingerprint. Each iris has a complicated pattern of stripes and gaps that an iris scanner can read to make a pattern like a bar code (below). Iris scans aren't perfect, though. Your irises change when you're ill, and you can hide your identity by wearing contact lenses.

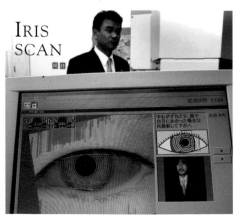

IRIS SCAN

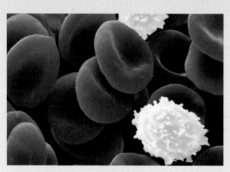

Your white blood cells can tell your cells apart from those of other people.

Your immune system can distinguish your cells from all others. If foreign cells (such as germs) get into your body, your white blood cells spot them and attack. Unfortunately, this system works so well that your body will try to **reject** organs transplanted from another person, even if you'd die without them. Organ transplants work best between close relatives, and best of all between identical twins, whose immune systems can't tell the difference between them.

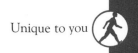

How would you prove you're the real *you*?

they're all based on the fact that everyone is **biologically unique**. Some of these tests are so effective that police can use them to catch criminals from the tiny clues left at the scene of a crime.

DNA VOICE SIGNATURE

A very good way of proving who you are is to get a **DNA fingerprint**. This is made by breaking a sample of your DNA into fragments and then letting these spread through a sheet of gel to make a pattern of bands. Police use DNA fingerprints to work out the identity of people from blood, hair, or other body tissues found at the scene of a crime. According to some experts, the chance of two people having the same DNA fingerprint is 1 in 5,000 billion billion.

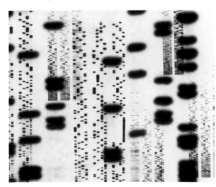

DNA banding patterns like this can be used to find out who your relatives are or to make unique DNA fingerprints.

"B A B Y"

Although your voice changes with your mood, with your choice of words, and with your age, there are certain tones that **stay distinctive** for life. A voiceprint analyzer can extract and recognize these sounds, even if you're talking on the phone. Some large banks use voiceprints to check the identity of their staff.

Voiceprint analyzers turn a person's voice into a pattern of lines on a computer.

Everyone has distinctive **handwriting**, and people called graphologists claim to be able to tell what kind of personality someone has from their handwriting. The traditional way of proving your identity is to write a signature. This is written in one quick action, exaggerating your style of handwriting in a way that makes the signature harder to fake. But signatures are not a foolproof way of proving your identity because they are usually judged by eye.

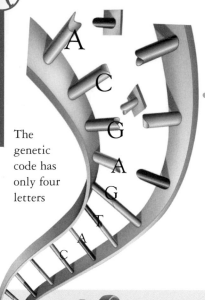

The genetic code has only four letters

What is a GENE?

The word gene has several meanings, but in essence, a gene is an instruction that tells your body how to work. The instruction is stored as a code in the molecule DNA.

DNA

Deoxyribonucleic acid

CHROMOSOMES

Nucleus

CELLS

You share 99% of your genes with a chimp, 85% with a mouse, and 50% with a banana!

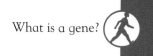

Gene can mean...

- a length of DNA • a code for making a protein
- an instruction that tells a cell what to do
- a controller that switches other genes on or off
- something you inherit from your parents—a unit of heredity

DNA CARRIES GENES. DNA is an amazingly long but ultra-thin molecule. It is shaped like a **twisted ladder**, the rungs of which make up a simple code with only four letters: **A, C, G,** and **T** (the letters stand for chemicals in the rungs). A gene is a segment of DNA containing a particular **sequence of letters**—a bit like a paragraph in a book. In most genes, the sequence of letters is a code for the sequence of different units (amino acids) in a protein molecule. Genes carry the code for many thousands of different proteins.

TCACCGTG
GTGGGCCTTGT
GGGTGCCTTCCGA
ATTCGAATTCCCTTG
TGGATGCCAATATAC
GCATATAGGCACAC
CGTGGTGGGCCT
TGTGGGTGCC
TTCCG

CHROMOSOMES CARRY DNA. Your DNA has to fit into a **tiny** space, so it is packed up in an ingenious way. Each molecule of DNA is coiled to make a thread, the thread is coiled again to make a cord, and so on (just as thin fibers can be wound together to make rope). The end result is a chunky, X-shaped structure called a **chromosome**. Chromosomes are far too small to see with the naked eye—you'd need about 100,000 of them just to fill a period. Even so, each chromosome contains a **whopping** 7 feet (2 meters) of DNA.

CELLS CARRY CHROMOSOMES. Each cell in your body (with a few exceptions) contains a set of 46 chromosomes squashed together inside the cell nucleus. The full set of 46 chromosomes carries **all your genes**, so you have a complete set of genes inside every cell. That's an **awful lot** of DNA! If you unraveled all the DNA from every chromosome in every cell in your body and laid the molecules end to end, your DNA would stretch to the Sun and back **400 times**. Yet all the information in your genes could be stored on a **single CD**.

ALL YOUR DNA = YOUR GENOME. The DNA in one set of chromosomes makes up your **genome**. There are only about 30,000 working genes in the human genome—the rest of the DNA is mostly **junk**. The human genome is very similar to that of many other species, even bananas! This is because all organisms share the same distant ancestors, and most of our genes are concerned with the nuts and bolts of making cells work. **Evolution** only has to tinker with a few genes to make a big difference in the way our bodies look and work.

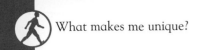

Where are my GENES from?

Your genes come from your parents, theirs come from their parents, and so on—all the way back to the first living thing that ever existed. Genes are passed down through families, and that's why you probably look a bit like your parents. Physical characteristics, like **long eyelashes, red hair, freckles,** or **blue eyes,** run in families because they are controlled by genes.

Half your genes come from your mother and half come from your father.

46
CHROMOSOMES

MOM

They were passed on to you in **chromosomes** carried by sperm and egg cells. Sperm and egg cells have only 23 chromosomes each—half the usual amount. When they meet and form an embryo, they create a new person with a full set of 46 chromosomes.

46
CHROMOSOMES

DAD

23 ARE PASSED ON TO YOU

46
CHROMOSOMES

YOU

ARE PASSED ON TO YOU 23

You actually have **two sets** of genes: one set from your mother and another from your father. These two **genomes** give you a mixture of your mother's and father's features—perhaps you have your mother's hair and your father's eyes, for instance.

Every child in a family is different because your parent's genes are **shuffled** and then divided in two before making each sperm and egg cell. So each child gets a unique set of genes (except for identical twins).

Your genome is a **mosaic** of genes from all your **grandparents**

What's a dominant gene?

Since you have two sets of genes, you have **two options** for everything. Take eye color, for instance. You get eye-color genes from both parents, but you might get a gene for brown eyes from your mother and one for blue eyes from your father. Sometimes one option takes priority over the other—we call it a dominant gene. The brown-eye gene is usually dominant over the blue-eye gene, for instance.

 +  =

If one of your parents has blue eyes...   ...and the other has brown eyes...   ...you'll *probably* have brown eyes, too.

Genes that are overpowered by dominant genes are **recessive**. For a recessive gene to have an effect, you'll need two copies—one from each parent. **Stick your thumb up**. If you can bend the tip of the thumb back, you have a "hitchhiker's thumb," which is caused by two recessive genes, one from each parent. Characteristics like this often skip a generation, appearing in grandparents and grandchildren but not in the parents.

What makes me a boy or a girl?

Two of your 46 chromosomes are special—they control your sex. These **sex chromosomes** are shaped like the letters **X** and **Y**. If you have two Xs, you're a girl (usually). If you have an X and a Y, you're a boy. In boys, all the genes on the X-chromosome have an effect whether or not they are dominant, because there isn't a matching X to complement them. This makes boys especially prone to genetic defects like color-blindness.

Boy

Girl

Some genes have a very simple and obvious effect. A single gene can make you color-blind or give you red hair, for instance. So you might think there's a gene for each of your characteristics, from the shape of your face to the length of your legs. However, the truth is not so simple. Many, perhaps most, of your characteristics involve lots of genes working together. Your height, your looks, the texture of your skin, the sound of your voice, the color of your hair, and so on, probably all depend on the combination of genes you have.

Things get even more complicated when it comes to genes that affect your brain. Genes can certainly have an influence on how smart, outgoing, adventurous, or creative you are. But they don't **determine** your personality—they just **influence** how it might develop. And so do many other factors, such as your family, your friends, the decisions you make in life, and luck.

Why can't I stand milk?

If you hate milk, you aren't alone. Most of the world's people are **lactose-intolerant**, which means that milk gives them stomach pain, indigestion, and worse. The cause is a **recessive gene**. Most Asian and Afro-Caribbean people have this gene, but people from northwest Europe usually don't. Scientists think Europeans evolved a different gene when they started herding cattle and drinking cow's milk thousands of years ago.

TEST YOUR GENES

1

TONGUE-ROLLING

Can you roll your tongue into a U-shape? (Don't cheat by squeezing your lips.)

2

BENT PINKIE

If the top part of your little finger bends toward the next finger, you have a "bent pinkie."

3

CONVEX NOSE

A nose that curves outward instead of inward is described as a convex or Roman nose.

5

CLEFT CHIN

A crease in the bottom of your chin is called a cleft chin. It's caused by a single dominant gene.

6

WIDOW'S PEAK

A widow's peak is a V-shaped pattern in your hairline, revealed when you brush your hair back.

7

FRECKLES

Freckles are spots of darker color on your skin. They are more pronounced when you're tanned.

9

DIMPLES

A dimple is a small dent that appears in one or both cheeks when you smile.

10

HITCHHIKER'S THUMB

If your thumb bends back more than 30°, you have a hitchhiker's thumb, which is caused by a recessive gene.

11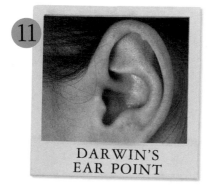

DARWIN'S EAR POINT

Feel the outer fold of your ear to see if you have a small point of skin called a Darwin's ear point.

Take the genes test. Most of these characteristics can be caused by a single dominant gene.

④

FREE EARLOBE

If your earlobe hangs free at the bottom, you have the dominant gene; otherwise, you have the recessive gene.

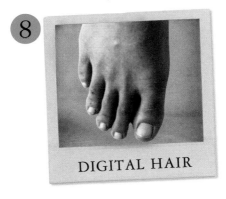

⑧

DIGITAL HAIR

If hair grows on the middle segment of your fingers or toes, you have the gene for "mid-digital hair."

⑫

HAND CLASPING

When you clasp your hands, which thumb is on top? The way that feels right is partly due to your genes.

WHAT DOES IT MEAN?

Blame your parents

All your genes come from your parents, so any characteristic caused by a dominant gene will probably also appear in one of your parents. If you can roll your tongue, the chances are that your mother or father can, too. And at least one of your four grandparents will have the dominant trait.

Be a DNA detective

With a bit of detective work, you can trace the path that genes take through your family by making a family tree. Collect photos of your relatives and glue them to a large piece of paper, with lines showing who is related to whom. Test everyone for the genes on this page and and write the results under the pictures.

Are you color blind?

If you can't see a number in this circle of colored dots, you might be color blind. Color blindness is caused by a **recessive gene** on the X-chromosome. Girls who inherit the gene usually have normal vision, but boys become color blind. Test your family for color blindness. If you or any of your brothers are color blind, the gene almost certainly came from your mother.

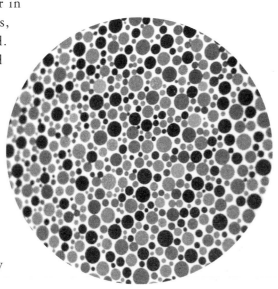

DOUBLE

Are **TWINS** *really*

Imagine what life would be like if there were two of you. That's a bit what being an identical twin is like. To scientists, identical twins are just like clones because they have the **same genes**. Because of this, twins give us a fascinating insight into how much genes can affect our personality.

FAQ

How do twins form?

Identical twins form when, for unknown reasons, an embryo splits and develops as two separate babies. **Fraternal twins** are different. They form when two egg cells are fertilized by two sperm. Like ordinary brothers and sisters, they share only half their genes—they just happen to develop at the same time and share the womb.

Jim and Jim

Identical twins who grow up separately often turn out to be uncannily similar. Jim Springer first met his twin Jim Lewis in 1979 at age 40. They had identical voices and were both overweight with high blood pressure, bitten nails, hemorrhoids, and migraines. They went to the same beach for vacations and both had a dog named Toy. They were good carpenters and both had built a white bench around a tree in the garden.

WHAT DO TWIN

Since identical twins have the same genes, any differences between them must be due to the environment in which they grow up (or chance). By studying the personality traits of lots of twins (especially twins who were adopted at birth and brought up in different families), scientists can actually measure how much of the variation in each trait is caused by genes. In other words, twin studies can help us begin to disentangle the effects of **nature** and **nurture**.

TROUBLE

IDENTICAL?

How identical are you?

Some identical twins are more alike than others. Most identical twins share 100 percent of their genes, but a few rare twins might share only 75 percent. These **half-identical** twins are thought to form when an egg cell splits *before* being fertilized by two different sperm. If the egg cell splits just *after* being fertilized, normal identical twins develop, each with its own placenta. But if the embryo splits 4–5 days after the egg is fertilized, the twins share a placenta and may become **mirror twins**. If an embryo splits around two weeks after fertilization, the cells may not separate entirely, resulting in **conjoined twins**.

What are mirror twins?

A quarter of identical twins are also mirror twins, which means that, in some respects, they look like mirror images of each other. Their fingerprints and the whorls in their hair look almost like reflections, and they may have the same pattern of moles or birthmarks, but on opposite sides of their bodies.

STUDIES TELL US?

THE RESULTS

Twin studies reveal that genes have a big influence on…

- what you look like
- your need to wear glasses
- your tendency to put on weight
- the medical problems you might have
- the main aspects of your personality (see p. 68)
- the fervor of your beliefs (but not what you believe)
- how long you might live
- your IQ

But genes have less influence on…

- whether you're right- or left-handed
- the food you like best
- your sense of humor

What are conjoined twins?

Conjoined twins are identical twins that don't completely separate and are born physically attached. Sometimes only a small patch of skin and muscle joins them, making it easy for doctors to separate them. In other cases, conjoined twins share vital internal organs such as the brain or spinal cord, which makes separating them very difficult and dangerous.

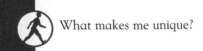

How did I DEVELOP?

Your genes control the amazing process of **development** that transforms you from a single cell into a body with 100 trillion cells. From the very beginning, your **environment** also plays a role in making you unique. And it continues to influence you for life as your brain keeps learning and changing.

How did I begin?

How fast did I grow?

When did my eyes start to appear?

When did my fingerprints form?

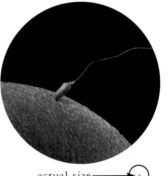

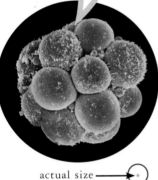

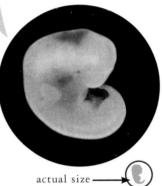

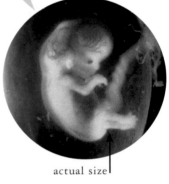

actual size
(look closely)

actual size

actual size

actual size

DAY 1

You spend the first half-hour of life as a single cell less than a tenth of a millimeter wide. This cell, called an **embryo**, forms when a sperm cell from your father fuses with an egg cell from your mother. The genes from your mother and father join together in the cell nucleus, giving you a unique genome.

3 DAYS

You don't grow much in the first few days. Instead, you divide. The single cell divides into 2, then 4, then 8, and so on, doubling in number each time. Within a week there are hundreds of cells, and over the next two weeks a body slowly begins to take shape. By three weeks, you have grown to the size of a **grain of rice**.

4 WEEKS

At 4 weeks, you look like a **shrimp** and have a tail. Your head is growing amazingly quickly and takes up nearly half your body. Arms are starting to form from buds, and dark spots mark the beginnings of your eyes. If your mother is undernourished at this stage, you are more likely to be overweight as an adult.

8 WEEKS

By 8 weeks, you are recognizably human but partly **transparent**. Your eyes, nose, lips, and even your teeth are forming, and your heart has started beating. By 12 weeks, you can move your arms and legs; your fingerprints have formed; you can swallow and urinate; and your brain is working.

When did
I first suck my
thumb?

When did I
start to
dream?

When did my
eyes open?

When did
I first
hear?

When did I
learn my mother's
voice?

What could I
do when I
was born?

16 WEEKS

You are now about the size of a **lemon** and have become much more active. You can clench your fists, suck your thumb, make facial expressions, and grasp the umbilical cord that connects you to your mother. You start to **hear** your first sounds, but your eyes are not open yet.

20 WEEKS

Your activity level begins to show at this stage. You might kick a lot and do somersaults, for instance. If so, you'll probably be noisy and active after birth as well. You can hear well, and loud bangs will make you jump. Your sense of taste has developed, and you have a preference for sweet things. Your entire body is covered by **fine hair** that will disappear later.

24 WEEKS

Between 22 and 24 weeks, your eyes open. You can't see much, though, because it's dark in the womb, but you might see sunlight as a pink glow. Your hearing is now so good that you can recognize your **mother's voice**. When you sleep, you spend most of your time dreaming.

BIRTH

You can breathe, suck, and swallow from the moment you are born. You can cry, cough, sneeze, and blink, and your senses of smell and hearing are very good. Your vision, however, is poor. Although you can distinguish colors and see faces, you can see things clearly only if they are very close. And, of course, you don't yet know what anything is.

How did I learn to speak?

When did I start to smile?

When did I begin to walk?

When did my personality start to show?

1ST 6 MONTHS

Your brain is already a quarter of adult size at birth, and it doubles in just 6 months. Your vision rapidly improves and is almost perfect by 6 months. You are fascinated by faces, and you can mirror your parents' **smiles** and frowns from birth. At 6 weeks old, you can stick out your tongue, at 5 months you recognize your name, and at 6 months you can sit up.

1 YEAR

Every day, your brain cells make billions of new connections as your brain learns to control your body and understand the world. Your brain is growing faster than the rest of you, and your **head is huge** compared to your body. You start walking at 12–18 months, but at first your balance is poor and your large head makes you top-heavy and unstable.

18 MONTHS

You've practiced language almost since birth, **babbling** in the vowels and consonants you hear around you. By 18 months you can understand hundreds of words and probably say a handful. Your personality is beginning to show. Your parents will know whether you're shy or sociable, noisy or quiet, nervous or calm.

2 YEARS

Your brain is three-quarters adult size, and you are learning faster than at any time in your life. If you're an average 2-year-old, you can say about 300 words and speak in sentences, but you may be hard to understand. Your **sense of self** begins to develop: you can recognize yourself in a mirror or photograph, and you start to use the words "me" and "mine."

When did my
memory begin?

When did
I start telling
lies?

How do I
know what I'm
good at?

How many
words did
I know at 3?

How did I
learn to read?

3 YEARS

You're learning up to
10 new words a day
and may already know
1,500 of the 40,000
or more you'll learn in
your life. Your brain
starts to lay down
long-term **memories**
that you can recall.
Your sense of balance
gets better, making
you less clumsy. Over
the next year or two
you learn to run, hop,
skip, catch balls,
and tie shoelaces.

4 YEARS

Your **social skills**
improve and you
become aware of
what other people are
thinking. This makes
you better at **lying**
and deceiving people.
Friendships become
important, and you
begin to see other
children as individuals
and play with them in
a cooperative way. But
you are very imaginative
and can also play alone.

5 YEARS

Your brain is now
almost adult-sized.
You have probably
started school, and
begun to learn to read
by understanding how
letters work together
to form words. You
now have a store of
long-term memories,
including exciting
times like vacations,
Christmas, and your
first day at school.
But your memories
go back only to age 3.

6–10 YEARS

During these years,
you master tricky
physical skills like
cycling, swimming,
skating, and ball
handling. You also
become skilled with
your hands, making
you better at writing,
typing, and drawing.
Your sense of identity
grows. You start
comparing yourself
to others, and you
become aware of
what you're good at.

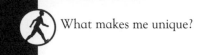

Why am I clumsy?

Why do my moods swing?

Why do I have such big feet?

Why am I changing shape?

11–12 YEARS

The years before the teens mark the beginning of **adolescence**—the period in which you change from child to adult. The point at which your sex organs start working is called **puberty**, and the age when this happens varies a great deal from person to person. Adolescence is a period of profound change—not just for your body but also for your brain.

GIRLS 13–17 YEARS

The female sex hormone **estrogen** is released by the ovaries. It causes a spurt of growth around age 11, and you may find yourself taller than boys of the same age for a couple of years. Once your periods start, you will grow no more than about 2.4 in (6 cm) taller. Puberty generally occurs at age 11 or 12, but it may be as early as age 8 or as late as 16. One of the main factors affecting the timing of puberty is your **weight**: girls start having periods when body weight reaches about 100 lb (45 kg).

- Your breasts start to develop.
- Your arms and legs get longer; your torso grows taller later.
- You start having periods.
- You grow pubic hair and, about two years after your periods start, hair grows under your arms.
- Your hips widen and continue to grow until your late teens.
- Your changing hormone levels are partly responsible for mood changes.
- You spend less time with family and more time with friends.
- You mix more with boys.
- You feel more **self-conscious**.

Am I a late developer?

Why am I so self-conscious?

Why do I have pimples?

Will I keep changing as I grow older?

BOYS 13–17 YEARS

18+ YEARS

The male sex hormone **testosterone** is released by the testes. It causes a spurt of growth around the age of 13, making you shoot up as much as 5 in (12 cm) in a single year. Growth happens from the **outside in**—first your hands and feet grow; then your arms and legs; then your torso. Bones grow faster than muscles, making you gangly, and your brain has to relearn how to balance your body, making you clumsy. Puberty is when you start making sperm, which happens on average when you are 13 or 14.

- You grow pubic hair.
- You start to produce sperm.
- Surges of testosterone can give you pimples (acne).
- Up to a third of boys develop slightly larger breasts in their early teens, before testosterone levels rise.
- Your voice deepens, often suddenly.
- About two years after pubic hair appears, hair grows on your face, legs, arms, and underarms.
- Your chest and shoulders broaden.
- Your face changes shape and your jaw becomes more square.
- Your body continues to fill out with muscle into your late teens.

By the time you reach your late teens, your brain and body stop changing so quickly, and you become more self-aware, independent, and socially confident. Your personality will continue to change throughout life as you develop a career, have relationships, and pursue your own interests.

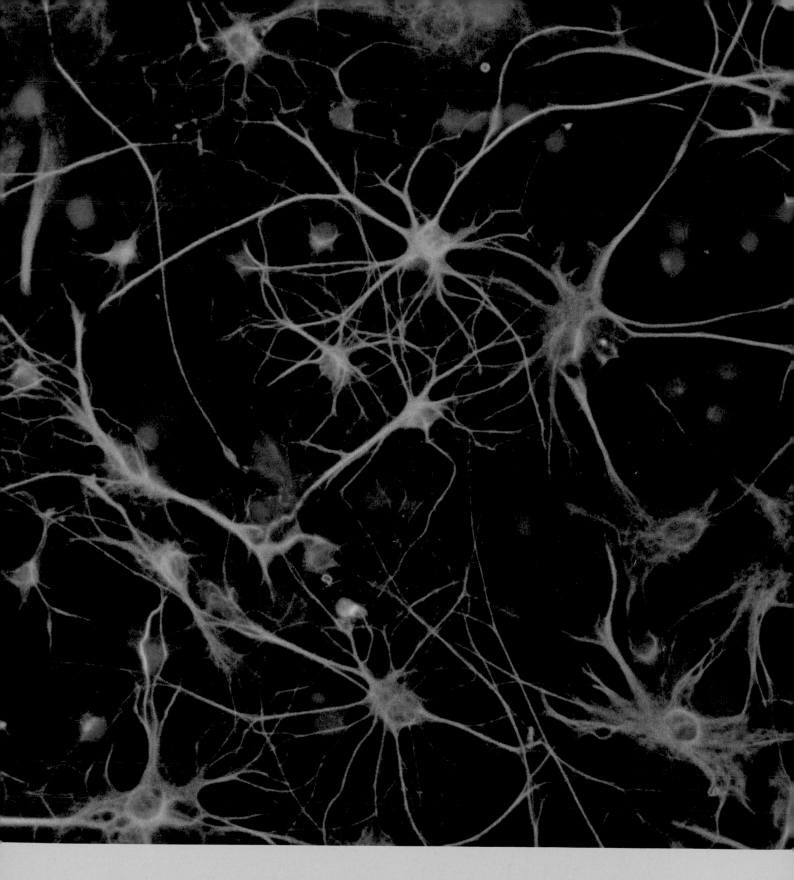

Your body: How does my **BRAIN** work?

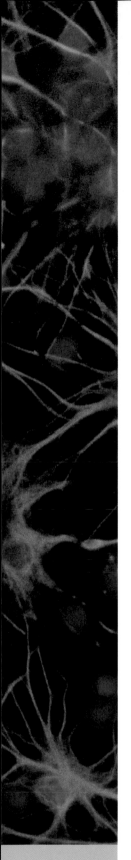

The brain is the organ that creates the real you.

All your thoughts, emotions, and memories—as well as everything you see and feel—are conjured up inside this cabbage-sized lump of tissue.

Exactly how it works is a mystery, but its secret seems to lie in the way its 100 billion neurons connect together, forming a maze of electrical circuits more complicated than any computer. And unlike any computer, your brain is continually rewiring itself and changing as it learns.

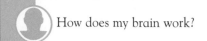

There are more possible circuits in

The **frontal lobe** is sometimes said to be the site of conscious thought, planning, and free will, but other parts of the brain also play a role in these functions.

FRONTAL

HOW DOES MY BRAIN WORK?

Your brain is pinkish-brown, about the size of two fists, and it has the consistency of gelatin. Its wrinkly surface is divided into **lobes**, which were once thought to specialize in different tasks, as organs do in the body. Although there's some truth in this, the brain is more complicated. It can spread tasks across lots of lobes and change the way it works if it's damaged.

One brain or two?

Each part of your brain is repeated on both sides, so you really have **two brains** in one. The two halves seem to have different characters and abilities, and they "talk" to each other. You need both halves to do many things. For instance, if you hear a joke, the left half understands the plot, but it's the right half that "gets" the joke.

your brain than atoms in the universe

The **parietal lobe** is important in movement, sensation, and orientation.

The **occipital lobe's** main job is to process information as it comes in from your eyes.

Cerebral cortex

The brain's wrinkly exterior is called the cerebral cortex. This is where **thinking** goes on, mainly at the front. Most of the rest of the cortex deals with information from your senses, especially vision and hearing. The cortex is split into left and right halves, each of which has four main lobes, as shown.

Cerebellum

The cerebellum helps to coordinate your body's **movement** and keep you balanced. But like most parts of the brain, it involves itself in lots of different tasks rather than specializing in one job. Recent discoveries show it plays a role in language, vision, reading, and planning.

Brain stem

At the very base of your brain is the brain stem, which is vital for basic life-support systems. It keeps your heart beating and your lungs breathing, and it helps control sleep and defecation. If your brain stem stops doing its job, you're said to be **brain-dead**.

LOBE

PARIETAL LOBE

TEMPORAL LOBE

OCCIPITAL LOBE

CEREBELLUM

BRAIN STEM

The **temporal lobe** deals with speech, language, and sound, among other tasks.

What's in the middle?

As a human, you have an amazingly big cerebral cortex, making your brain much smarter than that of any animal. Buried deep under the cortex, however, is what some people call your "animal brain"—the **limbic system**. This part of the brain generates basic emotions like fear and anger, and urges such as thirst and hunger.

Limbic system

How much of what YOU think and do

What's the subconscious?

The psychoanalyst Sigmund Freud was wrong about a lot of things, but he did get one thing right: much of what we do is controlled by hidden forces in the brain, which he called **subconscious**. The subconscious mind works behind the scenes, and we aren't usually aware of it. When you ride a bike, for instance, your subconscious mind takes over the job of pedaling, steering, and so on, leaving your conscious mind free to think about other things.

Is my world the same as yours?

Your experience of the world is **completely private**. Nobody can ever experience your thoughts and sensations. Some philosophers think that each of us might actually see the world in very different ways. What you see as red, for example, might look blue to somebody else, though they would know it as red. But since we can never look into somebody else's thoughts, we'll never know if this is true.

Where do my THOUGHTS come from?

We all have a sense of **inner self** inside our brains. The inner self is the real "you"—it has your thoughts and feelings, it sees the world through your eyes, and it vanishes when you go to sleep. Your inner self seems to make all your decisions, but is it really **in control**?

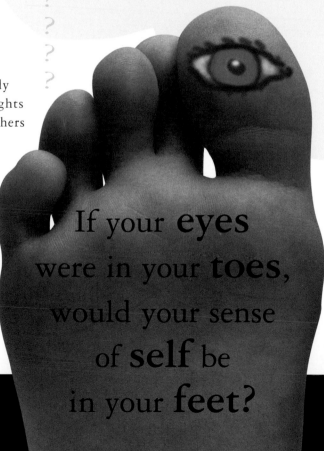

If your **eyes** were in your **toes**, would your sense of **self** be in your **feet**?

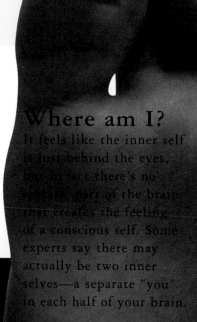

Where am I?
It feels like the inner self is just behind the eyes, but in fact there's no specific part of the brain that creates the feeling of a conscious self. Some experts say there may actually be two inner selves—a separate "you" in each half of your brain.

comes from hidden, subconscious forces?

Why do I daydream?

When you're bored or not concentrating, you'll quickly drift into an inner world and start to **daydream**.

Psychologists figure we spend up to 8 hours a day daydreaming

Like blinking, daydreaming happens all the time without our noticing it, and it probably has an important function. Most people have happy daydreams about things they want—like being rich and successful, **falling in love**, or becoming a hero. These positive daydreams can help focus your ambitions and motivate you. People often have **negative daydreams,** too, especially fantasies about taking revenge. These can be healthy because they help you let off steam.

What is consciousness?

The sensation of awareness that you feel while you're awake is called **consciousness**. Consciousness includes all the input from your senses, and it's dominated by vision—your top sense. It also includes the personal inner world that you can withdraw into and that nobody else can enter. Your thoughts, ideas, feelings, daydreams, and imagination are all part of consciousness.

FAQ

What's imagination?

Daydreams drift along without control, but you can also focus your thoughts and take control of the images in your mind. This happens when you use your imagination. For instance, try to remember how many rooms there are in your home. You can do this by imagining yourself walking through it.

What's my inner voice?

Thoughts sometimes take the form of an **inner voice** instead of images or feelings. When you're stuck on a difficult problem, you may even find yourself muttering as you speak your thoughts out loud. Talking to yourself like this doesn't mean you're crazy—it's just a good way of concentrating.

Everyone knows whether they're **right-handed** or **left-handed**, but do you know which is your dominant **foot**, your dominant **eye**, or your dominant **ear**? Because of the way your brain works, the two sides of your body are far from equal.

LEFT *or* RIGHT?

If you clasp your hands, cross your arms, or fold your legs, you'll probably always do it the same way, with either left or right on top. These asymmetries exist because your brain is split in two. The left half of your brain controls the right half of your body, and vice versa. For many tasks—whether physical or mental—one side of your brain is dominant.

IN MOST PEOPLE, THE LEFT BRAIN...

- is dominant for language, especially grammar, writing, and spelling
- is dominant for thinking logically
- is best at hearing the rhythm and pitch of music
- controls the right half of your body
- processes the right half of your vision

AND THE RIGHT BRAIN...

- is dominant at thinking spatially
- is best at appreciating music's melody
- is best at understanding jokes, sarcasm, and metaphors
- is best at recognizing objects
- controls the left half of your body
- processes the left half of your vision

◀ Which side of your BRAIN ▶ is the DOMINANT HALF?

Vision test

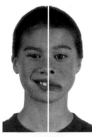

In many people, one half of the field of vision is dominant. Look directly at the nose in these two pictures. Does the girl look **happier** in one of them? Most people find the top face happier because the girl is smiling on the left, and the left half of the field of vision is usually dominant.

Which is your dominant foot?

Kick a soccer ball to see if you're right- or left-footed. About one in five people are left-footed. Many people are right-handed but left-footed.

Which is your dominant eye?

Hold up a finger and look past it to the distance. Close one eye at a time. The finger will jump with your weak eye and stay in place with your dominant eye.

WHICH HAND IS BEST?

What do **Bill Clinton**, **Paul McCartney**, and **Oprah Winfrey** have in common? Like 10 percent of the world's people, they are left-handed. Scientists have yet to figure out what causes people to become left- or right-handed. Identical twins are more likely to have the same preference, but the fact that they sometimes differ shows that genes aren't the only cause. Only babies can switch from one hand to the other, though by the age of two they develop a preference that sticks for life. Oddly, a lot of people aren't completely right-handed or left-handed. Some right-handers throw best with their left hand, for instance.

Most people are **right-mouthed**—they prefer to chew on the right side of the mouth

TEST YOUR HANDS

People who can use both hands are said to be **ambidextrous**. Take this test to see if you're ambidextrous. Hold a felt-tip pen in your right hand and see how many dots you can put in the white circles in exactly 15 seconds. Then try with your left hand. Go to page 270 to see what your results mean.

Left-hand start ↓

Right-hand start ↓

LOOK AT THESE FACES FOR 30 SECONDS, THEN TURN

MEMORY

Where are memories stored?

There isn't one specific place in your brain where memories are stored. However, there is a part of the brain called the **hippocampus** (which is shaped like a seahorse) that plays a key role in memory, apparently turning short-term memories into long-term ones. If the hippocampus is damaged, people suffer from **amnesia**, which means they can't lay down new memories or recall the past.

Where were you when ...

... the Army Public School in Peshawar, Pakistan, was attacked on December 16, 2014? Can you also remember who you were with and what you were doing when you heard the news? Our brains are especially good at remembering **shocking** events because the strong emotion makes the memory more vivid, more detailed, and easier to recall.

THE 4 TYPES OF MEMORY

SHORT-TERM

Shut your eyes and try to recite the last sentence you read. You're using your short-term memory. It last only **a few seconds** or minutes and then fades away, but it's vital for reading books and watching movies.

LONG-TERM

What did you get for your birthday? Now you're using long-term memory. Long-term memory can last for life. Strong **emotions**—such as joy or shock—can imprint permanent records in your long-term memory.

EPISODIC

Where did you go over summer vacation? Episodic memory is like a mental diary and has the **time and date** stamped on it. It includes whole experiences, including what you saw and how you felt.

FACTUAL

What's the world's tallest mountain? Now you're using your factual memory, which is a type of long-term memory. This is where you store what you learn in school. You need to keep **refreshing** your factual memories or they'll fade.

TO THE NEXT PAGE. CAN YOU SEE A NEW FACE?

Some memories fade with time, but others leave a permanent stamp on your brain. The first 3 years of your life are probably **blank**, but after that your memory began keeping careful records. Every experience you have leaves an impression somewhere in your brain, whether you can recall it or not.

HOW CAN I IMPROVE MY MEMORY?

There are lots of ways to improve your memory. One good way of memorizing schoolwork is to write notes as you read. This makes you concentrate on the most important facts, helping commit them to memory. Another effective technique is to reread your notes after a day, a week, and a month. Each time you refresh the memory, it becomes **easier to recall** and more permanent.

Memory tricks

Mnemonics are rhymes or phrases that help you commit facts to long-term memory. They work by linking boring information to something much more memorable. For instance, you can remember the order of the planets in the solar system with this mnemonic:

> **My very educated mother just served us noodles**

The first letter of each word stands for a planet, starting with the planet closest to the Sun: Mercury, Venus, Earth, Mars, Jupiter, Saturn, Uranus, Neptune.

To remember a list of numbers, convert each number into a mental image of a rhyming object, such as these:

1 bun
2 shoe
3 tree
4 door
5 hive
6 sticks
7 heaven
8 gate
9 wine
10 hen

Then combine the objects in an **imaginary scene**. For instance, to remember the year 1066, think of a hen with a pair of sticks poking out of its ears!

FAQ

I'm sorry—I forgot!

Forgetting is just as important as remembering. If your brain didn't forget, your memory would become clogged with irrelevant details and you wouldn't be able to think straight. So your brain usually filters out only **interesting** or **unusual** information and discards everything else.

Do some people have photographic memory?

Some people perform amazing feats of memory, such as recalling the sequence of all the cards in a deck after only one glance. But they don't have photographic memory—they've just trained themselves to use lots of clever memory tricks. Photographic memory probably doesn't exist.

CAN YOU SPOT THE NEW FACE? Your brain has a built-in

Test your MEMORY

TRY THESE TESTS TO SEE HOW GOOD YOUR MEMORY IS

1 **How's your memory for words?**
- Study the 12 words below for 30 seconds exactly.
- Close the book, wait a minute, and try to write them all down.
- Check how well you did and go to page 270 to see what your results mean.

Tip: visualizing the words and combining the images may help.

paper	salad	cup
	carrot	vinegar
chair		vomit
	carpet	dust
pebble	jam	camel

728345

Numbers can be harder to remember than

ability to recognize faces, so you should find this test fairly easy.

2 How's your visual memory?

• Study the objects on the tray for 30 seconds exactly.

• Close the book, wait a minute, and try to write down all the objects you saw.

• Check how well you did and go to page 270 to see what your results mean.

Tip: sketching the tray from memory may help.

736

words or images

3 Number cruncher

• Give yourself 15 seconds to memorize the number on the left.

• Close the book, wait a minute, then write it down.

• Check your result and see page 270.

Tip: keep saying the number to yourself.

When do I learn the most?

You learn some things best at certain ages—during **critical periods**. The critical period for **learning to see** is the first year of life. If a baby's eyes don't work properly during its first year, it may end up permanently blind, even if the eyes get better. The critical period for **learning to speak** is the first 11 years of life. You can learn to speak any language fluently during this period.

Why does practice make perfect?

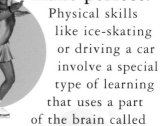

Physical skills like ice-skating or driving a car involve a special type of learning that uses a part of the brain called the cerebellum. When you start learning a tricky physical skill, you have to think hard about how to move each muscle. You use your cerebral cortex to consciously move your body, which takes concentration. After **practice**, however, the movements become second nature. Your cerebellum learns to take over, controlling your body like an autopilot.

Can I change my BRAIN?

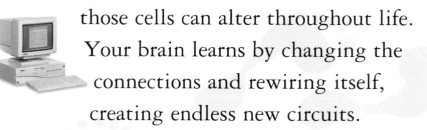

Your brain is **plastic**—it learns and adapts not by changing its software, as a computer does, but by physically changing its hardware. You were born with nearly all your 100 billion brain cells in place, but the **connections** between those cells can alter throughout life. Your brain learns by changing the connections and rewiring itself, creating endless new circuits.

The people you meet, the places you visit, the things you see, the skills you learn, even the dreams you have—all these things can change the **physical structure** of your brain. Your experience in life leaves its mark in the tangled web of connections inside your brain.

Since nobody has exactly the same life as you, nobody has a brain quite like yours

Your brain grows stronger

Whenever you learn a new skill or commit something to memory, you force your brain to rewire itself. And each time you practice the skill or refresh your memory, you make the new circuits **slightly stronger**, like wearing a path through a field.

When does my brain change most?

Your brain changes throughout life, but there are some periods when the rate of change is especially fast. In the first 2 or 3 years of life, a baby's brain cells grow connections at an amazing rate. But from the age of 3 onward, the brain starts pruning back, getting rid of connections it doesn't need and **killing brains cells** that don't get used. Another spurt of growth in connections happens at age 11–12, just before puberty. During adolescence, the new connections are pruned back once again.

Can I exercise my brain?

In some ways, your brain is like a **muscle**. If you exercise certain parts a lot, they grow stronger. Scientists have found that in violinists, a larger-than-usual area of brain is devoted to control of the left hand, which has the fiddly job of pressing the violin's strings while the right arm swings the bow. Likewise, in blind people who read Braille, an unusually large area of the brain is allocated to touch.

FAQ

Does sleep help me learn?

If you're trying to crack a tricky level in a computer game or master a difficult piano piece, you might find it easier to sleep on it and come back in the morning. Neuroscientists think there's a link between sleep and learning, especially for physical skills that require practice. There's also evidence that sleep can help you solve mental challenges, such as mathematical puzzles.

Stay focused

Learning is all about **attention**. Your brain takes in information only when it is interested and paying attention. If you get tired or bored and start to drift away, you stop learning.

Can the brain repair itself?

People who suffer brain damage after a stroke or injury often make what seems to be a **miraculous recovery**. A stroke can leave you paralyzed and unable to speak, yet several months later you can be walking and talking again. This happens because the brain is plastic. If the speech center in the left side of the brain is damaged, for instance, the right side of the brain can learn to do the same job.

and faster if you exercise it

What's IQ?

The IQ (intelligence quotient) test is the most famous way of measuring intelligence. It tests your spatial, verbal, and numerical skills and gives an overall score. The IQ test was originally devised to spot children who are struggling in school. It can give a good indication of how well you might do at school, but it doesn't necessarily show how successful you will be in life.

Is IQ genetic?

Studies of identical twins suggest that, among children brought up in stable, wealthy homes, most of the variation in IQ is related to **genes**. However, among children who grow up in underprivileged homes, most of the variation in IQ is caused by the **environment**. Though the results look contradictory, they show that genes and environment **both** have an influence on your IQ.

Am I a GENIUS?

WHAT ARE YOU BEST AT?

Intelligence can mean lots of different things, such as how good you are at math or how well you express yourself with words. The tests on the next few pages will give you an idea of what you might be best at.

SPATIAL intelligence

Thinking spatially means being able to see shapes in your **mind's eye** and turn them around. This type of intelligence is very useful in understanding machines and reading maps. On average, boys score higher than girls at spatial thinking.

VERBAL intelligence

This is a measure of your reading and writing skills. People with high verbal intelligence can read quickly and **take in information** easily. They can also express themselves well in writing. On average, girls score higher at this test than boys.

It takes 10,000 HOURS of

Is a smart person merely someone who knows lots of **facts**, or is intelligence about solving **logic puzzles** or being **imaginative**? And is it something you're born with or something you develop through practice?

NUMERICAL *intelligence*

High numerical intelligence is a sign of a logical, analytical mind. If you find math easy, you probably have high numerical intelligence. Some people score highly at this despite a low score for verbal intelligence.

LATERAL *intelligence*

Thinking laterally means using your **imagination** to solve a puzzle that may not have a logical answer. Lateral-thinking puzzles can be very difficult. If you're good at them, you probably have a very **creative** mind.

EMOTIONAL *intelligence*

If you're good at understanding how other people feel and think, you may have a high emotional IQ. People with high emotional IQ often become very successful in life, even if they score low on other types of intelligence tests.

FAQ

Can I change my IQ?

Your IQ isn't set in stone. If you study hard in school, your IQ will **go up**. The average IQ of whole nations has gone up over the last century, probably because of improvements in education. In Japan, average IQ has gone up about 12 points in the last 50 years. The change shows yet again that the environment can have a big impact on IQ.

What makes a genius?

A genius is someone who becomes exceptionally talented in a subject. **Albert Einstein** was perhaps the greatest scientific genius of all time. When he died, experts cut open his brain to see what was special about it, but it looked like any other brain. Even stranger, Einstein did badly at school and hated his teacher. His secret was probably his obsessive interest in science. **Obsession** is one thing that all geniuses have in common, and it often starts in childhood.

practice to become an *expert*

SPATIAL *intelligence* test

Try out this test, allowing yourself 20 minutes to complete it. Go to page 270 to check your answers.

1 If you want to cut a pizza into 8 equal portions, how many cuts do you need to make across it?
a) 8
b) 2
c) 16
d) 6
e) 4

2 How many edges does a cube have?
a) 8
b) 12
c) 16
d) 6
e) 4

3 Which shape matches the gray shape?

a   b   c   d   e

4 Which circle is the odd one out?

a   b   c   d   e

5 Which square is the odd one out?
a   b   c   d   e

VERBAL *intelligence* test

Try out this test, allowing yourself 20 minutes to complete it. Go to page 270 to check your answers.

1 India is to Asia as Italy is to
a) America
b) Africa
c) Europe
d) pizza
e) Jupiter

2 Ice is to water as solid is to
a) gas
b) ice
c) metal
d) liquid
e) vapor

3 Foot is to distance as pound is to
a) weight
b) gram
c) pound
d) ton
e) foot

4 Gigantic is to miniature as joyful is to
a) happy
b) ecstatic
c) bored
d) miserable
e) flea

5 Banana is to apple as cabbage is to
a) soup
b) cake
c) cherry
d) bowl
e) cauliflower

6 Which word is the odd one out?
a) eat
b) have
c) box
d) hold
e) smile

7 Which word is the odd one out?
a) eye
b) toe
c) ankle
d) tongue
e) giraffe

8 Which word is the odd one out?
a) shout
b) sing
c) talk
d) walk
e) whisper

6 Which of the objects on the bottom line comes next in the sequence?

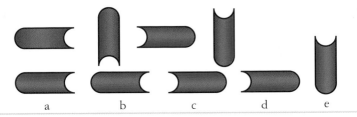

a   b   c   d   e

7 Which blue key fits the red shape?

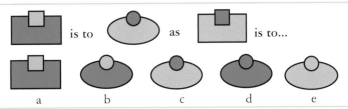

a   b   c   d   e

8 Which shape completes the sequence?

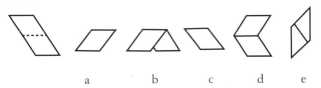

a   b   c   d   e

9 What shape is formed by folding the paper along the dotted line?

a   b   c   d   e

10 Which work of art contains the pattern below?

a

b

c

d

e

9 Which word is the odd one out?

a) agree
b) dispute
c) contradict
d) argue
e) disagree

10 Which word is the odd one out?

a) horse
b) cow
c) kangaroo
d) donkey
e) goat

11 Which word has a meaning similar to "construct"?

a) destroy
b) tower
c) brick
d) build
e) bridge

12 Which word has a meaning similar to "diverse"?

a) similar
b) spider
c) varied
d) calamity
e) abacus

13 Which word has a meaning similar to "essential"?

a) extra
b) harmonica
c) oil
d) surplus
e) vital

14 Which word has a meaning similar to "rotate"?

a) spin
b) encircle
c) invert
d) flip
e) collapse

15 If some gleebs are squmps, and some squmps are noomies, then some gleebs are definitely noomies. This statement is

a) true
b) false
c) sometimes true
d) sometimes false
e) none of the above

16 A cynic is someone who knows the price of everything and the ———————— of nothing.

a) size
b) value
c) meaning
d) circumference
e) opposite

NUMERICAL *intelligence* test

Try this test to see if you're good at numerical thinking. Allow yourself 30 minutes, then go to page 270 to check your answers. Be careful not to rush—it's harder than the other tests, and there are a few trick questions!

1 A farmer builds a 10-yard (or 10-meter) fence by stringing wire between wooden posts placed 2 yards (or meters) apart. How many posts does he need?
a) 10
b) 2
c) 4
d) 5
e) 6

2 The sum of all numbers from 1 to 7 is
a) 8
b) 15
c) 22
d) 25
e) 28

3 The day after tomorrow is two days before Tuesday. What day is it today?
a) Friday
b) Saturday
c) Sunday
d) Monday
e) Tuesday

4 What number comes next in the following sequence?

1, 2, 3, 5, 8, 13...
a) 15
b) 17
c) 19
d) 21
e) 23

5 If two cooks can peel two potatoes in one minute, how many cooks will it take to peel 20 potatoes in 10 minutes?
a) 1
b) 2
c) 3
d) 4
e) 5

6 1985516 is to sheep as 2315126 is to
a) wolf
b) horse
c) antelope
d) goat
e) cattle

LATERAL *thinking* test

You need to use your imagination to do this test. The questions are hard, so ask someone to help you if you're stuck. Don't be surprised if you get most of them wrong! Answers on page 270.

1 I live alone in a small house with no doors or windows, and when I leave I must break through the walls. What am I?

2 It's spring. You see a carrot and two pieces of coal together in somebody's front yard. How did they get there?

3 A man is lying dead in a field next to a backpack. How did he get there?

4 Two babies are born at the same time on the same day in the same month in the same year at the same hospital to the same biological mother. Why are they not twins?

7 Brian and Kevin collected 30 snails in a garden. Brian found five times more snails than Kevin. How many snails did Kevin find?

a) 6
b) 8
c) 3
d) none
e) 5

8 You're running in a race and you pass the person in second place. What place are you in now?

a) last
b) 4th
c) 3rd
d) 2nd
e) 1st

9 Jessica is taller than Nicole, and Maria is shorter than Jessica. Which of the following statements is correct?

a) Maria is taller than Nicole
b) Maria is shorter than Nicole
c) Maria is as tall as Nicole
d) It's impossible to tell
e) Maria is Nicole's sister

10 A group of ducks are walking in a line. There are two ducks in front of a duck, two ducks behind a duck, and a duck in the middle. How many ducks are there?

a) 1
b) 5
c) 3
d) 7
e) 2

11 What number is one-half of one-fourth of one-tenth of 800?

a) 2
b) 5
c) 8
d) 10
e) 40

12 The train trip from Centerville to Fairview is 300 miles. A fast train leaves Fairview at the same time as a slow train leaves Centerville. If the fast train goes at twice the speed of the slow train, how many miles will the slow train have traveled when they pass?

a) 100 miles
b) 150 miles
c) 200 miles
d) 133 miles
e) 266 miles

13 David is 4 years old and his sister Sarah is three times older. When David is 12 years old, how old will Sarah be?

a) 16
b) 20
c) 24
d) 28
e) 36

14 What number comes next in the following sequence?

144, 121, 100, 81, 64...

a) 55
b) 49
c) 36
d) 16
e) 9

15 A car travels 23 miles in 30 minutes. How fast it is traveling?

a) 23 mph
b) 30 mph
c) 46 mph
d) 52 mph
e) 60 mph

5 Why is it better for utility covers to be round instead of square?
Clue: think about turning them.

6 A man went to a party and drank some of the punch. He then left early. Everyone else at the party who drank the punch subsequently died of poisoning. Why did the man not die?
Clue: there was poison in the punch.

7 What's more powerful than God; the rich need it, the poor have it,

8 Three switches in the basement are wired to three lights in a room upstairs. How can you determine which switch turns on which light with just one trip from the basement to the room?
Clue: there are light bulbs in the lights.

9 A man lives on the tenth floor of a building. Every day he takes the elevator to the ground floor to go to work. When he returns, he takes the elevator to the seventh floor and walks the rest of the way. If it's raining, he takes the elevator all the way up. Why?
Clue: he owns an umbrella.

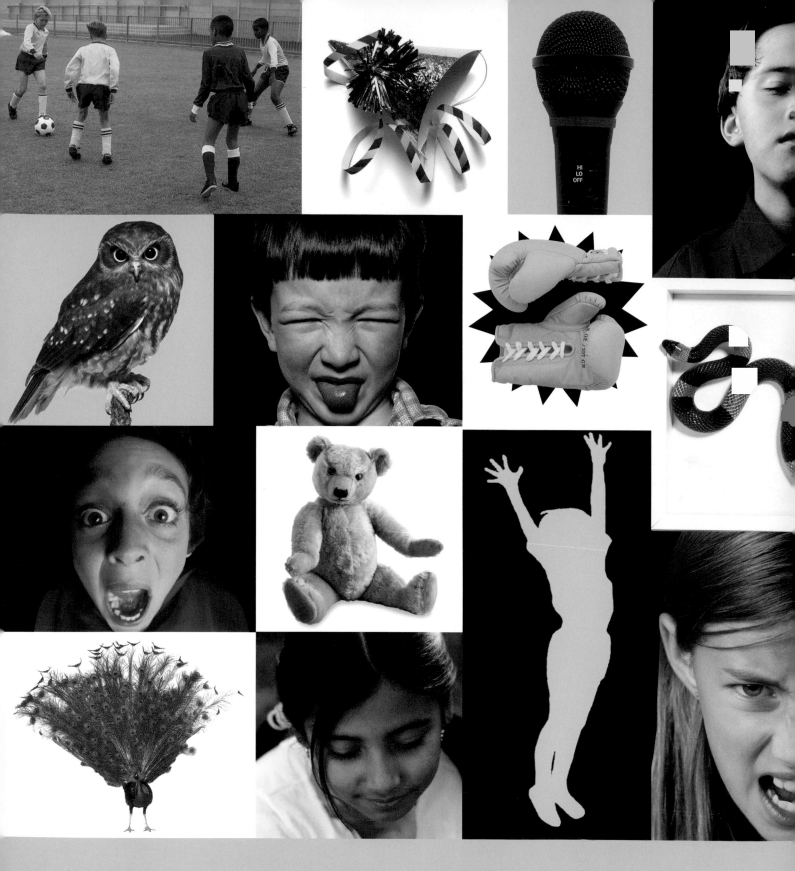

Your body: What kind of PERSON AM I?

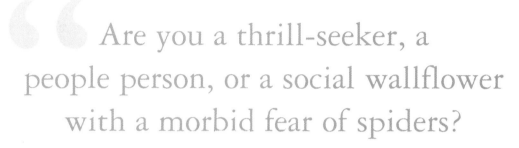

"Are you a thrill-seeker, a people person, or a social wallflower with a morbid fear of spiders?

Do you like to party and stay up late, or would you rather go to bed early and bury your head in a book? And if so, who's to blame— your parents or your genes?

Everyone has a unique personality, with a combination of habits and foibles unlike anyone else's. More than any other thing, it's your personality that makes you *you*."

Test your PERSONALITY

1. Do you like doing things that are a little dangerous?

2. If you don't like someone, are you afraid to tell them what you think of them?

3. Do you like having long conversations on the phone?

4. Are you good at remembering people's birthdays?

5. Would you rather hang around with a large gang than just one or two friends?

6. Are you very sensitive to criticism?

7. Do you get bored with hobbies easily and keep trying new ones?

8. Do you enjoy talking to new people and getting to know them?

9. Do you usually do your homework on time?

10. Do you feel sorry for people who are unhappy?

11. Are you good at staying calm under pressure?

12. If someone upsets you, do you usually forgive and forget?

13. Would other people describe you as shy?

14. Do you usually plan what you're going to do over the weekend?

15. Do you keep your room neat and clean?

16. Is it rare for you to get into arguments with people?

ADD UP YOUR SCORES BELOW

OPENNESS Score 2 for a "yes" to questions 7, 17, 20, 24, 26. Score 2 for a "no" to question 14. Score 1 for a "not sure" to 7, 14, 17, 20, 24, 26. Add your scores. 3 or less = low; 4–8 = medium; 9 or more = high.

CONSCIENTIOUSNESS Score 2 for a "yes" to questions 4, 9, 15, 19, 21, 29. Score 1 for a "not sure" to 4, 9, 15, 19, 21, 29. Add your scores. 3 or less = low; 4–8 = medium; 9 or more = high.

EXTROVERSION Score 2 for a "yes" to questions 1, 3, 5, 8, 22. Score 2 for a "no" to question 13. Score 1 for a "not sure" to 1, 3, 5, 8, 13, 22. Add your scores. 3 or less = low; 4–8 = medium; 9 or more = high.

Take this test to find out more about your personality. For each question, write down your answer as "yes," "no," or "not sure." There are no correct answers in this test—just try to be **as honest as possible**. Follow the instructions at the bottom of the page to add up your scores, then turn to the next page to find out what your results mean.

17 Do you like exploring strange places?

18 Are you scared of what other people might think about you?

19 Do you ever offer to help with the dishes?

20 Would you consider yourself a bit of a rebel?

21 Do you usually do things to the best of your ability?

22 Would you like to try bungee jumping, skydiving, or white-water rafting?

23 Do you often get angry about small things?

24 Does your taste in music and clothes keep changing?

25 Do you find it easy to trust people?

26 Do you like artistic or creative hobbies?

27 If you disagree with someone, would you keep quiet about it?

28 Would you describe yourself as carefree and relaxed?

29 Do you finish most books you start reading?

30 Are you someone who gets anxious easily?

Remember, you can answer "not sure" if you want

AGREEABLENESS Score 2 for a "yes" to questions 2, 10, 12, 16, 25, 27. Score 1 for a "not sure" to 2, 10, 12, 16, 25, 27. Add your scores. 3 or less = low; 4–8 = medium; 9 or more = high.

NEUROTICISM Score 2 for a "yes" to questions 6, 18, 23, 30. Score 2 for a "no" to 11 and 28. Score 1 for a "not sure" to 6, 11, 18, 23, 28, 30. Add your scores. 3 or less = low; 4–8 = medium; 9 or more = high.

TURN THE PAGE TO FIND OUT MORE ...

What's my
PERSONALITY?

Some people are loud and popular, others are quiet and shy. Some people **fly off the handle** easily, others never get worked up. Personality is something we judge intuitively, warming to some people but not others, so how can you study it scientifically? Psychologists tackle this problem by breaking down personality into different dimensions.

You need *a bit* of all these

If you scored highly for conscientiousness, you're probably sensible, reliable, and **hard-working**. Conscientious people strive to do their best at everything and are usually very neat and tidy, though sometimes a little fussy. If you got a low score, you're probably a bit disorganized and find things like homework and washing dishes very tedious.

Extroverts love excitement and fun. If you scored highly here, you're probably very confident, talkative, and like mixing with people. You may also be a **thrill-seeker** with a taste for danger. If you got a low score, you're more likely to be an introvert. Introverts tend to be shy and wary. They prefer being with friends they know well to being in a crowd.

Neuroticism is a measure of how **highly strung** and emotionally sensitive you are. A neurotic person gets upset, worried, or excited more easily than other people. The opposite of a neurotic person is someone who's very calm and relaxed, seldom gets emotional, and may sometimes seem to be indifferent to the world.

THE BIG FIVE

One of the most common tests psychologists use to study personality is the **Big Five** test, which breaks down personality into the five dimensions below. These dimensions are independent, which means that your score in one dimension has no bearing on the others.

You might be very extroverted, for instance, but quite disagreeable

To do the Big Five test properly, you need to work through questionnaires designed by psychologists. The test on the previous page can only give you a hint at your true scores, so don't worry if the results seem disappointing.

Is personality in the genes?

Studies of identical twins suggest that genes do have a big influence on everyone's personality. In one major study, genes accounted for about **40 percent** of the variation in people's Big Five scores, and the environment accounted for about **35 percent** of the variation. (The remaining 25 percent was due to sampling error.)

personality traits

AGREEABLENESS

Agreeableness is a measure of how easy you are to get along with. If you scored highly, people probably find you cooperative and **good-natured**. If you got a low score, you might be too outspoken or argumentative sometimes. People tend to become more agreeable as they get older.

OPENNESS

If you're very open, you like **new experiences** and change. You make decisions on the spur of the moment rather than following plans, and you tend to dip into things rather than immersing yourself in one hobby. People who score low on openness prefer familiar surroundings and routines, and they may become highly absorbed in one hobby.

FAQ

Can I change?

If you think you have a bad personality, don't panic. Personality changes during life, even in adulthood. In your 20s and 30s, your agreeableness and conscientiousness will probably go up. In women, neuroticism and extroversion go down with age. In men they stay the same, though they start off lower.

What job will suit me?

Different careers suit different personalities. If you're very shy, you may be happier in a career that's task-oriented rather than people-oriented. Understanding your personality can help you identify your **strengths** and work out which career might suit you best. But remember that people change; many people overcome shyness as they grow older, for instance.

Does birth order matter?

Some people say your position in a family has a strong influence on personality. The **oldest child**, for instance, often seems to be the most sensible, while younger children are more likely to be risk-takers. Careful study, however, suggests that these effects apply only **within the family**. When you're away from home and with friends, the way you behave has nothing to do with your family's birth order.

FAQ

Why am I shy?

Introverts can feel awkward or nervous in social situations, and this can make them avoid other people. There's nothing wrong with feeling shy—it's an important defensive **instinct**. Everybody feels shy from time to time, though most people become good at hiding it and acting confident as they get older. People also become less shy and more socially skilled as they grow out of their teens and start feeling less self-conscious.

Are you an ambivert?

Most people aren't complete extroverts or introverts. They're **ambiverts**, which means they're somewhere in the middle. An ambivert might be shy with strangers but very confident and outgoing with friends and family.

How many friends should you have?

Many people worry about how **popular** they are, especially during their teens. Extroverts always seem to be surrounded by a crowd of friends, while introverts might spend their time with just one best friend. There's no right answer to how many friends you should have—all that matters is that you enjoy spending time together.

One way of thinking about your personality is to decide whether you're an **extrovert** *or* an **introvert**. Do you devote your attention to the outer world of people and activities or

Introvert

OR

IF YOU'RE AN INTROVERT, YOU ARE...

- Quiet and reserved
- Serious and cautious
- Sensitive and reflective
- Happy on your own

Introverts tend to **think things through** before talking and acting, and are good at listening to others. They are shy and quiet, which sometimes makes them seem **aloof** or unfriendly. Introverts do well in jobs that involve working independently, thinking carefully, and analyzing information.

Ideas, people, adventure, books, parties ..

the inner world of ideas and experiences? Do you crave **excitement** and company, or do you prefer spending time on your own, away from the crowd?

EXTROVERT

IF YOU'RE AN EXTROVERT, YOU ARE...

- Outgoing and communicative
- Adventurous and risk-taking
- Confident and assertive
- Easily bored

Extroverts are energized by others. They are confident and **make friends easily**, and they can be great fun. Sometimes, however, extroverts can come across as shallow or loud. Extroverts do well in active jobs that involve meeting lots of people, and they can make **great leaders**.

FAQ

Are you a party animal?
Extroverts love going to **parties** and socializing with lots of new people. The "life and soul of a party" is much more likely to be an extrovert than an introvert. Extroverts are confident talkers and quickly get to know people, which can make them popular. But, like introverts, they probably have only a few friends who are really close.

Are you a thrill-seeker?
Some psychologists think extroverts have a gene that makes them **less sensitive** to stimulation than introverts. According to this theory, introverts are so easily stimulated that they can find social situations stressful, so they shy away from people. Extroverts, in contrast, seek out stimulation to avoid getting bored. So extroverts are more likely to be thrill-seekers who take part in dangerous sports, like skydiving or bungee jumping.

TAKE THE LEMON JUICE TEST

To see if you're more introverted than a friend, drop some **lemon juice** on both your tongues and then collect your **saliva** in glasses. Introverts tend to make more saliva than extroverts because they are more sensitive to stimulation.

FAQ

Do male and female brains look different?

Men have slightly bigger brains than women, even allowing for their larger bodies, but the average IQ of men and women is the same. In women, the connection between the two halves of the brain is a little thicker. Some people say this means women are better at using both sides of the brain together.

What's testosterone?

The male sex hormone testosterone,  which triggers puberty in boys, has a big impact on behavior and personality. When animals are given extra testosterone, they become more **aggressive** and **competitive**. Testosterone has the same effect in humans, making boys generally more aggressive and competitive.

Take the finger test

Testosterone is present in the body throughout life, in girls as well as boys. It even affects the way an unborn baby develops. If you had a high level of fetal testosterone, your **ring finger** may be longer than your index finger, and you're more likely to have a **male brain**.

index finger   ring finger

What SEX is

IF YOU HAVE A FEMALE BRAIN, YOU'RE GOOD AT:

- skills that use the **left side** of your brain, such as language, reading, and writing
- understanding people's feelings
- telling when someone is lying
- reading body language
- noticing the bigger picture

You might be a girl who's good at male skills like fixing computers, or you might be a boy with good social skills

Psychologists think male and female brains have different skills. The differences are not huge or absolute—they are based on **averages**. On average, female brains are better at **empathizing** skills, such as understanding people's feelings. On average, male brains are better at **systemizing** skills, such as understanding how machines work. And these differences seem to be present from birth—they don't occur just because boys and girls are brought up differently.

If you have a BALANCED BRAIN you are

my BRAIN?

IF YOU HAVE A MALE BRAIN, YOU'RE BETTER AT:

- skills that use the **right side** of the brain, such as thinking about shapes or understanding maps and diagrams
- understanding technical matters
- memorizing lists of facts
- noticing small details

Generalizations can be misleading because very very few people are perfectly average

Gender is a bit like a **spectrum**, with the typical male brain at one end and the typical female brain at the other. Where you fall on the spectrum depends on your own skills and abilities. Most people are somewhere in the middle, where male and female skills **overlap**. As a result, you might have a mix of typically male and typically female skills. You might have great social skills, for instance, but also be good at fixing computers. Then again, you might be hopeless at both.

Am I a people person?

If you're good at understanding people and putting them at ease, you're a people person. This is a typically female skill. Some scientists think evolution has given women better social skills (on average) because they tend to spend more time than men caring for children and families.

The extreme male brain

Some people seem to have an exaggerated type of male brain, with very poor social skills but sometimes enhanced systemizing skills. Such people are said to be **autistic**. Autistic children have difficulties relating to other people, and they sometimes develop obsessive interests in unusual subjects, such as memorizing car license plates or copying pictures perfectly.

AZN 885

The bike test

To find out how male someone's brain is, ask them to **draw a bike** from memory in only 30 seconds. Men tend to draw accurate bikes, like the blue one. Women are more likely to draw bikes that couldn't possibly work, like the pink one, but might include a rider.

equally good at **MALE** and **FEMALE** skills

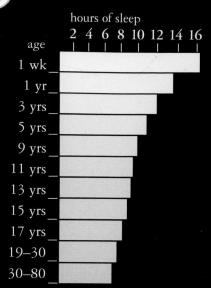

hours of sleep

age	2 4 6 8 10 12 14 16
1 wk	
1 yr	
3 yrs	
5 yrs	
9 yrs	
11 yrs	
13 yrs	
15 yrs	
17 yrs	
19–30	
30–80	

How much is enough?

As the chart above shows, you need less sleep as you get older. Teenagers need about **two hours more** than adults and suffer much more from the effects of sleep deprivation. So don't be surprised if you find it hard to get out of bed in the morning!

What's the point of sleep?

We spend **a third** of our lives asleep, but experts are still scratching their heads about what sleep is for. One theory is that sleep allows our brains to correct **chemical imbalances** that build up in the day. Another theory is that sleep allows our brains to build new **connections**, laying down memories and learned skills.

How long can I last without sleep?

Rats die sooner of sleep deprivation than starvation, and we probably would, too. The longest anyone claims to have lasted without sleep is 18 days in a **rocking-chair marathon**. But the claim may be fake—people who don't sleep at night probably catnap in the day without realizing it.

IF YOU'RE AN OWL, YOU...

- Sleep through your alarm clock
- Stay awake well past midnight
- Enjoy sleeping in

Are *you* an OWL

If you find it hard to get out of bed in the morning, it doesn't necessarily mean you're lazy—it could be down to your genes. Your genes have a big influence on how much sleep you need, and so does your age.

Your body has a kind of inner clock that controls your daily rhythms. It tells your body when to release **hormones** that make you alert or slow you down. Some people have such a reliable **body clock** that it wakes them at exactly the same time each day, like a built-in alarm clock.

The average **person** has a *body clock* of *24 hours* and *18 minutes*

74

IF YOU'RE A LARK, YOU...

- Jump out of bed early in the morning
- Don't like staying up late
- Fall asleep easily

OR a LARK?

The length of the clock varies from person to person and depends partly on your **genes**. On average, it's 24 hours 18 minutes (maybe that's why most people always want more sleep in the mornings). If your clock is short, you're a **lark**—someone who's full of energy early in the day. If your clock is long, you're an **owl**—and you probably like staying up late.

Can I reset my clock?

When you fly across the world, your body clock goes haywire, giving you **jet lag**. The clock no longer matches the true time, so you have to reset it. Bright light can help. When light enters your eyes, it triggers a signal that tells your brain it's daytime. Likewise, darkness tells your brain that it's night—and time to release the hormones that help you sleep.

Am I sleep-deprived?

It should take 10–15 minutes to fall asleep. It if takes less, you're **sleep-deprived**, which means you aren't getting enough sleep. Sleep deprivation makes you miserable and **bad-tempered**, slows your learning, and can even cause hallucinations. If you're sleep-deprived at school, you might nod off in class. Sleep-deprived drivers can fall asleep at the wheel and crash.

TAKE THE TEST

1 **When your alarm clock wakes you up, do you:**
a. Get out of bed right away?
b. Switch it off and get up slowly?
c. Put the alarm clock on snooze?
d. Switch it off and go back to sleep?

2 **What time do you go to bed on Friday evenings?**
a. 8:00–9:00 pm
b. 9:00–10:00 pm
c. 10:00–11:00 pm
d. after 11:00 pm

3 **What time do you get up on Saturday mornings?**
a. before 9:00 am
b. 9:00–10:00 am
c. 10:00–11:00 am
d. after 11:00 am

4 **How hungry are you when you eat breakfast?**
a. Very hungry
b. Only slightly hungry
c. Not really hungry but you make an effort to eat
d. Disgusted by the thought of food

5 **At what time of day do you feel most energetic?**
a. Mornings
b. Afternoons
c. Evenings
d. Late at night

6 **How quickly do you usually fall asleep?**
a. In 10 minutes
b. 10–20 minutes
c. 20–30 minutes
d. More than 30 minutes

See page 270 to get your results.

What are nightmares?

The part of your brain that creates **emotions** is very active in dreams. If it creates a feeling of fear, the dream becomes a **nightmare**, and the rest of your brain makes up a story to go with it. You might think you're falling from a height or trying to escape and hide from something scary, for instance. Nightmares are natural and everyone has them, but they get less common as you get older.

Why don't I know I'm dreaming?

One of the odd things about dreams is that when you're in one, you can't tell it's a dream—even though the strangest things keep happening. This is because you have no sense of **self-awareness** in dreams. Your brain's frontal lobes, which create your sense of self, are mostly shut down.

Do animals dream?

Many animals experience REM sleep, so perhaps they dream as well. Oddly, the amount of time they spend in REM sleep depends on how immature they are at birth. The **platypus**, which is tiny and helpless at birth, appears to dream for **8 hours** a day. Dolphins and dream, and birds seem to dream in song—their brain waves in sleep are the same as when they sing.

Why do I DREAM?

Dreams can be **terrifying**, bizarre, and fantastic, but what in the world are they for? Despite decades of research, dreams remain one of the brain's biggest mysteries.

When do I dream?

When you sleep, your brain goes through cycles of activity, alternating between **deep** and **shallow** sleep every 90 minutes. Most of your dreams happen in the shallow part of the cycle, when you're nearly awake. During these shallow periods, your **eyes dart around** under your eyelids as though you're watching something. This is called REM (rapid eye movement) sleep. If you wake someone in REM sleep, there's an 80 percent chance that they'll remember being in a dream.

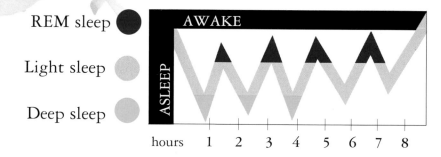

REM sleep
Light sleep
Deep sleep

AWAKE

ASLEEP

hours 1 2 3 4 5 6 7 8

How much do I dream?

Most people don't realize how much they dream. There are two good reasons for this. First, unless you wake in a dream, you won't remember anything about it. And second, **dreams distort time**. If someone splashes your face to wake you, you might wake up thinking you've been dreaming of rain for hours. Sleep scientists think we dream about five times a night and spend **1–2 hours** in dreams. Most dreams happen in REM sleep, but some people think we can dream in deeper sleep as well.

The average person dreams

You'll spend around five years of your life in dreams

Do dreams have a purpose?

There are lots of theories about why we dream, but the truth is that nobody really knows. Some experts think dreams help lay down **memories**, but there are people who never dream and have perfectly good memories. Other experts say dreams help sort out the experiences of the day, but unborn babies spend nearly half their time in REM sleep, and they have no experiences to sort out. And if dreams are simply for sorting information, why are they so **strange**?

What do my dreams mean?

The psychoanalyst **Sigmund Freud** thought dreams were a window into our hidden, **unconscious** desires, and he spent years talking to patients about their dreams and thinking up complicated meanings for them. Most people now think Freud read too much into dreams. The strange events in a dream might just be **meaningless** stories that your brain invents out of memories because it's active but starved of input from the senses.

Can I move during a dream?

When you dream, your body is literally **paralyzed**. This is a safety feature to stop you from acting out your dreams. Your brain keeps sending messages to your muscles to try to move them, but your **spinal cord** blocks the messages. Messages do still get through to your eyes, lungs, and heart, though, and that's why your eyes dart around and your heart rate and breathing become irregular. Sometimes people partially wake from dreams while still paralyzed and find themselves pinned to the bed, unable to move and **utterly terrified**.

about 1,825 times a year

FAQ

What's the lurch?

Have you ever dreamed that you're falling, only to wake with a lurch just before you hit the ground? This happens most often when you're right on the verge of falling asleep, and it's called a **hypnagogic startle**. It's caused by your brain suddenly waking again.

Why do people sleepwalk?

Some people get out of bed and walk around when they are fast asleep—they are **sleepwalking**. Sleepwalkers are not acting out their dreams. In fact, they are not dreaming at all. Sleepwalking usually happens as a cycle of very deep sleep comes to an end. Many people move around in bed or mumble at this point, but sleepwalkers get up and walk around. Sleep scientists call it a **partial awakening** because the brain is half awake and half asleep.

Keep a dream diary

Dreams are hard to remember, but if you write them down as soon as you wake up, your notes will help you recall them later. Try to answer these questions by writing down your dreams:

- Do you dream in color?
- Can you hear in dreams?
- Can you control dreams?
- Can you fly in dreams?
- What emotions do you feel?
- Can you sense time?

Can you control your
EMOTIONS?

FEAR   ANGER   JOY

Fear makes the eyebrows shoot up and pulls up the eyelids, exposing the whites of the eyes above the iris. At the same time, the lower eyelids rise. The mouth opens with a gasp and the lips pull back tensely. Blood drains from the skin, making it turn pale.

Muscles pull the eyebrows down and inward, causing vertical wrinkles to appear between them. The eyes narrow and take on a **glaring** expression that doesn't waver. The mouth may close tightly or open and snarl with rage, exposing the teeth. Blood rushes to the face, making it red.

A true smile affects the whole face, raising the cheeks and making crow's feet appear beside the eyes and bags appear under them. The mouth opens and the top lip pulls back, exposing the upper teeth. Smiling also sends **feedback signals** to the brain, intensifying the feeling of joy.

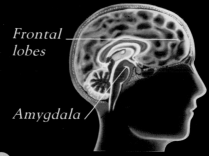

Frontal lobes

Amygdala

Temper, temper!

Strong emotions are triggered by a part of the brain called the **amygdala**, in the limbic system. More advanced parts of the brain called the **frontal lobes** act as policemen, enabling us to hide emotions and resist the urge to act on them. The frontal lobes take a long time to develop and don't reach maturity until we are in our twenties. As a result, children and teenagers are prone to **tantrums** and flashes of temper. Their amygdalas generate strong feelings, but their frontal lobes are not sufficiently mature to control them.

The way we show **emotions** in our faces is the same **all over the world**—a smile means the same thing in the Sahara Desert or the Amazon jungle. Psychologists think there are 6 primary emotions, each with a characteristic facial expression. These facial expressions are **programmed** into our brains by our genes.

Like primary colors, emotions mix together.

SURPRISE SADNESS DISGUST

Surprise can look similar to fear, but there are subtle differences. The eyebrows not only shoot up but become strongly arched. The jaw drops open, making the mouth look slack, and the eyes widen, exposing their whites. Surprise is difficult to hide, but fear can be masked.

In a sad face, the ends of the mouth droop and the inner ends of the eyebrows rise, creating a triangular shape above the nose, often with wrinkles higher up. The eyes may water or redden in preparation for tears, but often a sad person will turn away or cover their face to hide this telltale sign.

When a person feels intensely disgusted, strong wrinkles spread across the bridge of the nose and forehead. The eyes narrow, eyebrows come down, and cheeks rise. The sight of intense disgust in someone's face can also trigger a **feeling** of disgust in anyone watching.

Keep a feelings diary

Your emotions may not always be accurate: you may be highly strung and overreact sometimes. Try this exercise to find out how reliable your emotions are.

- Next time you have a strong feeling about something, try to work out exactly what the feeling is and what caused it. Write your conclusions in a "feelings diary." Keep doing this every time you feel strongly.
- After a few days, look back at what you've written. Were your feelings justified? Write down any comments in your diary.
- After two or three weeks, review your diary. Were your feelings accurate or were you overreacting? Were some feelings more reliable than others? Take note of how much to trust your feelings in the future.

What makes you AFRAID?

Powerful emotions like fear, anger, surprise, and disgust are basic **instincts** that protect you from danger and help you survive. They don't just affect your state of mind—they prime your whole body for action by triggering a state known as **arousal**. This happens so amazingly quickly that your body is on red alert before you even have time to think about what's happening.

SEE

REACT

FEEL

THINK

HOW DOES FEAR AFFECT THE BODY?

Your digestive system is put on hold and blood rushes away from it to supply your muscles, giving you butterflies in the stomach. Adrenaline also stimulates your bowels. In wild animals, this reflex causes weight loss to help the animal flee.

Your eyes widen and appear to flash.

Blood rushes to your muscles.

Your breathing rate suddenly rises, making you gasp for air.

Your heart speeds up with a jolt, making your chest pound. The faster heart rate helps deliver extra oxygen to your muscles.

THE FIRST SECOND

Fear is the most powerful emotion of all. Lightning reactions are vital, so the fear pathway takes a **shortcut** through your brain, bypassing consciousness. This is what happens in the first split second, as you freeze in terror:

1 A signal passes from your eyes or ears to your **limbic system**, which makes a very quick analysis and sends a danger signal to your body.

2 Your body is put on red alert by the nervous system and the hormone **adrenaline**. The body sends feedback signals to your **frontal lobes**, making you feel fear.

3 A slower signal from your eyes or ears goes to your **sensory cortex**, which works out what you've really seen and sends a message to your frontal lobes.

4 The frontal lobes use **thought** and **memory** to decide whether the threat is truly dangerous. If it isn't, it sends signals to the limbic system to make your body calm down.

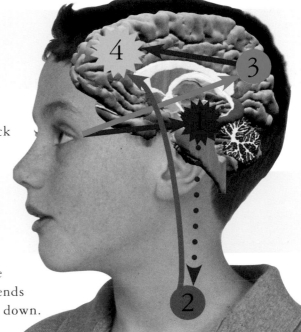

Fear has a profound and instant effect on your whole body. It increases your level of arousal by stimulating your **sympathetic nervous system**. This gets your heart, lungs, and muscles ready for action. The hormone **adrenaline** has the same effect, but it lingers in your blood, making you feel shaken after the moment of danger passes.

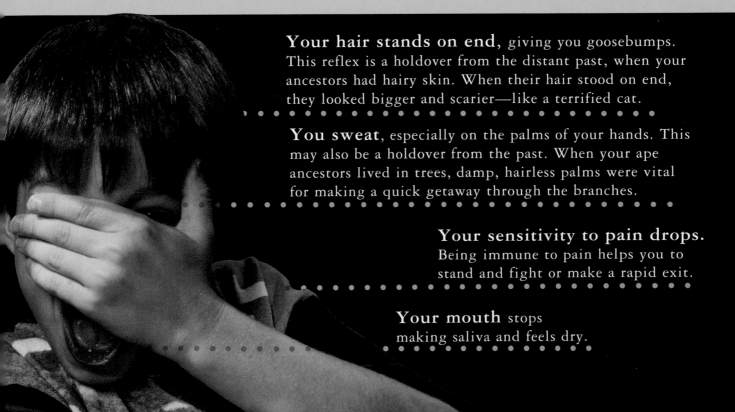

Your hair stands on end, giving you goosebumps. This reflex is a holdover from the distant past, when your ancestors had hairy skin. When their hair stood on end, they looked bigger and scarier—like a terrified cat.

You sweat, especially on the palms of your hands. This may also be a holdover from the past. When your ape ancestors lived in trees, damp, hairless palms were vital for making a quick getaway through the branches.

Your sensitivity to pain drops. Being immune to pain helps you to stand and fight or make a rapid exit.

Your mouth stops making saliva and feels dry.

A phobia is like a *car alarm* going off by accident

Do you have a

What is phobia?

Someone who has a **specific phobia** suffers from a full-blown feeling of terror when they see a certain trigger, such as a snake or a spider. Before they have time to think, the **limbic system** in the brain has put the body on red alert and caused all the symptoms of fear, including a racing heart, a queasy stomach, and a feeling of utter **dread**.

Why snakes and spiders?

People have an inborn tendency to develop phobias of **animals**. Psychologists think this is because poisonous or aggressive animals were serious dangers in our distant, evolutionary past, and we still carry the genes that can trigger fear of them.

Why are phobias irrational?

Fear happens below the level of conscious thought, and this is why phobias can be triggered by things we know are not really dangerous. It is possible to suppress the feeling of fear with thought, but the initial **gut reaction** is hard to prevent.

phobia?

What gives people phobias?

According to some surveys, as many as one in ten people have a phobia. Identical twins often have the same phobia, which suggests that genes play a role in causing phobias. But most phobias are probably learned. As children, we learn what to fear by **watching other people**. If we see someone reacting in terror to something, we are quite likely to become afraid of it ourselves.

Do you have...

... a fear of spiders, blood, or heights? Most true phobias involve animals, disease, or dangerous situations:

 gephyrophobia
fear of crossing bridges

 aerophobia
fear of flying

 musophobia
fear of rats

 myrmecophobia
fear of ants

 batrachophobia
fear of frogs, toads, and newts

 vertigo
fear of heights

 amaxophobia
fear of vehicles

 alektorophobia
fear of chickens

 arachnophobia
fear of spiders

 ichthyophobia
fear of fish

 ailurophobia
fear of cats

 hemophobia
fear of blood

Some "phobias" are really just dislikes. The phobias below don't cause genuine fear:

 pogonophobia
fear of beards

 xanthophobia
fear of yellow

 chronometrophobia
fear of clocks

 blennophobia
fear of slime

 scopophobia
fear of being stared at

octophobia
fear of the number 8

 panophobia
fear of everything

 arachibutyrophobia
fear of peanut butter sticking to the roof of the mouth

 iophobia
fear of poisons and rust

 didaskaleinophobia
fear of going to school

 pteronophobia
fear of being tickled by feathers

 geniophobia
fear of chins

HOW TO SPOT A LIAR

People don't just lie with their voice—they also use phony expressions and gestures. But there are a few giveaway clues:

Blushing

Some people blush involuntarily when they're lying or embarrassed about being caught out.

Microexpressions

Skilled liars can look convincingly happy or sad, but if you watch carefully, you might see true expressions appear fleetingly— for less than a fifth of a second.

Suppressed expressions

Less skilled liars can sometimes be seen trying to **suppress** facial expressions—they might try to hide a smirk, for example.

Honest muscles

Some muscles in the face are more honest than others, especially those around the **eyebrows**. A liar might be smiling, for instance, but an eyebrow might rise or twitch because they feel uncomfortable.

Touching the face

Small children often cover their mouths when lying. Adults and older children use similar but more subtle gestures, like touching the nose or scratching a lip.

Can you read FACES?

Head movements are usually easy to interpret. A slightly tilted head can be a sign of **interest**, while a head resting on a hand suggests boredom. Turning the head away can be a sign of rejection, but it is also a sign of concentration. If someone tilts back their head slightly, it might mean they think they're **superior**.

Eyes give away a lot. If you follow someone's gaze, you'll often see what they're thinking about. When someone is excited, their pupils **dilate**, and this is impossible to fake. Exposing the whites of the eyes above the iris is a sign of fear or shock. Rolling back the eyes to show the lower white is a sign of **contempt**, often done secretly behind someone's back.

Normal pupil　*Dilated pupil*　*White of eye exposed*　*Rolling the eyes*

Mouth movements play a role in many obvious expressions, including frowns and smiles, but they can also give away hidden feelings. Tightly closed lips show **suppressed anger**, for instance, and a yawn may be a sign of fear or nerves rather than tiredness. Sucking a pen or biting a fingernail can be signs of tension, and lopsided smiles show lack of interest.

Smile　*Thin lips*　*Yawn*　*Nail-biting*

Psychologists think we have about 7,000 different facial expressions, and these can flit across our faces with amazing speed, often without our realizing it. To a large extent, your social skills depend on how good you are at reading people's faces and decoding their inner thoughts and feelings—especially when they are hiding something or being dishonest.

Eye contact is the key to good communication,
but how much is the right amount? Prolonged eye contact can be a sign of aggression or **attraction**; very little eye contact may mean dishonesty, shyness, or dislike. In most conversations, eye contact is a matter of give and take, with frequent breaks. When people are **flirting**, eye contact lasts longer and the eyes rove down the face.

Eyebrows are among the most honest parts of the face.
Watch the skin above and between them—when someone is worried or uneasy, small wrinkles appear without their realizing.

Eyelids show several emotions. Rapid blinking indicates tension
or fascination, but blinking may stop altogether if someone is lying or angry. A spasm of **eyelid fluttering** is a sure sign of nerves.

Raised eyebrow

Furrowed brow

Blinking

Nose movements usually show negative emotions.
When the nose and brow wrinkle up severely, a person is disgusted. A faint wrinkling merely shows dislike, and a twitch to the side might show disagreement. If a person's nostrils flare open, they may find you attractive.

Twitch to side

Slightly wrinkled

Very wrinkled

Flared nostrils

HOW TO SPOT A FAKE SMILE

The trick to spotting a fake smile is to look at the smiler's eyes.

- A real smile spreads across the **whole face**, raising the cheeks and making the eyes wrinkle up.

- Crow's feet form beside the eyes, bags appear under them, and the eyebrows are lowered. In a fake smile, the mouth moves but the eyes stay **cold and neutral**.

- Fake smiles tend to be somewhat mistimed. They can appear too quickly and **end abruptly**. They may also last too long (a frozen smile) or be too short (on–off smile).

- Real smiles are usually very **symmetrical**, but fake smiles can look **crooked** and painful.

CAN *YOU* SPOT ANY FAKES?

1

2

3

4

5

6

See page 270 for the answers.

What's your BODY LANGUAGE?

People enter our **social zone** in public places, such as stores or sidewalks.

The **personal zone** is used for polite conversation.

Heads facing but bodies turned away can be a sign of conflict.

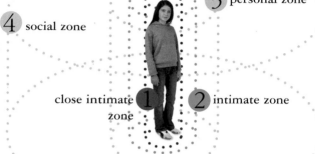

4 social zone

3 personal zone

close intimate zone 1

2 intimate zone

The **close intimate zone** is for physical contact.

Personal space

How close to us we allow other people to come depends on how well we know them. Strangers usually get no closer than the social or personal zone, and only best friends and family can enter the intimate zones. The limits of your zones depends on your personality and the culture you grow up in.

Words and facial expressions aren't the only way we **communicate**— we also use our bodies. Some of our gestures are deliberate, but a lot of our body language is **unconscious**. We also read body language

This boy has a relaxed and **open** posture—a sign of confidence or perhaps arrogance.

Politicians sometimes use the **power grip** during a speech.

Hiding the hands and looking down both show submissiveness.

These girls are unconsciously copying each other.

DOMINANCE

Someone who feels superior or **powerful** shows it with a relaxed posture. Relaxing is normal when with friends and family, but in the company of strangers, it can appear cocky.

SUBMISSION

Submissive is the opposite of powerful. A submissive person stands still or sits upright, with their hands held down.

MIMICKING

When two people get along very well, they often **mimic** each other's body language without realizing it.

By keeping their bodies facing each other, these two people are **excluding** the third person.

As well as turning toward each other, these girls are pointing with their feet. The boy feels shut out.

This girl secretly likes the boy with red hair.

Aggression

When a fight is brewing between boys, they will **square off**, with faces facing but bodies turned away a little. Their eyes glower and they stop blinking.

POINTING WITH THE BODY

In a social situation like a party, the direction your body faces is important. Two people can make a third person feel **unwelcome** by keeping their bodies turned toward each other. Even if they occasionally turn their heads to be polite, the third person will feel excluded and awkward. People may unwittingly point with a part of the body toward someone or something they are secretly thinking about.

unconsciously—you might get a feeling that someone likes or dislikes you without knowing why. Body language sends **powerful signals**, and it can give away your secret feelings.

Rubbing an eye

Fidgeting hand and foot

Pulling an ear

Crossed ankles and clenched hands

Folded arms and legs

DISHONESTY

People usually feel uncomfortable when they lie, and this can make them **fidget** or touch themselves. As well as touching their faces, liars might shift in their chairs or start moving a foot restlessly.

DEFENSIVENESS

When people feel anxious or defensive, they unconsciously adopt **closed** postures. Crossed ankles can mean someone is hiding negative feelings. The **foot lock** (center) is a typically female gesture that reveals a defensive attitude.

FAQ

How did I learn to speak?

Babies have an **instinctive** ability to pick up language without being taught. They listen intently to voices, even before they are born. At birth they can babble in all the vowels and consonants of all the world's languages, but by 6 months this has narrowed down to the language they hear. By age 3 they've picked up most of the important words in this language.

Where does my accent come from?

The language you speak and your accent depend on **where you live**. Most people pick up their accent (as well as slang words) from their friends rather than their parents, so the way you speak might be quite different from your parents. In childhood, you can pick up any accent and learn any language fluently, but by about the age of 11 the circuits in your brain that pick up new sounds wither away. As a result, the accent you have in your teens will probably stick with you for life.

How big is my vocabulary?

The words you know depend on your age, how much you read, and the language you speak. The average American high-school student knows about **40,000 words**, which is barely a tenth of the total number of words in the English language. Even so, it's more than enough —most people use only one or two thousand words in everyday life.

Do you have a way with

WORDS?

Your genes build the basic apparatus you need for speech, but almost everything about the way you speak depends on your upbringing, from your **accent** and **language** to your choice of **words**—and even your sense of humor!

Where does my voice come from?

Your voice comes from your **vocal cords**—two vibrating cords of tissue in your voice box, deep in your throat. **Touch your throat** while you speak to feel your vocal cords vibrate. Try the same thing when whispering and you won't feel a thing because you're only using your mouth to make sound. Your mouth is vital to all speech. It shapes sound to make vowels— look in a mirror as you say **ooo, eee, aaa**. You also use your lips, tongue, and teeth for consonants. Try reading this sentence out loud without closing your lips to see why.

Yikes, a leopard!

CAN ANIMALS TALK?

Animals communicate in lots of ways —by growling, singing, squeaking, scent-marking, and using all sorts of body language. Some animals, such as meerkats, even have a small **vocabulary** of calls to warn each other of different predators, such as eagles, leopards, and snakes.

But there's one thing that humans alone are capable of: grammar. Using the rules of grammar, we can arrange words in different combinations to create sentences, each with a unique meaning that can be clearly understood.

The only voice you never hear properly is *your own*

What does my voice sound like?

You hear your own voice partly as vibrations in your skull, so you never hear it properly. Record it and play it back to see what it really sounds like. The basic sound and pitch of your voice depend on the size and shape of your voice box and mouth. But the vowels and consonants you can say depend on your language and culture.

FAQ

What are gestures for?

To see how important hand gestures are to speech, try describing a spiral in words alone, or try keeping your hands still next time you're on the phone. We pick up gestures by unconsciously **copying** the people around us as we grow up. The way you walk, stand, sit, and move your hands all probably come from copying your family.

What makes you laugh?

According to studies of identical twins, your sense of humor— like your accent and language— comes from the environment you grow up in and not from your genes. Laughter is a vital part of the way we communicate because it strengthens social bonds. Some scientists think it has the same physical effect as **grooming** does in monkeys. Monkeys spend hours every day grooming the fur of relatives and best friends. Doing so triggers the release of brain chemicals called **endorphins**, which relieve tension.

What's dyslexia?

Some people find learning to read and write unusually difficult because of a problem known as **dyslexia**. A dyslexic person might find it very difficult to tell the difference between the letters "b" and "d" or the numbers "6" and "9," for instance. Dyslexic people are just as intelligent as other people and often go on to be very successful in life.

What's my POTENTIAL?

Play to your STRENGTHS

Achieving your potential is all about knowing what you're good at and playing to your strengths. Psychologists recognize at least seven different areas of natural ability, or "intelligence." What **skills** do you have?

- **Interpersonal** Are you quick to see what other people are thinking or feeling?
- **Intrapersonal** Do you truly understand your own feelings and emotions—do you have "self-knowledge"?
- **Physical** Are you quick to master physical skills like driving, skiing, sports, or new dance steps?
- **Musical** Can you hum a song after hearing it once, and can you sing in perfect tune?
- **Spatial** Do you find reading maps and tinkering with machines easy?
- **Verbal** Are you an avid reader or good at writing?
- **Logical** Do you find things like math and computers easy to understand?

What about my WEAKNESSES?

Being bad at something often doesn't matter. If you can't draw, it's unlikely to stop you from becoming a CEO or an Olympic athlete. There are some areas of ability, however, that are important for everyone and worth trying to improve. All of us come in contact with other people at home and at work or school, which makes interpersonal skills very important. People with good interpersonal skills have a **head start** in life and often rise quickly through the ranks in their profession. People with less ability may struggle to succeed unless they learn to behave in a more socially skilled way. And these skills can certainly be learned—and are indeed learned by almost everyone as they grow up.

Can I be a SUCCESS?

You need only two things to be a success: a certain amount of natural ability, and the willingness to **persevere**. Even geniuses need to work very hard to succeed. As the inventor Thomas Edison said, "genius is one percent inspiration and 99 percent perspiration." The composer Mozart was a musical genius, but only after years of training. In fact, he had already spent 5 years performing by the age of 12. Likewise, Albert Einstein spent his childhood reading very difficult books on mathematics and philosophy. Real top-quality genius isn't just about hard work, though—it also requires **creative thinking** and leaps of imagination. A genius breaks the mold and discovers new ways of doing things that everybody else copies. So what's the secret of creativity? Psychologists figure it takes about **10,000 hours** of practice at something to become so good that you are truly creative. It sounds like a lot, but it's only 5 years!

What is the secret of HAPPINESS?

What's the point of being successful if it doesn't make you happy? For most people, the ultimate ambition in life is to be **happy**. People have been searching for the secret of happiness for thousands of years, and recently psychologists have joined the hunt. If their research is right, the secret of happiness is actually very simple. First of all, it helps if you enjoy meeting people and don't spend too much time alone. Second, you're more likely to be happy if your expectations aren't too high. And third, don't forget to look on the bright side of things!

The secret of *success* is to know what

Do you feel destined for **FAME** and **FORTUNE**, or do you worry that you won't be able to use your abilities to gain the success you deserve?

you're good at and play to your **STRENGTHS**

Your Brain
Introducing the BRAIN

For centuries, people thought the heart or soul were where thoughts and feelings came from and regarded the brain as *useless gunk*. Thanks to a few gruesome discoveries, the truth about that mysterious gunk in our heads slowly began to emerge. Today, we know more about the brain than ever, yet it remains a *riddle wrapped in a mystery*. It's the very organ we use to understand itself, yet it's the only organ we don't *really understand*—and perhaps never will.

Discovering the BRAIN

If it weren't for scientists and about 8,500 years of history, you might not even know you had a brain in your head. From realizing we have a brain . . .

I'm the greatest!

Ancient Egyptians gave the brain a name but otherwise had little time for it. Before making a mummy from a dead body, they'd carefully preserve its heart. But the brain was scraped out through the nostrils and thrown away.

What's that smell?

Herophilus, a Greek doctor, kicked off the science of anatomy by prizing open dead bodies and sketching what he found inside. After making detailed studies of the eye and nerves, he realized the brain was the body's control center.

6500 BCE	1077 BCE	400 BCE	300 BCE	0

Trepanning was boring old brain surgery—literally. Used from the Stone Age onward, it involved drilling holes in the skull, more or less at random. It was used to "treat" many types of illness, from mild headaches to out-and-out insanity.

I needed that like a hole in the head...

Aristotle, a Greek thinker, was the world's first great scientist, but he had some wacky ideas about the brain. He thought the heart was in charge of our emotions, while the brain was little more than a radiator that stopped the body from overheating.

. . . to figuring out precisely what this squishy, head-mounted "computer" actually does has been a long and slow but fascinating process.

Andreas Vesalius

Andreas Vesalius gave us the first detailed drawings of the brain. One of the sketches was from a murderer who'd been hanged and beheaded. As if that weren't enough, Vesalius chopped up his body in public, reassembling the bones later for display at the local university.

Phineas Gage

Phineas Gage was a hard-working and reliable railroad worker until an accident at work blew a metal spike through the front of his brain. Suddenly, he became rude, careless, and aggressive. This famous case revealed how damage to the brain's frontal lobe can cause a dramatic change in someone's character.

That's given me a headache!

1543   **1637**

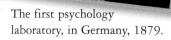

The first psychology laboratory, in Germany, 1879.

1848 1850

René Descartes

René Descartes was a French philosopher who liked to scribble away in bed until noon. His famous idea was that the mind and body were totally separate things that could, nevertheless, work together. He's best remembered for saying "I think therefore I am."

Shh, I'm thinking!

Hermann von Helmholtz

Hermann von Helmholtz helped make psychology into a science. His experiments on how people see colors and hear sounds were the first scientific studies of perception. Wilhelm Wundt built on his work to found experimental psychology (studying behavior using scientific methods).

95

Paul Broca was a French doctor

who discovered where speech is produced in the brain. One of his patients was nicknamed "Tan" because that was the only word he could say. When Tan died, Broca examined his brain and found damage to the left front side. Broca realized the damaged part (now called Broca's area) must be involved in moving the mouth to form words. This was the first time anyone had really tried to find which parts of the brain did what.

Tan, tan
tan, tan!

Sigmund Freud, a hugely influential Austrian doctor,

believed mental problems could be traced back to experiences in childhood. According to Freud, people are driven by "unconscious" forces they aren't aware of, except in dreams and nightmares. Freud invented a treatment called psychoanalysis, where patients lay back on a cozy couch and moaned about their lives while the analyst listened patiently, explained what was wrong, then gave them a huge bill. Some of Freud's ideas have now fallen out of favor for being unscientific, but he is still regarded as a great thinker.

*Tell me about
your childhood...*

1861 1870   1900   1914

Dr. Eduard Hitzig, a German neurologist,

conducted shocking experiments on injured soldiers. When he poked a tiny electric needle into different parts of their brains, he noticed the soldier's body jerked around. Repeating the experiment on dogs, he found he could move different parts of a dog's body by poking different parts of its brain. Prodding the left side of the brain made the right side of the body jerk, and vice-versa.

Left brain controls
right side of body

Right brain
controls left side

Henry Dale,

a British scientist, discovered neurotransmitters (chemicals that relay signals between nerve cells) in 1914. As a student, Dale took part in public experiments on live animals that led to protests about cruelty. Animal experiments, which have led to many important discoveries about the brain, are now more strictly controlled to minimize suffering.

Gordon Holmes was an Irish doctor who specialized in studying damage to the rear part of the brain, including the cerebellum and brain stem. By examining the head wounds of more than 2,000 soldiers in World War I, Holmes reached the conclusion that we see things in an area at the back of the brain that we now call the **visual cortex**.

I can see clearly now.

Brain stem

Cerebellum

Visual cortex

Lobotomies were a drastic kind of brain surgery, popular from the 1930s to the 1950s, intended to help people with mental illness or brain diseases such as epilepsy. The operation involved cutting the connections between the frontal lobe (a part of the brain vital for careful thinking) and the rest of the brain. It was quick and easy and could be done by hammering a knife into the brain through the eye socket. Although it often cured the patient's symptoms, it also caused unwanted changes in personality, and many doctors considered the operation barbaric. Thousands of people had lobotomies until the early 1970s, when newly invented drugs provided alternative treatments. Lobotomies are still performed today, but much less frequently.

1919   1920   1934   1938

Electroencephalography is the detection and recording of "brain waves"—electrical waves from the brain—using an instrument worn on the head. Brain waves were first properly studied by Hans Berger, a German scientist who thought they might shed light on telepathy.

Burrhus Frederic Skinner, an American psychologist, thought we could understand how animals (including humans) behave without worrying too much about the brain. Called behaviorism, the theory was that animals do things because they're given rewards or punishments. This idea dominated psychology for years and put many scientists off studying the brain until the 1960s.

I smell a rat...

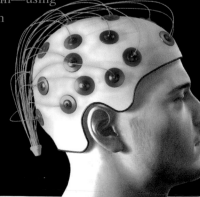

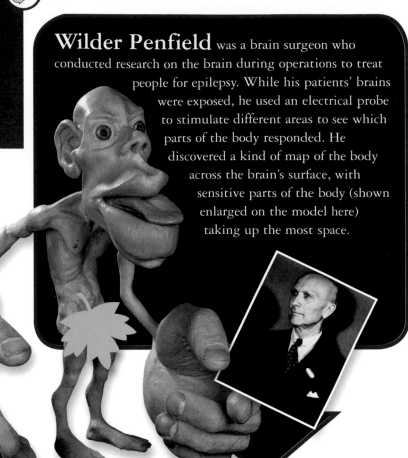

Wilder Penfield was a brain surgeon who
conducted research on the brain during operations to treat people for epilepsy. While his patients' brains were exposed, he used an electrical probe to stimulate different areas to see which parts of the body responded. He discovered a kind of map of the body across the brain's surface, with sensitive parts of the body (shown enlarged on the model here) taking up the most space.

Cognitive psychology was a
new way of studying the brain that took off in the 1960s. Until the 1960s, psychologists had studied behavior and ignored what went on inside the brain. Now the psychologists began trying to figure out the brain's inner workings. They thought of the brain as a machine following simple rules that were programmed into it. The goal of cognitive psychology was to reveal the hidden rules underlying language, vision, memory, and other mental processes.

Whirr, whirr, click...

1951–1953

1960s

Who am *I?*

Henry Molaison
(known as "H. M.") had the world's most exhaustively studied noggin. After undergoing brain surgery to cure his epilepsy in 1953, he could no longer remember new things. He spent his remaining years as a patient, helping scientists to unravel the mysteries of memory.

Jose Delgado
invented the first radio-controlled brain, in 1964. After sticking an electronic implant in a bull's brain, he stepped into a ring with an electronic controller and waited for the bull to charge him. Then he calmly pressed a button, zapped the bull, and brought it to a screeching halt.

I don't know if I'm coming or going.

Roger Sperry studied people

who'd had surgery to separate the left and right halves of the brain—a last-resort cure for epilepsy. This drastic operation resulted in two "selves" controlling different parts of the body and sometimes disagreeing with one another!

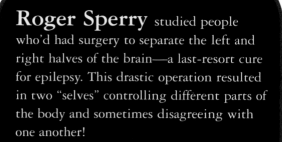

"The great pleasure and feeling in my right brain is more than my left brain can find the words to tell you."

Neuroscience

is the modern term for the scientific study of the brain. Neuroscientists think of brain cells (neurons) as electrical components that connect together to form complicated circuits. Neuroscience involves bits and pieces of many different areas of science, from biology and medicine to math and computer science.

Neuroscience is all about being well connected!

1970s   1980s   1995

Brain scans made it

possible to look into the brain without smashing open the skull. This was great news for doctors (and for patients!) as it made detecting and treating illnesses such as brain tumors much easier. Scientists also began using brain scanners to see which parts of the healthy brain are most active when people do all kinds of tasks, from reading books to seeing someone smile.

Mirror neurons, which might

enable us to understand each other's behavior and feelings, are among many exciting discoveries made in brain science. But lots of big questions remain, such as what sleep is for, how genes program the brain, how the brain changes through life, and how brain changes cause mental illness.

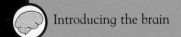

Why have a BRAIN?

You might *think* you can't survive without a brain, but MANY ANIMALS FARE PERFECTLY WELL WITHOUT ONE, and no one has found so much as a nerve, let alone a brain, in a plant or a micoorganism. So what is the point of brains? And why are human brains so huge that they use up one-fifth of our body's energy?

These have no brains

YUM YUM

Couch potato

????

PLANTS

While animals tend to lead active lives, moving around and exploring the world, plants spend their lives rooted to one spot. As a result, they don't need sophisticated sense organs or rapid reactions, so plants have no nervous system. And because they have no nervous system, they have no brain. Even so, plants can sense and respond to things. They can detect light and grow toward it, for instance, though their movement is usually so slow that we barely notice it.

Some sea animals spend their lives rooted to one spot, a bit like plants, and so have no need for a brain. A sea anemone is a brainless animal that lives stuck to a rock, waving its sticky tentacles to catch food particles drifting by in the water. Although it has no brain, a simple network of nerves coordinates its movements and enables it to scrunch up into a ball if anything disturbs it.

NO HEAD, NO BRAIN

Starfish, sea urchins, jellyfish, and other headless animals don't think anything because they have no brains at all. They do not have a front end or a left or a right side. When they move, left is just as good as right or backward—it makes no difference to their body direction. They have nerves, but like those of sea anemones, the nerves form a simple network spread throughout their bodies— nowhere are they bunched into a brainlike bulge.

Beginnings of brains

Animals with heads

Perhaps 1 billion years ago, wormlike animals began moving purposefully, with one part of their body—their front end, or head—leading the way. As they evolved and became better explorers, their eyes and other sense organs clustered on the head, because it was good to get sensations (food, danger, light, saltiness) as early as possible. It was convenient to have a bundle of nerves there, in the head, to analyze all the sense information that was pouring in. That bundle became a brain and the worms evolved into every animal with a front end alive today.

Which brain is in charge?

Octopuses are surprisingly smart, but they don't have a single, large brain. They do have a main brain, but two-thirds of their brain cells are spread out into their tentacles, making, in a way, a total of nine brains. With its own mini-brain, each of the octopus's arms works fairly independently, without having to report back to the main brain. So the octopus doesn't get direct feedback from its arms and cannot "feel" where they are—that's the arm's job. The only way an octopus can be completely aware of what its arms are doing is actually to look at them.

These animals have brains

A word on the wise

Then do you know what she said to me?

Unbelievable!

An owl has a big brain by bird standards, but this does not make it wise. The largest parts of its brain are those used for processing vision and hearing from its excellent eyes and ears, and for the precise movements of flying. It doesn't learn very much. Its brain usually acts automatically by instinct, following preprogrammed patterns of preening, sleeping, and feeding its chicks when they beg for food.

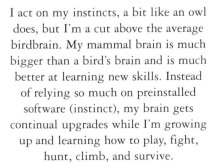

I act on my instincts, a bit like an owl does, but I'm a cut above the average birdbrain. My mammal brain is much bigger than a bird's brain and is much better at learning new skills. Instead of relying so much on preinstalled software (instinct), my brain gets continual upgrades while I'm growing up and learning how to play, fight, hunt, climb, and survive.

BIG-BRAINED GOSSIPS

Humans brains are six times larger than those of similar-sized mammals. Why so big? Like other primates (monkeys, apes, and relatives), we live in social groups, and it pays to get along socially. Gelada baboons have the biggest social groups in nature and spend 40 percent of their lives grooming one another, nurturing their social bonds. Like humans, they have a huge frontal lobe—the thinking part of the brain. Perhaps humans have big brains because it takes brainpower to keep track of relationships with many other intelligent, unpredictable beings. Some experts think human gossiping evolved from grooming. Gossipers, like groomers, bond with one another, but they also get useful information about other people.

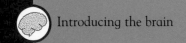

Brain *bits*

Push your fists tightly together—that's how big your brain is. And just like a pair of fists, your brain is divided into two equal halves and has a bumpy, folded surface. The surface is the part of the brain that makes humans smart.

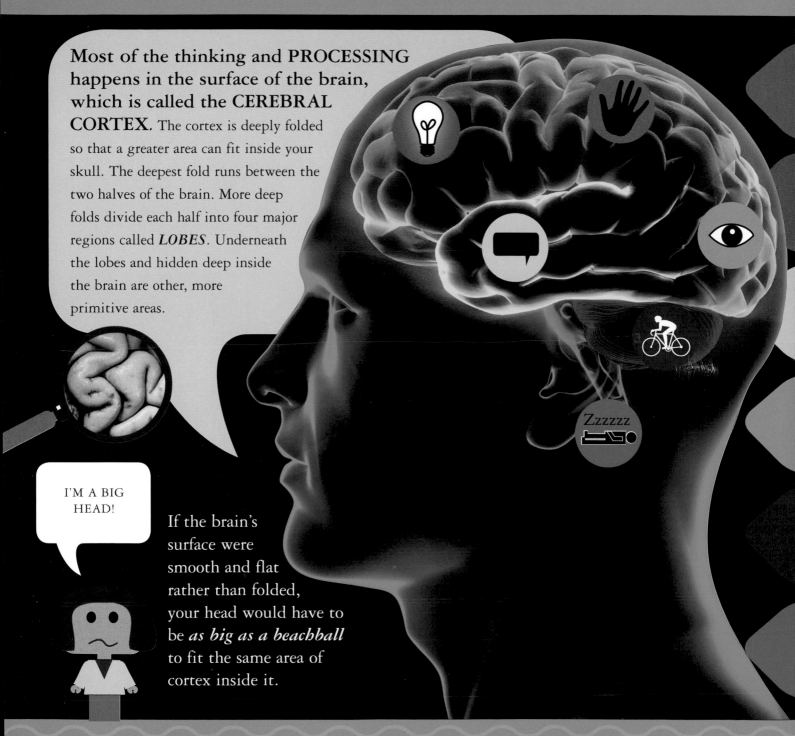

Most of the thinking and PROCESSING happens in the surface of the brain, which is called the CEREBRAL CORTEX. The cortex is deeply folded so that a greater area can fit inside your skull. The deepest fold runs between the two halves of the brain. More deep folds divide each half into four major regions called *LOBES*. Underneath the lobes and hidden deep inside the brain are other, more primitive areas.

I'M A BIG HEAD!

If the brain's surface were smooth and flat rather than folded, your head would have to be *as big as a beachball* to fit the same area of cortex inside it.

Question: What percentage of *the brain* is water?

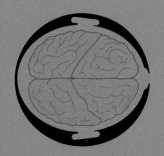

Two brains in one

The main part of your brain is split into two halves or **CEREBRAL HEMISPHERES**. These are a mirror image of each other, giving you (in some respects) two brains in one. This is a handy arrangement because if one side gets damaged, the other side may be able to take over (though not always). It's a little like having two ears and two eyes—you've got a spare. The left hemisphere controls the right side of your body and sees the right side of your visual field, while the right hemisphere takes care of the left side.

FRONTAL lobe (front lobe)

Much of your thinking happens in this lobe. You use it for PLANNING, REASONING, figuring out people's thoughts, and hiding your own.

PARIETAL lobe (top lobe)

Among other jobs, this lobe processes INFORMATION coming from *senses* such as TOUCH, TASTE, AND PAIN.

TEMPORAL lobe (side lobe)

The temporal lobe plays a very important role in hearing, SPEECH, and in laying down long-term *memories*.

OCCIPITAL lobe (back lobe)

This part of the brain is where *information* from your eyes is processed so your brain can build an inner IMAGE of the world.

CEREBELLUM Tucked under the back of the two hemispheres is a single, separate structure, the CEREBELLUM. It COORDINATES your muscles so they all work in perfect time, like a conductor directing the musicians in an orchestra.

BRAIN stem Nerves from your body join the brain at its base in a structure called the BRAIN STEM. The brain stem controls *vital functions* that keep you alive, such as HEARTBEAT and BREATHING.

BRAIN SIZE

Human

Chimp

Monkey

Rat

It's not the size of a brain that makes it smart—it's the area of the cortex. Human brains are so big and folded they have **four times** as much **cortical area** as chimpanzees, our closest relatives. If the cortex of your brain were unfolded and laid out flat, it would be about the same area as four pages of this book.

LIMBIC SYSTEM

Deep inside the brain is a complicated set of structures that look very different from the folded cortex. Called the "limbic system," these parts of the brain generate powerful, instinctive emotions like fear and excitement. The human limbic system is much like that of other animals, and some scientists see it as a very ancient part of the brain where primitive "animal urges" come from.

BLOOD SUPPLY

The brain is a *very* hungry organ. It takes up only 2% of your weight but it uses **20% OF YOUR ENERGY**. (Don't panic—it runs on only 20 watts, about the same as a low-energy bulb.) To keep the brain fueled with the sugar and oxygen it needs, the heart pumps 20% of the body's blood supply to it.

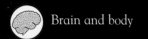

Brain *cells*

To find out what your brain is really made of, we need to zoom in with a microscope until we can see individual cells. The cells in the brain are called nerve cells or NEURONS. They are connected to each other in a complicated maze and make your brain work somewhat like a computer.

A computer chip is made up of a few million transistors, each with three or four connections.

PROCESSING POWER

The human brain has 100 billion neurons, each with up to 10,000 connections. That gives the human brain a staggering 500,000 times as many connections as the most advanced computer chip. On top of that, the human brain can effortlessly do what computer scientists call "massively parallel processing," which is like running thousands of computers together to work on the same task.

What is more powerful...

Supercomputer

The brain can *rewire* itself, **pruning** unused connections

NEURONS

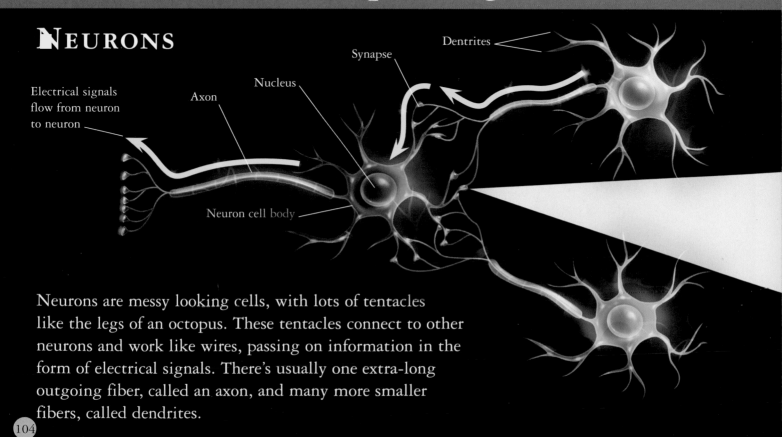

Electrical signals flow from neuron to neuron

Axon

Nucleus

Synapse

Dentrites

Neuron cell body

Neurons are messy looking cells, with lots of tentacles like the legs of an octopus. These tentacles connect to other neurons and work like wires, passing on information in the form of electrical signals. There's usually one extra-long outgoing fiber, called an axon, and many more smaller fibers, called dendrites.

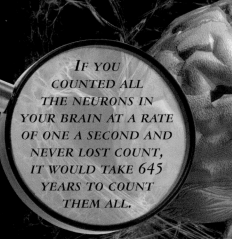

IF YOU COUNTED ALL THE NEURONS IN YOUR BRAIN AT A RATE OF ONE A SECOND AND NEVER LOST COUNT, IT WOULD TAKE 645 YEARS TO COUNT THEM ALL.

It's all gray and white

If you cut a slice through a dead brain, you'd see that the outer part is a yellowy gray color, while the inner area is paler. These two areas are known as gray and white matter. White matter is made up of axons bundled together like electric cables. These run across the brain connecting different areas together. Gray matter consists of neuron cell bodies and billions of dendrites, and this is where most of the heavy computation takes place.

supercomputer or mouse?

The world's **top** *supercomputer* is only about as powerful as HALF A MOUSE BRAIN yet it takes up more than *a million times* as much space.

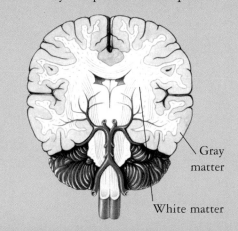

Gray matter

White matter

and **building** new ones as it LEARNS and *adapts*.

Electricity in the body

Neurons carry electrical signals, but they work in a different way from electric wires. When a neuron is resting, it pumps positively charged sodium atoms (from sodium chloride—ordinary salt) to the outside of the cell, where they build up like water behind a dam. When an electrical signal arrives, the floodgates open and the charged atoms rush back inside the cell, causing an electrical charge to shoot along the axon at speeds of up to 370 mph (430 km/h).

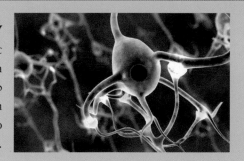

Neurons connect to each other at junctions called **SYNAPSES**. The electrical signal can't flow across the synapse because there's a tiny gap. Instead, the synapse releases special chemicals, called NEUROTRANSMITTERS, that travel across the gap and trigger an electrical impulse in the next neuron.

Neurotransmitters

SYNAPSE

Neurons and synapses come in many different shapes, sizes, and varieties, making the brain all the more complicated and its computing powers even greater.

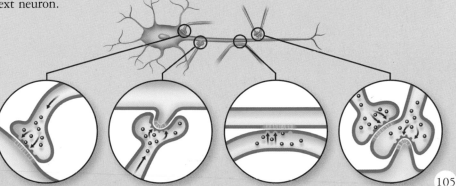

Mapping the *mind*

For centuries, people have been trying to find out what the different parts of the brain are for. Does each part *specialize* in a particular task, like a blade on a Swiss Army knife, or do the parts work together, their cells TEAMING UP in ever-changing **networks**? It's a puzzle that science has yet to solve.

A BUMP ON THE HEAD

A German doctor named Franz Joseph Gall announced in the 1790s that he could tell a person's character by feeling their skull for bumps. Gall's theory was that the parts of the brain we use most grow larger, like muscles, making the head bulge in certain places. His system was called PHRENOLOGY and it became all the rage, though there wasn't a shred of evidence that it worked. He divided the brain into "organs," which he gave long names such as "amativeness" (jargon for being loving). Gall believed he could say whether a person was a loving parent, a devout Christian, or a calculating murderer just by feeling their head.

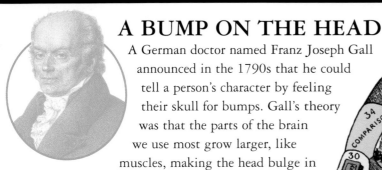

The cartoonist who drew this picture of a phrenologist at work in 1826 thought phrenology was an absurd craze.

1. Amativeness	7. Secretiveness	13. Benevolence	19. Ideality
2. Parental love	8. Acquisitiveness	14. Veneration	20. Mirthfulness
3. Inhabitiveness	9. Constructiveness	15. Firmness	21. Imitation
4. Friendship	10. Self-esteem	16. Conscientiousness	22. Individuality
5. Combativeness	11. Approbativeness	17. Hope	23. Form
6. Destructiveness	12. Cautiousness	18. Spirituality	24. Size

25. Weight		
26. Color		
27. Locality		

28. Calculation
29. Order
30. Eventuality
31. Time
32. Tune
33. Language
34. Comparison
35. Causality
36. Alimentiveness
37. Concentrativeness

A. Union for life
B. Sublimity
C. Human nature
D. Agreeableness
E. Vitativeness

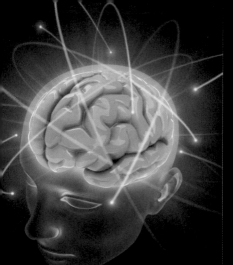

Mapping the mind

"A PIECE OF THOROUGH QUACKERY FROM BEGINNING TO END."

Scottish anatomist John Gordon's opinion of phrenology, printed in the Edinburgh Review, 1815

THE MAN INSIDE YOUR HEAD

A large part of the brain's surface forms a kind of map of the body. American brain scientist Wilder Penfield (1891–1976) made this discovery in the 1950s. While treating patients with epilepsy, he used an electric needle to test a section of their brain's surface called the sensory cortex (which monitors sensations). As Penfield moved the needle around, the patients felt things in different parts of their bodies. When Penfield drew his findings onto a plan, he discovered the brain has much more space for some body parts, such as the lips and tongue.

MODERN MAPS

When brain scanners were invented in the 1970s, they began to reveal that different parts of the brain do indeed have different functions, so there was a grain of truth in phrenology after all. Modern scanners used by brain scientists detect where brain cells are using up energy most quickly and show these areas of activity as colored highlights on an image. Although scanning has shown that some actions, such as speaking, are controlled by specific areas, it has also revealed the brain to be highly interconnected, with memory, perception, pain, and many other functions involving huge areas of the brain firing in complex circuits.

The brain scans above show parts of the back of the brain lighting up as a person spots a happy face.

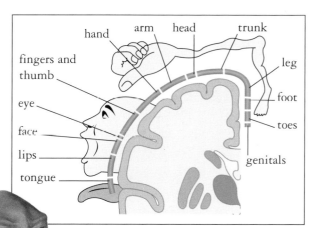

The sensitive bits

This hideous creature is what you look like according to your own sensory cortex—that part of your brain that receives touch information. It is a 3-D version of the mental body map discovered by Penfield. The sensory cortex doesn't have much space for the trunk and arms because it doesn't care much about them. It is more interested in touch information from sensitive parts, such as the fingers and lips, so they are huge in its "mind's eye."

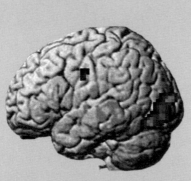

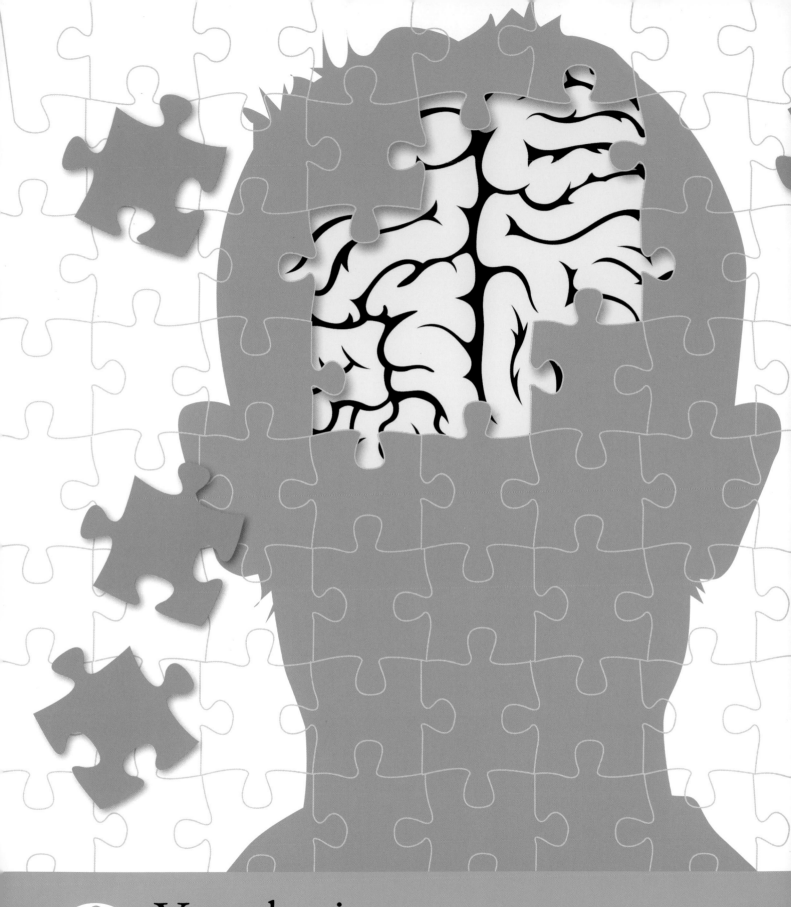

 Your brain:
Brain and **BODY**

Your brain consists of an *intricate maze* of electrical circuits, but those circuits aren't confined to your head. Your brain is WIRED INTO EVERY PART of your body through a vast network of neurons that reaches down your spine and extends out to the tip of *every finger and toe*. These neurons monitor the world around you and send the data back to the brain to give you *senses*. And they direct your body's every action, governing your movements and coordinating the daily cycle of activity and sleep.

Nervous *system*

The brain doesn't work alone—it is part of an extensive *network* of neurons called the nervous system, which runs throughout the body, directing and coordinating every activity. The nervous system performs two jobs: it takes information in through the SENSES and, after the *brain* has processed the information, it sends out new signals telling the body how to react.

The nervous system's control center is called the **CENTRAL NERVOUS SYSTEM** and consists of both the brain and the spinal cord—a thick bundle of nerves that runs down the spine. From the spinal cord, nerves reach out to every part of the body, forming the **PERIPHERAL NERVOUS SYSTEM**.

Much of the peripheral nervous system is under your **control**, but some of it is **involuntary**. When you're scared, the involuntary branch of your nervous system sends the message to your heart to speed up. Vital functions like your heartbeat and breathing are controlled by the brain stem—the part of the brain joined to the spinal cord. The brain stem can keep your body *alive* even if the rest of the brain is dead.

> I WISH I COULD SEE WHERE I'M GOING!

ALMOST BRAINLESS
An American chicken named Mike survived for 18 months after a botched attempt to decapitate him left part of his brain stem behind.

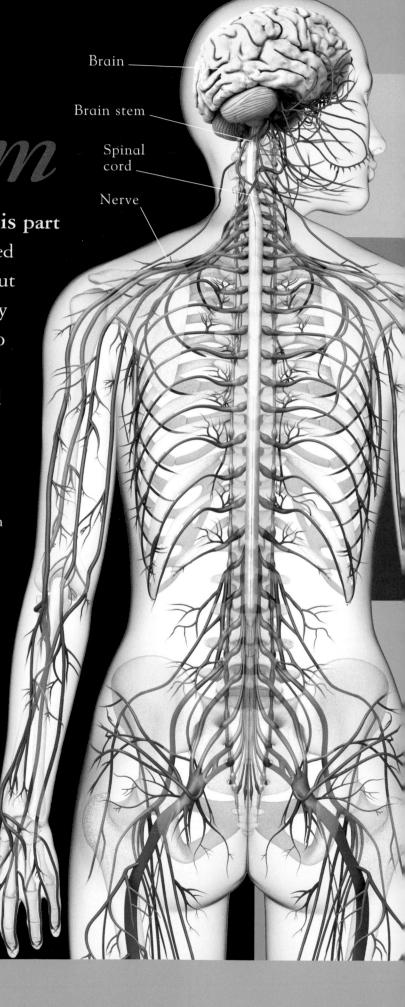

Brain

Brain stem

Spinal cord

Nerve

THE SENSES

Vision

When the neurons in our eyes are struck by light rays, they send signals to the brain, creating the sense of vision. Vision is our most important sense, with a huge area of the brain dedicated to processing what we see.

Hearing

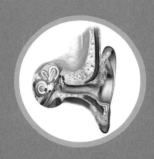

Our ears detect air vibrations that we call sound. Sound waves are funneled into the ear and are transmitted across the middle ear by a tiny drum and series of levers. These vibrations set off nerve cells in the inner ear that send signals to the brain.

Smell

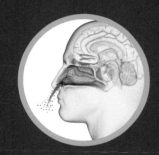

The sense of smell enables you to detect odor molecules. The lining of the nose and passages behind it are full of sensors that can detect between 4,000 and 10,000 different smells. Your brain puts the signals together to tell you what the smelly object is.

Taste

The tongue can detect only five tastes: sweet, sour, salty, bitter, and savory. Combining these with smell signals helps the brain tell the difference between cherries, cheese, and toast.

Touch

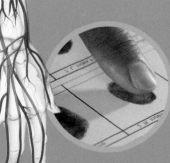

The skin is full of sensors that respond to different touch sensations, such as firm pressure, stroking, light touch, and vibration. Your sense of touch is so good that you can figure out what objects are with your eyes closed.

SPECIAL SENSES

In addition to the five main senses, humans have a number of other senses that play an important role in how our bodies work and how we interact with the environment around us. Many of them work without us even being aware of them.

GRAVITY affects tiny sensors in your ears called otoliths, which tell your brain which way is up and which is down, helping you balance.

MOTION is also picked up by sensors in your ears. You can confuse these sensors by spinning around very fast until you feel dizzy.

POSTURE is detected in your muscles and joints by stretch receptors that tell your brain the position and movement of the parts of your body.

HEAT sensors respond to a rise in temperature, whether it's caused by the Sun's rays, a hot cup of coffee, or a fever brought on by an illness.

COLD receptors react to low temperatures, causing goosebumps on your skin as body hairs rise to try and keep you warm.

PAIN is a special sense that warns you about things that might cause injury or affect your health. Itching and tickling are related to pain.

DIRECTION is a sense humans probably don't have, but many animals do because they can tune into Earth's magnetic field to find their way.

CALLS OF NATURE involve stretch sensors in organs like your bladder and bowels that tell you when they're full and ready to let go.

Vision

The light-sensitive retina inside the eye is wired to the back of the brain via a cable called the optic nerve.

Visual cortex

Optic nerve

Retina

Eye

The sense of vision is the *main* way in which your brain takes in INFORMATION about the world. Your eyes are extensions of your brain, *small periscopes* that poke through holes in your skull to let **light** onto the brain's surface. Lining the back of each eye are *125 million* light-sensing neurons forming a layer called a RETINA.

LIVING CAMERAS

An eye works much like a camera, but its lenses are made of clear jelly or fluid rather than glass. Like a camera, it uses curved lenses to focus captured light rays onto a light-sensitive film (the retina) on its back surface, forming an upside-down image. Cameras adjust their focus by moving the lens in and out, but eyes use muscles to stretch an adjustable lens.

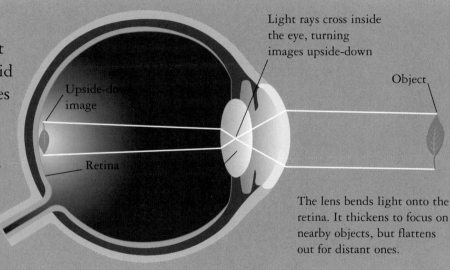

Light rays cross inside the eye, turning images upside-down

Upside-down image

Retina

Object

The lens bends light onto the retina. It thickens to focus on nearby objects, but flattens out for distant ones.

See *inside* your eyes!

This trick lets you see your own retina. You need a dim flashlight with the bulb exposed and a piece of black paper. In a dark room, hold the paper so it fills your field of vision. Hold the flashlight ½ in (1 cm) in front of and below your eyes (taking care not to poke an eye) and stare at the paper. A treelike shape will appear—the shadow of your retina's blood vessels.

Rods and cones

The photoreceptors on the surface of the retina come in two main types: rods and cones. These have different strengths and weaknesses. Cones can see color and fine details, but they need bright light to work. Rods work in very dim light, but they see in black-and-white and pick up less detail. When you try to see in the dark, only your rods are working and so the world becomes colorless. Switch on a light and your cones switch on, too, flooding the image in your mind with color and detail.

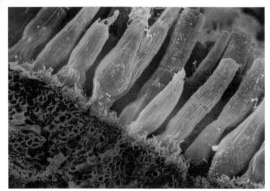

The retina contains around 20 times more rods (shown in artificially colored blue) than cones (blue-green).

The eye's spotlight

When you look directly at something, such as this word, you see it much more clearly and sharply than things elsewhere in your field of vision (your peripheral vision). This is because you use a special part of the retina—the fovea—to see objects in the middle of your field of vision. The fovea is packed with cones and has few rods, giving better color and detail than any other part of the eye.

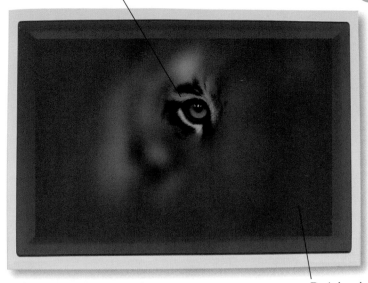

Center of visual field

Peripheral vision

The fovea isn't very good in the dark. To see faint stars at night, look away from them slightly so you see them with your peripheral vision, where there are more rods.

COLOR *on the edge*

Your peripheral vision is lousy at seeing color. Ask a friend to move a colored pencil slowly from behind you into your peripheral vision while you stare straight ahead. Tell them to stop moving it as soon as you see it. What color is it? It will look black at first, but move it a little farther and its color will appear.

THE VISUAL PATHWAY

The light your eyes capture is converted into electrical signals that pass to the back of the brain to be processed in the visual cortex. The rods and cones that pick up light from the left side of the visual field are wired into the right half of the brain, and vice versa. People with brain damage to one half of the brain may not see the whole visual field—so may eat all the food on the left of the plate, but not see any on the right.

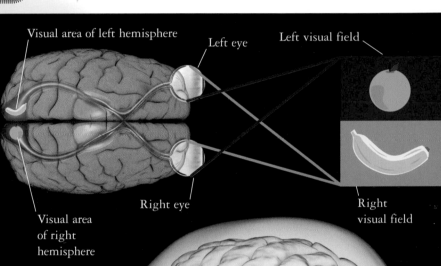

Visual area of left hemisphere

Left eye

Left visual field

Visual area of right hemisphere

Right eye

Right visual field

EYES IN THE BACK OF THE HEAD

During World War II, aptly named British doctor Henry Head discovered that soldiers with shrapnel injuries in the back of the brain had strange blind spots in their field of vision. Henry Head had discovered the visual cortex—the part of the brain that processes images. As signals from the eyes pass through the visual cortex, different strips of cortex detect different pieces of information, such as edges, colors, motion, angles, and simple shapes. Bit by bit, the image is broken down into a set of clues that are forwarded to other parts of the brain so that objects can be recognized.

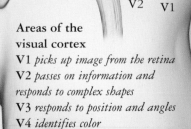

V3
V4
V2
V1

Areas of the visual cortex
V1 *picks up image from the retina*
V2 *passes on information and responds to complex shapes*
V3 *responds to position and angles*
V4 *identifies color*

113

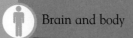

PERCEPTION

The image of the world that we see in our mind's eye is not simply a snapshot like a photograph. The complex patterns of light and shade captured by our eyes are processed by the brain to give the images *meaning*. Perception involves not just vision but also memory, experience, expectations, and even imagination.

WHAT ARE *THESE*..?

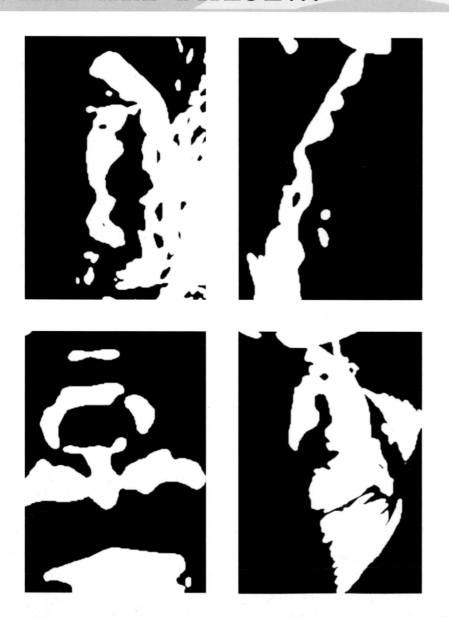

If you're stuck, turn the page upside down. You can *see* the images whichever way up they are, but you don't *recognize* them until they're the right way up. Human brains are programmed to recognize faces—provided they are upright—from the sketchiest of details. We can even perceive the sex, race, age, and mood of the people in the images from nothing more than a few white squiggles. This skill depends on a part of the brain's temporal (side) lobe called the fusiform face area. The visual cortex sends signals here so we can quickly identify people and assess their mood. Damage to the fusiform face area causes a rare condition called prosopagnosia, in which a sufferer can't even recognize family members.

A human face on Mars..?   ... The "face" revealed.

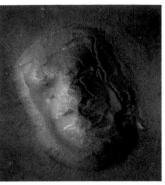

Face on Mars

Our brains are *so* good at spotting **faces** that we can see some that aren't even there. In 1976, the Viking spacecraft took a photograph of what appeared to be a huge sculpture of a human face on Mars. This led to outlandish theories about *alien visitors* or ancient Martian civilizations. Around 22 years later, the Mars Orbiter sent back a new image of the face showing it was just a TRICK of the light.

Mona Lisa by Leonardo da Vinci

The *Mona Lisa's* secret?

Is the *Mona Lisa* smiling? This enigma has baffled people for years, but one scientist thinks she may have solved the riddle. According to Professor Margaret Livingstone of Harvard University, the *smile* only appears when you look away from her face. Livingstone says that when we look away, we see the face with our peripheral vision, picking up shadows and patterns that suggest she's smiling. But when we look *directly* at her mouth, we use our **fovea**, the sharpest point of vision, which picks up finer details (such as the flat mouth) that suggest she isn't smiling.

LOOK at this painting of the countryside in summer and, before you read on, think of four or five adjectives that describe it.

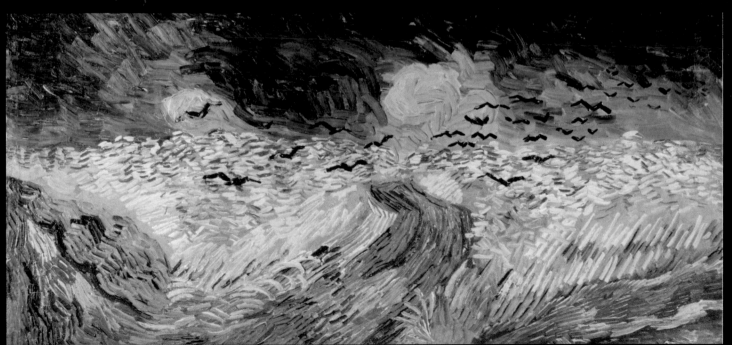

Wheatfield with Crows by Vincent van Gogh, 1890

You might have thought of words like sunny, tranquil, or natural. Now take another look, bearing in mind that the artist van Gogh painted this scene just before he killed himself as a result of depression. Does the scene now appear gloomy, dark, or disturbing? What we see depends on our expectations. Knowing that van Gogh was suicidally unhappy when he painted the field gives the image an emotional meaning and focuses our attention on its DARKER elements: the stormy sky, the black crows fleeing, and the lonely emptiness of the field.

STOP! What are you *really*

An Unexpected Visitor by Ilya Repin, 1884.

SEEING WITHOUT SEEING

It takes only a fraction of a second for the brain to process an image from your eyes and make you consciously aware of what you're looking at. But this isn't always fast enough. What if a rock is hurtling toward you or a snake lunges up from the grass? In dangerous situations where rapid reactions are vital, the brain relies on a processing shortcut known as the **low road** that causes the body to react before you're conscious of what you've seen. On the way to the **visual cortex**, which creates conscious vision, signals from your eyes pass through the **thalamus**, which recognizes simple threats such as snakelike objects and sends a signal to the **amygdala**, triggering a "fight or flight" reaction.

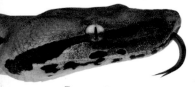

LOOKING at?

By tracking eye movements when people view images such as the painting on the left, scientists have found out how the brain takes in a scene. We don't simply take in a snapshot in one glance, as you might think. Instead, our eyes dart around quickly and instinctively, gathering information as the FOVEA (the high-resolution part of the retina) rests briefly on one detail after another. The brain directs the eyes to parts of the scene it considers significant—especially faces—and disregards much of the rest. Why faces? To humans, faces are a vital source of information about people, their relationships, and their intentions.

Above: Eye-tracking studies record eye movements, revealing which parts of the painting viewers look at in the first few seconds.

Below: In addition to focusing on faces, we follow each person's gaze to see what they are looking at (and therefore thinking about).

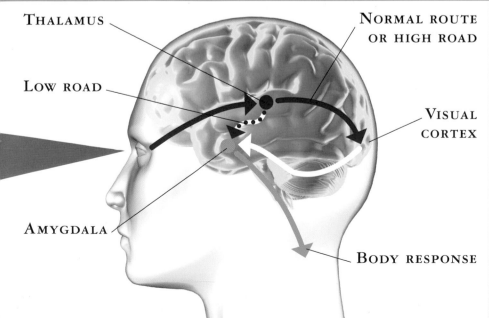

THALAMUS

NORMAL ROUTE OR HIGH ROAD

LOW ROAD

VISUAL CORTEX

AMYGDALA

BODY RESPONSE

OUT OF SIGHT

Watch the gaps

You're blind for about 90 minutes every day with your eyes open. When your eyes dart from place to place (a saccade), your brain temporarily ignores signals from the retina, otherwise your vision would be blurry. You don't notice because your brain fills in the gaps, but you can prove the blindness happens by looking alternately at your left and right eyes in a mirror. You won't be able to spot the motion—it's impossible.

Stopping time

Have you ever glanced at a clock and thought the second hand was frozen, only for it to start moving after what seems like more than a second? This is called the "stopped clock illusion" and is caused by your eyes saccading to the clock and your brain filling in the gap by "backdating" the image of the clock, making that second seem longer than a second.

Constant movement

In addition to darting around, our eyes vibrate back and forth by a tiny amount up to 40 times a second. These movements, called microsaccades, are essential as the retina responds only to *changes* in light. If the image is frozen by floating a tiny viewing device on a person's eye, the image fades in seconds. The blood vessels on the retina are invisible to us because they move with the eyeball.

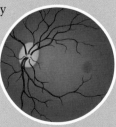

Blood vessels in the retina

SEEING IN 3-D

To catch a ball, jump over a fence, or pour a cup of coffee, it helps if you can SEE in 3-D. Three-dimensional vision allows us to **judge** DEPTH and d i s t a n c e, telling our brains *exactly* how far we need to move to pick something up or avoid collisions.

SEEING DOUBLE

Hold your finger in front of your face and close your right eye. Now close your left. Your finger appears to have moved! We have two eyes, so we see the world twice, at two different angles. The nearer an object is, the more different it looks to the right and left eye. The brain uses these differences to work out where an object is and create an awareness of 3-D. 3-D movies use a similar idea: each scene is filmed by a pair of cameras set apart like eyes. Viewers wear special glasses so that each eye sees only what it is meant to.

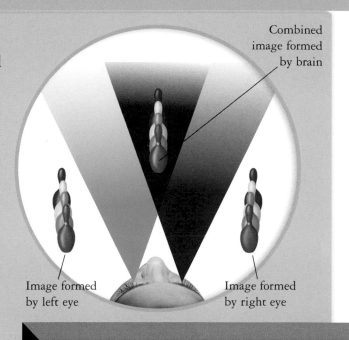

Combined image formed by brain

Image formed by left eye

Image formed by right eye

One giant leap—off the page!

You don't need special glasses to see in 3-D: this stereogram allows you to see the Moon landing in 3-D simply by crossing your eyes (which may take a bit of practice). First, hold the pair of pictures about half an arm's length away from your eyes. Stare into the middle and cross your eyes so you see three images. They will be blurred at first, but hold your attention on the central blurry image. Slowly, it will come into focus, revealing the scene in dramatic 3-D.

Hidden images

Autostereograms contain hidden 3-D images. Hold the page close and relax your eyes to look through the image so it's blurred. The repeating patterns of dots seen by your right and left eyes will slide around as your eyes change their focus. Be patient, and the repeating patterns might overlap so they match, fooling your brain into thinking the image is in focus. When that happens, the hidden object will slowly appear.

3-D CLUES

Stereo vision isn't the only source of 3-D information our brains use. There are many other clues as well. Artists exploit these clues to give depth to scenes or to trick your brain into seeing the impossible.

1 When we see parallel lines that converge (draw together), our brains assume the lines are **receding** (going into the distance).

2 **Shadows** reveal the shape of 3-D objects.

3 Details **fade with distance**—so separate leaves become a blur of green.

4 If one object is **behind** another, it must be farther away...

5 ... And if there are several objects we know to be the same size (such as people) then the smaller ones must be **farther away.**

Motion clues

A spitting cobra swings its head left to right to pinpoint its prey

Even with one eye closed you can judge depth by moving your head from side to side, because distant objects seem to keep still while nearby objects move more.

Distance fog

Computer games use fog to create distance

Outdoors, distant objects such as hills usually appear hazy and bluish, with less color than nearby objects. This is because dust in the air filters out much of the light.

Depth of field

The pig appears 3-D next to the blurred car

When you focus on a nearby object, things in the background are blurred. Photographers blur objects in the background to draw attention to those in front, making them stand out.

Ice see it now

It looks like a glacier has split apart, sending chunks of ice tumbling a long way down—but this clever illusion is simply a chalk drawing on the sidewalk. The artist has used shading, converging lines, and other tricks of perspective (angle of view) to make a two-dimensional image trick our brains into seeing a three-dimensional world that isn't there.

This amazing 3-D street art was created by artist Edgar Mueller.

Illusions

In order to *make sense* of the images captured by our eyes, the brain must extract clues from the images and then interpret the clues correctly by using rules of thumb about the world. Illusions reveal what those rules of thumb are by breaking the rules and making us see *impossible or nonsensical images*.

Which is bigger?

Believe it not, the yellow lines on the left are exactly the same size, and so are the tigers on the right. So why does one look bigger? When we see straight lines that taper together, it's usually because they're getting farther away. Our brains use this rule of thumb to perceive distance. We see the third tiger as farther away, so we also see it as bigger.

Which is darker?

Does square A look darker than B? They're exactly the same, as the smaller picture proves. The main rule of thumb being tricked is that objects in the shade reflect less light. Our brains compensate for this effect by telling us to perceive B as brighter than it really is. For the same reason, a snowball always looks white to us—even when we take it indoors and it actually becomes gray.

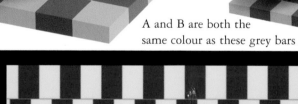

Rules of thumb our brains use:
1. Objects in shadow reflect less light.
2. Shadows usually have soft edges.

A and B are both the same colour as these grey bars

Slanted or straight? The horizontal lines are absolutely straight but appear to slope. This illusion works by exploiting a flaw in the way neurons in the brain's visual cortex process patterns of bright and dark shade. For complicated reasons, we see the gray lines between the squares as sloping in our peripheral vision, making the whole pattern look crooked.

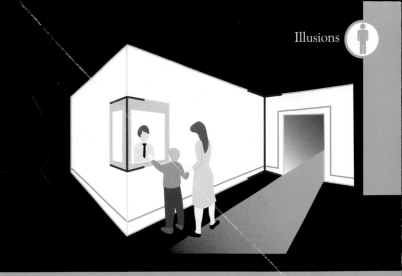

Which line is longer?

Neither—they're just the same. The best explanation for this famous illusion is that the arrows trigger our brain's 3-D perception system. The top line resembles a nearby edge, whereas the bottom line resembles a more distant edge, which we therefore perceive as wider since it's farther away. The picture on the right shows the same red lines superimposed on walls, making the 3-D effect even more powerful.

WHICH LEANING TOWER LEANS THE MOST?

Is one of these towers leaning more than the other? No, it's the same photo and they're leaning at the same angle. Why the apparent difference then? In the real world, two parallel towers would appear to *converge* (point together) if you stood at the bottom looking up, just as parallel railroad lines converge as they run into the distance. But here the towers don't converge— they remain parallel. So our brains assume they must be *diverging*, and we see one as leaning farther than the other.

Rule of thumb our brains make:
1. Lines that are truly parallel always appear to converge as they run into the distance.
2. Lines that run into the distance but are parallel on the retina must be diverging.

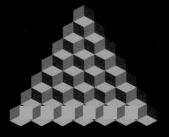

If you stare for long enough at the image on the left, it will suddenly change. The cubes will flip upside down, and the corners that stick out will suddenly point inward. The illusion happens because there are two ways your brain can process the picture to create a 3-D mental image. These two interpretations can't coexist in your brain at the same time, so your perception flips between one and the other.

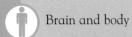

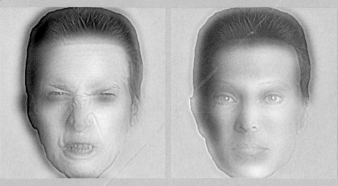

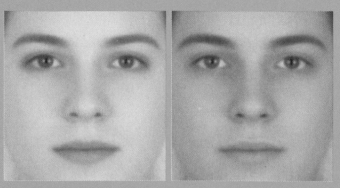

Who's angriest? Now prop the book up, walk 10 ft (3 m) away and look again. Mr. Angry becomes Mr. Nice, and vice versa! Each image is a hybrid of two faces, one made of fine details and another made of coarser shadings. Your eyes pick up the fine details only when close. The hidden blurry face emerges when the fine details are too far away to see.

Which is male and female? We see the right face as male and the left as female, but they're actually both the same photograph of a man. The contrast between the eyes, mouth and skin has been exaggerated in the left image, producing a darker mouth and eyes. Makeup creates the same high contrast, so we see the left face as female.

Do the blue spots move around when you read these words?

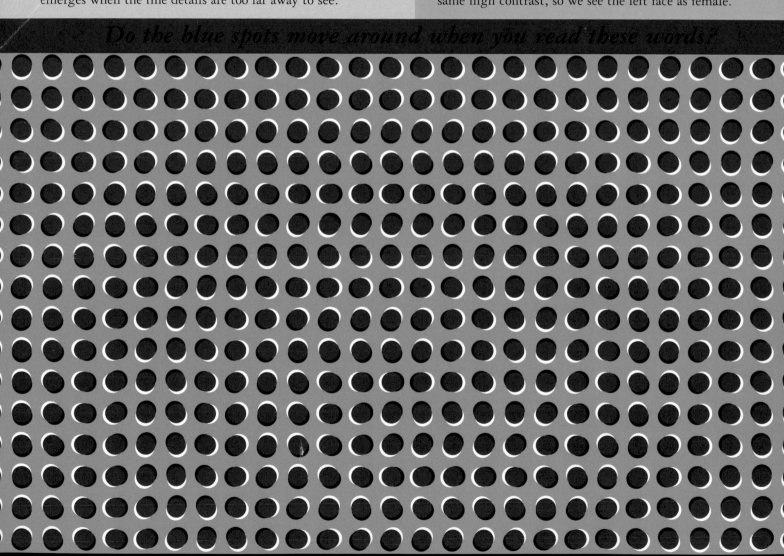

The blue dots appear to move in the corner of your eye but freeze when you look straight at one. The motion happens only in your "peripheral vision"—the parts of your field of vision that you aren't looking at directly—and only while your eyes are moving. It's caused by the pattern of repeating bright and dark bands. Bright areas are processed slightly faster by the brain's visual system. As a result, when your eyes move, the bright areas are perceived as having "gotten there first." The repetitive pattern also makes it hard for your brain lock on to the image and prevent the imaginary motion.

Without turning the page

Without turning the page upside down, see if you can figure out the difference between the *Mona Lisa* here and the one on page 115. Now turn the page around. Surprised? The facial recognition area in the brain is tuned to detect upright faces only and cannot process upside-down faces, so we don't spot the flaws in this image. However, the parts of the brain that recognize eyes and mouths still work and perceive those parts of the image as normal. As a result, we don't see what a weird image this truly is until we turn it around.

Seeing double?

This illusion can make your head spin. When we look at faces our brains measure the shape of the triangle made by the eyes and mouth. This image confuses the facial recognition system by giving it two conflicting triangles. Our attention flickers from one to the other as the brain tries to lock on to the image, making us feel slightly dizzy.

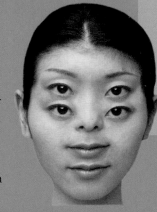

ARE THE PEOPLE BELOW REAL PEOPLE OR TINY MODELS?

No it's not a tiny model, it's a real station full of real people. So why do they look so small? The photographer has used a special lens that focuses only on objects within a narrow range of distances, blurring everything else and creating what photographers call "narrow depth of field." Normally, we only experience a narrow depth of field when looking at small objects close to our eyes (hold a finger up to your eyes and the background will look blurred). Our brains interpret narrow depth of field as a clue that objects are miniature, so we perceive the people as tiny models.

Body *ILLUSIONS*

BODY SENSES

The amazing sense that makes you aware of your body and its movements is called PROPRIOCEPTION. Special sensors inside different parts of your body tell your brain what every part of your body is up to without you having to think about it.

Joints

Sensors in every joint tell the brain exactly where all our bones are. This helps the brain to decide which movements are safe to make. If we don't pay attention to our sensors, we may get hurt!

Muscles

Whenever we move, our muscles stretch and contract, triggering stretch sensors buried deep inside them. These send signals to the brain, too.

The inner ear

Tiny gravity sensors in the inner ear help us to know which way is up or down, while tiny motion sensors inside three fluid-filled loops in the inner ear sense movement in any direction.

Cerebellum

This part of the brain is like the conductor in an orchestra. It stores learned sequences of movement and coordinates and fine-tunes messages from elsewhere in the brain to create fluid body movements.

Balance

To help us balance, our brain has to coordinate all the visual signals from our eyes, sensory information from our ears, and proprioception signals from our muscles.

AMAZE

Eye–hand coordination

1 We tend to use our eyes to guide our hands, but you can *almost* manage with proprioception alone. Test this by drawing a square with your eyes closed. As long as you keep pen on paper it's quite easy, because your brain can rely on feedback from your hand and arm muscles to sense how it's doing.

2 Now draw a house with your eyes closed. As soon as you take your hand off the page to add details, you'll find you can't put them exactly where they need to go. It's hard to put your hands precisely where they need to be unless you have visual feedback from your eyes.

3 Now try drawing the same house in a mirror. (Don't cheat—look into the mirror the whole time.) This is surprisingly difficult because the signals your brain gets from your eyes *conflict* with those from your hand, leaving your brain confused about what to do. The secret to drawing in a mirror? Close your eyes. You'll do much better!

Your external senses of touch and vision work together with a special internal *body sense* to keep your brain aware of where every bit of your body is and how it's moving. The TRICKS on this page not only show how your internal body sense works but also show you *how to fool it, too*!

YOUR FRIENDS WITH THESE MIND-BENDING TRICKS!

Cross your fingers

The Aristotle illusion is one of the oldest known body illusions. Cross your fingers, then touch your nose with both fingers at the same time. Does it feel like you have two noses? Try the same trick with a marble or a pea.

> Your brain receives sensory signals from the outside edges of both fingers. Because they don't usually rub against each other, your brain concludes that you must be touching two objects.

Hopping mad

Ask your friend to close his eyes. Tap him quickly four times on the wrist, four times on the elbow, and four times at the top of his arm. Does it feel like a small rabbit is hopping up his arm?

> Scientists aren't sure why we feel taps *all* along the arm, instead of in just three places, but it is thought that what the brain *expects* to happen overrides what it feels is taking place.

Hard to resist

❶ Ask a friend to stretch out his arm. Tell him to resist as you press down on his wrist with two fingers. He should find it easy to resist the pressure.

❷ Now ask your friend to put one foot on a low pile of books or a step and repeat the test.

❸ This time, your friend won't be able to resist the pressure and you'll find it easy to force his arm down.

Pinocchio nose

❶ Blindfold yourself and then stand behind a friend.

❷ At the same time, and with identical movements, stroke your own nose with one hand and your friend's nose with your other hand for a couple of minutes. Does your nose seem longer all of a sudden?

> Your brain receives identical sensory signals from both hands and is confused into thinking you are only touching one nose. Because of a lack of visual clues and since one arm is outstretched, it concludes your nose has grown.

Levitating arm

❶ Stand straight against a wall and push your arm against it as hard as you can for 60 seconds—the harder you push, the better the final effect!

❷ Now move away from the wall. Does your arm rise up on its own?

> You are tensing your arm muscles as you push against the wall. The muscles and brain adapt to this constant tension, so that when you stop, your muscles remain slightly tense and your arm rises. And if you *expect* your arm to rise, it will rise all the more.

> When your friend raises one foot, his brain thinks that the spine is in a vulnerable position. In order to protect the spine from damage, the brain "turns off" the messages to the arm muscles that are making it resist, and the arm lowers.

Nothing grabs your attention quite like a sudden pain. And that's exactly what it's supposed to do. Pain is a warning sign that something is wrong with your body and that you need to do something about it before you do any further damage. Ongoing pain is a reminder not to overdo things while the injury heals.

In each *square inch* of skin there are **1,300** *pain sensors*

WHERE'S THE PAIN COMING FROM?

Our skin, muscles, and internal organs are full of sensors that respond to things such as pressure, heat, and chemicals. If any of these start to damage the body, they trigger pain sensors, which send electrical signals up the spinal cord and to a part of the brain called the thalamus. The thalamus directs the signals to other parts of the brain that figure out where the pain is coming from, what it means, and how unpleasant it should feel. The brain sends messages back to the spinal cord telling your body how to react.

3 FEEL
The brain receives the signal and interprets what kind of pain it is, how strong it is, and how much damage may have been done. Armed with this knowledge, the brain then decides what to do next.

2 REACT
The spinal cord reacts almost instantly, before the pain signal reaches the brain. It sends a new signal to your leg muscles to lift your foot off the pin.

1 DETECT
If you step on a pin, pain sensors in your skin immediately send a message about the injury to your brain. Touch sensors also send signals about what's causing the pain.

Pain is a special sense that makes an alarm ring inside your brain

Natural born painkillers

One of the brain's responses to pain is to send messages to nerve cells near the injury that contain substances called endorphins. These are released into the synapses and are taken up by the neurons that are transmitting the pain signal. Endorphins block the signal and prevent it from traveling to the brain. Endorphins have a similar chemical structure to morphine, which is used as a painkiller in hospitals. Morphine is one of several natural painkillers produced in the seed heads of the opium poppy.

Pain under strain

Acute stress can have an amazing effect on pain. Soldiers injured in battle can fight on despite the pain because their bodies are pumping out a powerful combination of stress chemicals, including epinephrine and cortisol, which trigger the release of endorphins. People have even been hit by bullets and not felt a thing. The effect doesn't last, but it is often long enough for a person to reach safety.

No pain, no gain

Psychology plays an important part in how we respond to pain. Positive thinking can have as much effect as powerful painkiller drugs. Athletes can train themselves to endure pain that would have lesser mortals in bed for a week. This ability to put "mind over matter" and block out pain is what enables people to walk over hot coals or lie on a bed of nails. By "psyching themselves up" they can reduce the amount of pain they actually feel.

Sugaring the pill

Doctors have found that giving harmless sugar pills or saltwater injections to people in pain can have the same effect as giving them real painkillers. This is known as the "placebo effect." The patient's belief that they have been given a real medicine is so strong that the pain really goes away. Brain scans even show that placebos dampen down the parts of the brain that become active during pain in just the same way as real painkillers.

Rub it better

Not all pain signals go directly to the brain. Weaker signals may be filtered out by special "gatekeeper" nerve cells in the spinal cord. Gatekeeper cells are also affected by nerve fibers that transmit touch sensations. If you sprain your ankle, it's instinctive to rub the injury. Rubbing activates touch sensors, whose signals swamp the gatekeeper cells and reduce the number of pain signals they can send to the brain. That's why rubbing the injury really does make it feel better.

PAINFUL FACTS

• Chile contains a substance called capsaicin that causes a burning pain. Some people think the endorphins this pain releases are responsible for the pleasurable sensation caused by eating spicy food.

• Swearing really can help reduce the pain you feel when you hurt yourself. Scientists think that anger triggers the stress response, which releases chemicals that help lessen the pain. Just remember not to do it in front of Grandma...

@ % &
* # £ * !

• A faulty gene prevents some people from feeling any pain at all. It might sound great but feeling no pain can be lethally dangerous. Pain is good for you!

FAQ

Where is the body clock?

The main body clock is near the base of the brain, next to the nerves that carry signals into the brain from the eyes. It consists of two clusters of brain cells called the suprachiasmatic nuclei (SCN). Special genes in these brain cells switch themselves on and off like clockwork, keeping time. The SCN controls wakefulness by triggering the release of hormones such as melatonin, which make us feel sleepy or alert.

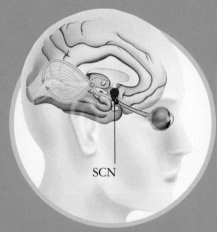

SCN

Are you an owl or a lark?

The human body clock works on a 24-hour cycle, but the length of the cycle can vary from person to person, perhaps largely for genetic reasons. People with a clock shorter than 24 hours find it easier getting up early in the morning and are known as larks. People with a longer body clock tend to stay up late at night and are called owls.

DEEP INSIDE the human brain is a living clock that acts as your body's timekeeper, telling you when to wake, sleep, rest, and play. Understanding your body clock can help you get the most out of each day.

8:30 a.m. Bowel movement most likely.

8:00–11:00 a.m. Heart attacks are most likely in the morning because the blood is sticky, blood vessels are stiffer, and blood pressure rises steeply after waking.

11:00 a.m. We are now fully alert and active, except for teenagers, who have a late-running body clock and are not fully alert until the afternoon. This late clock makes it hard for teenagers to get up early.

Noon Around lunch, wakefulness and body temperature dip naturally, whether or not we've had a meal. "Microsleeps," where people accidentally nod off for a few seconds, can happen. In some countries, people take a siesta in the post-lunch dip.

2:00 p.m. This is the time of day when car crashes are most likely. Many highway crashes are probably caused by drivers having microsleeps at the wheel.

4:00 p.m. Alertness and body temperature rise again. Reaction times are fastest around this time, making it the best part of the day for sports performance.

6:00 p.m. Although the working day is over, the body clock is still in prime time, keeping us active and alert. A good time for socializing.

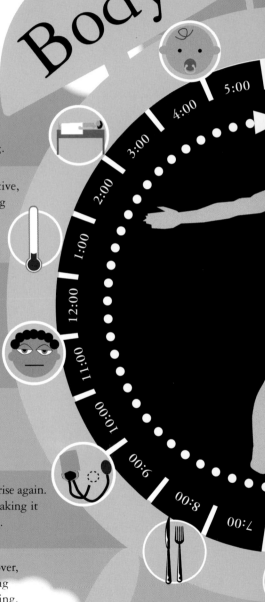

Body

The *deadliest hours* of the

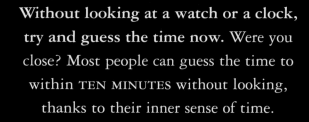

Without looking at a watch or a clock, try and guess the time now. Were you close? Most people can guess the time to within TEN MINUTES without looking, thanks to their inner sense of time.

7:00 p.m. Fading daylight is detected by our eyes and brain, which then tell the body that night is drawing in and start preparing us for sleep.

8:00 p.m. Many people eat their main meal of the day around now, though the hormone insulin, which clears digested sugar from the blood, is more effective in the mornings. Some scientists think we should have our main meal at breakfast and only a snack at night.

8:00–10:00 p.m. Body temperature and blood pressure fall and we feel more tired. Teens and young adults, however, may continue to feel energetic into the late hours.

2:00 a.m. Deepest sleep.

2:00–4:00 a.m. Body activity and temperature drop to a low point to conserve energy during sleep. These are the hours in which the very sick or very old are most likely to die.

3:00–5:00 a.m. Most births occur around this time. This is true of other primates, too. Giving birth in the dead of night may be an evolutionary adaptation that protects the infant, since primates tend to be somewhere safe at night—like up a tree!

FAQ

Can you reset the clock?
The SCN keeps time on its own but is also continually reset by light entering our eyes. The light triggers the release of chemicals onto the clock cells, tweaking it so it matches the 24-hour day. Too little light in the early morning (sunrise) or too much in the late evening (sunset) can upset the clock, putting it out of sync.

Why is it hard getting up?
The cycle of activity controlled by our body clocks changes as we get older. Young children start the day very early in the morning, but between 13 and 21, getting up early and being active in the morning is much harder than at any other time of life. An adult's need for sleep falls with age, making early mornings easier as we get older.

Temperature
One of the main effects of the body clock is to control our temperature, which is 98.6°F (37°C) on average but rises and falls over the course of a day. It peaks between 11 a.m. and 7 p.m., except for a post-lunch dip, when we feel sleepy.

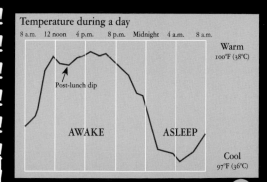

Temperature during a day

| 8 a.m. | 12 noon | 4 p.m. | 8 p.m. | Midnight | 4 a.m. | 8 a.m. |

Warm 100°F (38°C)

Post-lunch dip

AWAKE ASLEEP

Cool 97°F (36°C)

day are just BEFORE DAWN

Time *travel*

Why does time fly when you're having fun? An hour spent doing something you love feels like a minute, but a minute spent doing something you hate feels like an hour. The passage of time that we feel—called SUBJECTIVE TIME—is not the same as the time that clocks and watches measure. ***It seems to speed up and slow down according to our state of mind.***

WHY DOES LIFE *SPEED UP* AS WE GET OLDER?

One of the reasons that time seems to speed up as we age is that our lives become less varied and active, with fewer new memories to look back on. Another reason is simply that one year of our life becomes a smaller fraction of the total. Using some clever mathematical trickery, a scientist used this declining apparent length of a year to adjust a human lifespan into subjective years, revealing that by the time we're 10 years old, we're already more than halfway through our subjective life! But don't take it too seriously—the research only made it into the ***Journal of Irreproducible Results***, a magazine of scientific jokes.

| 0 | AGE IN ACTUAL YEARS | | 1 | | 2 | | 3 | | 4 | | 5 | | 10 |

| 0 | AGE IN SUBJECTIVE YEARS | 10 | | 20 | | 30 | | 40 | | 5 |

SLOWING DOWN TIME

Extreme thrills can slow down subjective time, stretching out each second for longer. This happens because the neurons in the brain's dopamine pathway (see page 152) fire more frequently when we're excited, allowing the brain to process more moments of experience with each second. In car crashes, victims sometimes report that events seemed to happen in slow motion at the moment of crisis. Time also seems to slow down when we're bored or impatient for something to happen—such as the ringing of the school bell at the end of a dull class.

Time-keeping neurons

Tasks that require an accurate sense of rhythm, such as dancing, depend on special neurons in our brains that keep time. Scientists discovered these in the prefrontal cortex and striatum of monkeys' brains. They fire at specific intervals, such as 10 times a second, and may enable our brains to "time-stamp" memories, allowing us not only to recall events but also sense when they originally took place.

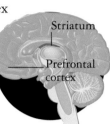
Striatum
Prefrontal cortex

15 20 30 40 50 60 70 80
60 70 80

SPEEDING UP TIME

When your brain is busy focusing on a complicated task, such as playing a tricky level on a computer game, it pays less heed to the passage of time. As a result, time passes without you noticing it and so seems to flow more quickly. Time also seems to move faster if you're rushing to get something finished by a tight deadline.

TIME ILLUSIONS

Now is an illusion

Your brain is very good at making you feel like things are happening *right now*, but that's merely an illusion. It takes about a fifth of a second for an image on your retina to get sent to your brain's visual cortex, recognized, and processed as a conscious experience. As a 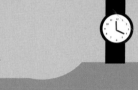 result, the "now" you experience is always slightly in the past. Fortunately, the brain is an expert at predicting what's about to happen from moment to moment, so it always has the right "reaction" up its sleeve and seldom gets caught out by the delay. In fact, our brains are so good at predicting that much of what we "experience" is simply what we expect and not what really happens.

Time standing still

We rely on our memory to sense the passage of time through life, but some people suffering from brain damage can lose this ability. One famous patient with this problem, called Korsakoff's syndrome, developed memory loss when he was a young sailor in 1945. For the rest of his life he believed himself to still be a young man and was horrified when he looked in mirrors to see an old man staring back. Fortunately, as soon as he looked away from the mirror he'd forget how old he looked.

SLEEP DISORDERS

Sleepwalking

Do you sleepwalk? It's very common, and may run (or walk!) in the family. Sleepwalking isn't caused by dreaming—it is unconscious movement that happens in the deepest sleep, and you don't remember it in the morning. Some people write, draw, and have even committed crimes in their sleep.

Sleep apnea

Your body is relaxed when it's asleep, which is the safest state for it—unless you have sleep apnea, when your throat muscles are so relaxed they collapse and block your airways so you can't breathe. It can be very dangerous, but in most sufferers, their brain wakes them up, usually with a loud snore.

Insomnia

It's normal to wake up a few times during the night, but if you have trouble falling asleep again, it could be insomnia. It's caused by many things, including stress and drinking caffeine. If you find it hard to fall asleep, try to relax before bed (maybe read a book or take a bath), and make sure there's not too much noise or light around you.

Narcolepsy

For some people, it doesn't matter how much they sleep, they want more—sometimes suddenly collapsing into a sleep attack between 30 seconds and 30 minutes long during the day. Narcolepsy can be extremely dangerous: imagine suffering an attack that paralyzes you while driving a car.

Sleepy HEAD

We spend one-third of our lives asleep. We know that babies need more sleep than adults, and that teenagers can't get up in the morning, but science doesn't really know what sleep actually does, or even what dreams are for.

TIME FOR BED!

You sleep in a cycle of light and deep sleep that repeats every 90 minutes or so. Brain activity is slowest during deep sleep. During the lightest stage of sleep (REM sleep), your brain creates memorable dreams and is as active as when you're awake. REM stands for "rapid eye movement"—your eyes move around rapidly under their lids in this stage of sleep.

■ REM SLEEP
■ LIGHTER SLEEP
■ DEEPER SLEEP

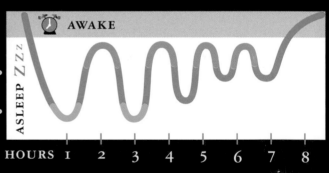

I don't WANT to go to bed!

EVERYONE NEEDS SLEEP. How much depends on how old you are—the older you are, the less you'll need. While no one knows why we sleep, it's easy to see the effects of too little sleep. If you don't sleep enough, you'll be tired and confused during the day. Continued sleep deprivation will make you feel unwell physically and mentally, causing

THE STUFF DREAMS ARE MADE OF

Almost everyone dreams. You will have more than 1,800 dreams in an average year, but you won't remember most of them unless you wake up while you're dreaming. Dreams do strange things: they change time—you may feel a dream has lasted hours, but in reality it has taken minutes. Also, dreams feel real—you can't tell that you're in a dream, even if really weird things are happening. Your brain's frontal lobes are mostly shut down when you sleep, so you have no sense of reality.

Going without

In 1959, American DJ Peter Tripp broke the then-world record for staying awake. He chatted, played records, and was kept awake by nurses and doctors for 201 hours (8 days). But after just a few days, he began to hallucinate, imagining cobwebs, mice, and kittens, and looking for money that wasn't there. He never fully recovered from the sleep deprivation and became aggressive and paranoid.

But WHAT are they *for*?

No one knows why we dream. One theory suggests that it's a way of storing memories; another is that dreams sort experiences from your day. Some dreams are triggered by noises you hear in the night or feelings you have. (Have you ever dreamed of having to go to the bathroom and woken up to realize you actually need to go?) Alternatively, dreams could simply be your own imagination working overtime.

What a *nightmare*

Dreams can feel very scary. This is because the part of your brain that produces emotions is very active when you're asleep. Sometimes it creates a sense of fear, which the rest of your brain weaves into an upsetting dream—a nightmare.

Z z z

vision and speech problems and lowering your immune system. And if you don't sleep at all—not even a nap—for several days, you will die. No one knows how many days of sleep deprivation will kill you because humans haven't been tested. However, rats that were tested died sooner from lack of sleep than lack of food.

 2  3  4

 Your brain:
I think **THEREFORE** I am

"I think therefore I am," said the philosopher René Descartes about 400 years ago. Descartes had realized that the mere act of thinking was proof of his own existence. Just like Descartes, all of us have a powerful sense of an *inner self* that exists within us and has thoughts, feelings, and sensations. That sense of self is a crucial part of a mysterious human phenomenon we call CONSCIOUSNESS. Our inner self is also utterly unique. Our minds are built and shaped by a set of genes and experiences that are ours alone, giving each of us a *unique personality*.

The *curiosity* that is CONSCIOUSNESS

Pay attention!

Can you feel your socks on your feet? The conscious mind is very good at focusing on one thing at a time—a bit like a mental spotlight—and ignoring everything else, such as the sensation of socks on feet. We call this mental spotlight *attention*. You can choose to focus your attention on something, such as this book, but certain things can capture it against your will. If a mouse scurries across the floor in the corner of your eye, or if you hear someone mutter your name, your attention will move in a flash.

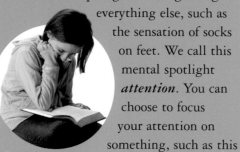

The mirror test

Do animals have consciousness? It's impossible to answer this question, since we can't get inside animals' minds to look. However, there is a way of testing whether animals might be self-aware. The test simply involves putting a dot of red paint on an animal's face and showing it a mirror. If the animal recognizes itself, it will touch the red dot. Human beings pass this test from the age of 18 months onward. Only a few animal species pass, including chimps, dolphins, magpies, and (in a variation of the test) pigs—all animals we think of as being intelligent.

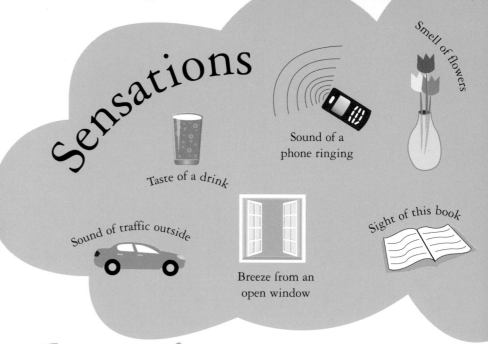

Sensations

Taste of a drink

Sound of a phone ringing

Smell of flowers

Sound of traffic outside

Breeze from an open window

Sight of this book

Consciousness is a

What is consciousness?

When you're in a deep sleep, consciousness VANISHES. When you wake up, it SWITCHES ON like a light, making you aware of the world. Although we all experience consciousness, it's difficult to say what it *actually is*, and even scientists can't agree on a meaning. That's one of the reasons it's such a puzzle.

Think of consciousness as a movie playing in your head. The movie includes not only sound and pictures but also smells, tastes, and sensations. There's more still: consciousness includes a secret INNER WORLD of thoughts, feelings, and wishes. Right now, you might even hear the words on this page being spoken by an INNER VOICE. It might sound a little like a another person, but at the same time, you know it's *you*.

This SENSE OF SELF is an important part of human consciousness. We all feel as though there's a secret inner self living inside our heads, making decisions.

Every moment you are awake, something mysterious is happening in your brain. The information you get from your senses, the thoughts you have, your ideas, feelings, and memories all come together to form *consciousness*. Understanding how it works is one of the big mysteries of science.

Thoughts and feelings

Worrying about exams

Feeling bored

Z z z z

Thinking about clothes you want to buy

sense of *awareness*

Unconscious processes

We like to think we have conscious control of our minds and bodies, but lots of things are beyond our conscious control or even beyond our awareness. You don't have to make a conscious effort to breathe or blink, for instance, although both these processes are controlled by your brain.

 Your heart beats nonstop, speeds up, and slows down automatically.

 Your lungs pump air nonstop without you having to think about it.

 Sensations that don't matter, such as the feel of socks, disappear from consciousness.

 Complicated muscle movements become almost unconscious when you've learned a skill such as tying your shoes.

Where does it happen?

As far as we can tell, there isn't a specific part of the brain that creates the sense of consciousness. Brain-scanning studies reveal that many areas of the brain's cortex are crucial in creating consciousness but none of them can do it on their own. Some people believe that the conscious mind is separate from the physical universe—a kind of spirit or soul. Most scientists, however, think consciousness is simply the result of brain activity.

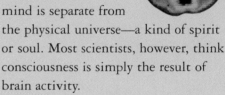

Conscious or not?

Serious head injuries that damage the brain can cause people to stay deeply asleep for days or weeks, a state known as a coma. In some cases, patients wake again but are completely unresponsive, as though they have lost all awareness. Such people are said to be in a "persistent vegetative state" (PVS), but are they conscious? Scientists recently scanned the brain of a woman in PVS while asking her to imagine playing tennis. The scan showed the same brain activity as in healthy people thinking of tennis, suggesting that she truly understood and responded to the question.

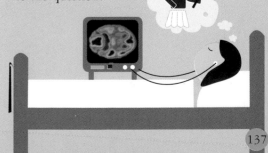

THINKING *without*

SIXTH SENSE

Ever had an odd feeling that something wasn't right *but you couldn't say why?* Perhaps you went to your room and felt something was wrong... A few seconds later, you realize a poster is missing. This is your unconscious mind at work. Without you even noticing, your brain takes in a lot of information and makes a superfast assessment. If there's a problem, first of all it sends a warning signal to the emotional part of your brain, creating that "something's up" feeling.

Conscious thinking is the tip of an iceberg—just a small fraction of what goes on in our brains. Most mental activity is unconscious, happening behind

First impressions

We rely on unconscious thinking to size other people up. Within a few seconds of meeting someone for the first time, we've jumped to all sorts of conclusions and immediately sensed whether we trust them, though we're often unable to say why. Even the size of a person's pupils can strongly affect our reaction to them: larger pupils make people more attractive.

Unconscious thinking

... or ESP, sixth sense, gut instinct...

If you get bitten by a rat, the you will instinctively avoid it, even

Analysis paralysis?

Is it better to think things through slowly and carefully, or go with your gut instinct and make a snap decision? Imagine you're comparing three new phones, each with lots of different features. Weighing up all the options consciously is extremely difficult, so most people go with their gut. Dutch psychologists have found this often leads to the right answer. They carried out experiments in which people had to use 12 facts to choose the best car from a group and discovered that people made sounder decisions when they were distracted and unable to focus consciously.

THINKING

the scenes and beyond our awareness. This unconscious processing can be amazingly powerful and fast, but it can also make mistakes.

The more experience you have, the greater your sense of intuition = intuition... next time you see one if you can't remember why

THE POWER OF INTUITION

We call our ability to think unconsciously "intuition." People with lots of experience develop a strong sense of intuition. In one case, a fire chief in a burning building had a gut feeling something was wrong and ordered his crew out; seconds later, the floor collapsed into the basement, where the raging fire had started. The chief put his hunch down to ESP (extrasensory perception), but the truth is that experience had honed his instincts.

Priming

Intuition isn't always right, and experiments have shown that unconscious thinking can be swayed by trivial or even irrelevant things, an effect known as priming. For instance, people have been found to clean a room more thoroughly just because they could smell disinfectant, or to play games involving money more competitively just because they saw a briefcase in the room. In one recent study, it was found that students rated nonsensical articles about the brain as reliable simply because the articles were accompanied by pictures of a brain scan, while students given the same articles with graphs instead of brain scans found them unconvincing.

Free to CHOOSE?

When we make decisions, we feel as though an inner self is using free will to make a choice. But this may just be an illusion. Ingenious experiments suggest that unconscious parts of our brains make decisions for us up to *10 seconds before* our conscious mind is aware of deciding. In one experiment, a person presses a button whenever they wish while watching letters flash on a screen, noting the letter that's visible when they decide to press the button. Brain scans detected the neural activity that led to the finger movement 10 seconds before the chosen letter appeared. Scientists could even predict the letter the person would choose before they knew themself.

When does he *really* decide to press the button?

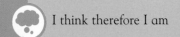
Reading MINDS

How do my parents *always*

Be *very careful* if you lie to your parents. They can tell when you're doing it BY PICKING UP ON SUBTLE SIGNALS that you may not realize you're sending out.

1 READING YOUR FACE

Facial expressions give away our inner emotions, even when we're trying to hide or suppress them. You may fake a smile to try to look pleased, but if your eyes remain cold and neutral they will give you away. One of the more honest parts of the face is your forehead—crinkled brows show something is annoying you, even when you're trying not to look bothered.

2 FOLLOWING YOUR EYES

One of the easiest ways to find out what someone is thinking about or what somebody wants is to follow their gaze. People look at things they want, giving away what's on their mind. If you try to hide your thoughts by deliberately looking down or away, that may be obvious, too.

FURTHER READING...

Mirror, mirror

Our ability to read minds may involve special brain cells called mirror neurons. Scientists discovered these by accident in monkeys while studying a part of the monkey brain that activates when a monkey grasps food. The scientists found that the same parts of the brain became active when the monkeys were watching the scientists handle food, as though the monkeys were replaying the sensation in their minds. It's likely mirror neurons exist in the human brain, too.

Mirror faces

Mirroring may play a role in the way we use facial expressions to communicate. When we see someone smile with joy or gasp with fear, we not only feel a flicker of the same emotion ourselves but also make the corresponding facial expression to go with it.

According to some scientists, large brains evolved in humans to make us better at UNDERSTANDING EACH OTHER. Success in life requires an ability to figure out what other people think and want—we need to *read their minds*.

know when *I'm* LYING?

③ BODY LANGUAGE

Are your muscles tensed or relaxed? Are your arms folded defensively? We give away a host of clues with our posture and gestures. One subtle form of body language is the way we mirror each other. When we agree with or like someone, we copy their movements; when we disagree or dislike each other, body language falls out of step.

④ INTONATION

The tone of your voice can carry more meaning than the words you actually say. The loudness, pitch, and pattern of breathing all give away your emotional state. Studies have shown that listeners can even figure out how a foreign-language speaker feels without understanding a word they say.

⑤ SELF-AWARENESS

Your parents' main secret weapon is self-awareness. They were once your age and told the same lies to their parents—they know all the tricks. When you try it on, they see their younger selves in you. Their own self-knowledge makes you easy to figure out.

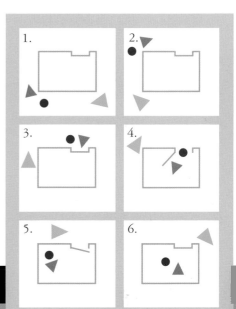

I feel your pain

Watch someone stub their toe and you'll wince in pain, too. Watch them make a fool of themselves and you may cringe with embarrassment yourself. We have an amazing ability to step into other people's shoes by experiencing an echo of their own feelings, an ability that helps us read minds. Brain scans even show similar areas of the human brain light up in a person watching someone feel pain as in the person feeling it.

Catching a yawn

Look at the photo and count to ten... Have you started yawning? Yawning is so catching that you can make other people do it without realizing why, simply by standing in front of them and yawning yourself. Why this happens is a bit of a puzzle, but one theory is that yawning is a social signal that tells the rest of the group to get ready for action—by taking a deep breath.

Seeing intentions

Humans beings have a built-in tendency to see intentions in the behavior of other people or in animals—an ability that helps us predict what other people are going to do. The tendency is so strong that we can even see intention in lifeless objects, such as these colored shapes. If you read them like a cartoon strip, these images suggest a chase in which the red and purple shapes *run away* from the green shape and *hide* inside the rectangle.

Personality

Are you loud or quiet, neat or messy? The way you think, act, and interact with others is unique to you and makes up your *personality*. But where does your personality come from—is it set by your genes or molded by your experience?

What type of person are you?

We all have strong opinions about each other's personality, but our opinions aren't very scientific, since they're strongly colored by who we like or dislike. To assess personality more fairly, psychologists have devised a range of systems that classify people according to different elements of personality. One of the systems is shown below. In the middle of each arrow is a question, and at the two ends of the arrows are opposite answers to the questions that different kinds of people tend to prefer. You can use this system to take a personality quiz on page 144 and find out a bit more about yourself.

WHAT GIVES YOU THE MOST ENERGY?

Interacting with other people and playing outside.

Having time on your own to concentrate on something.

WHAT DO YOU TEND TO NOTICE?

Important details. Things that are real and actually there.

The bigger picture. Things that you imagine could be there.

HOW DO YOU PREFER TO MAKE DECISIONS?

By thinking things through and weighing up all the important facts.

By thinking about how other people might feel.

HOW DO YOU LIKE TO LIVE YOUR LIFE?

By staying organized and planning what to do next.

By deciding on the spur of the moment and not being too strict.

Find out more about *your own*

NATURE... OR NURTURE?

Where does your personality come from? Well, you could blame your parents. Scientific studies show that your genes have a big influence on your personality. Identical twins (who share almost identical genes) who have been adopted into different families often grow up with similar personalities despite their different environments. Likewise, biological brothers or sisters are more alike than adopted brothers and sisters.

However, even identical twins don't have identical personalities, so there must be more to personality than genes. Your personality is shaped by your experiences in life (nurture), such as the people you mix with, from members of your family to your friends and teachers. Even what you watch on TV could have an effect on your personality.

The DNA molecule stores genes as a simple code.

Growing up

If you're always in trouble and think your personality is to blame, don't worry. As we grow up, we become much better at understanding our own personalities and those of other people. This knowledge helps us to avoid or to deal with difficult situations such as disagreements. Understanding your own personality can also be a big help in choosing a career that will suit you.

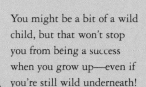

You might be a bit of a wild child, but that won't stop you from being a success when you grow up—even if you're still wild underneath!

Multiple personalities

Is it possible to have more than one personality? Some psychiatrists claim to have patients with up to 16 different personalities that take turns occupying the same body, each with a different name, accent, and no knowledge or memory of what the other personalities get up to. Not all experts are convinced, however. Almost all cases of "multiple personality disorder" have occurred in North America, where movies and books featuring the problem have made it famous, perhaps leading psychiatrists to diagnose it too readily or leading patients or criminals to fake the condition.

Testing, testing

The study of personality has involved some very unscientific methods. For centuries, astrologers have used the stars to assess personality, while graphologists study handwriting, but there's no scientific evidence that either technique works. Some psychologists give people ink blots and ask what they can see in them, but many regard this test as unreliable, too.

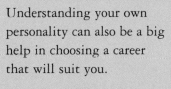

Ink blot

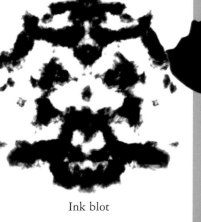

In the novel *Strange Case of Dr. Jekyll and Mr. Hyde*, Hyde is Jekyll's murderous alter ego (second personality).

personality type on the next page

What are YOU like?

Psychologists use **PERSONALITY** questionnaires to help find out what *kind* of person you are. The questionnaires don't tell you what you **can** or **can't do**, they just reveal how you *prefer to be*. Finding out more about your personality can help you understand **why** and **how** people act *differently* to you.

The questions here can help you identify some of your personality preferences. If you find yourself thinking "I like both the options," try to decide which option seems to describe you best.

QUESTIONS

1 **When you first get in from school what do you prefer to do?**

A) Find someone to talk to about your day.
B) Think through your day, maybe in your room while watching TV or listening to music.

2 **At school do you prefer to work...**

A) In a team?
B) Alone, in private study?

3 **When you are given a new board game or computer game would you rather...**

A) Read all the rules before you start to play?
B) Start playing and only look at the rules if you need to?

4 **Think about a bike. Take a piece of paper and write down what you're thinking. What did you write?**

A) A list of facts about the bike, such as its color, size, what type of bike it is, how many gears it has, if it has lights, and so on.
B) A description that includes where you could go on the bike, how it can get you to places you want to go to, how it is good exercise, and so on.

5 **Think about a time that a friend came to you with a problem. Did you...**

A) Try to help them by solving their problem?
B) Ask them how they are feeling, say how sorry you felt, put your arm around them, and try to make them feel better?

6 **When a friend asks you to read their homework do you...**

A) Tell them how they could improve it, so that they will get a top grade?
B) Tell them what you like about it and what they did well?

7 **Look in your closet. What is it like?**

A) Neat and organized—a place for everything, and everything in its place.
B) A bit messy. You know where everything is but no one else does!

8 **When you do your homework, do you prefer...**

A) To plan out your work and work until it's finished?
B) To leave it until it really needs to be done, because this is when you do your best work.

IF YOU PICKED As: You may have a preference for *Extraversion* (E). This means you get your energy from being with other people, and may prefer to spend as much time with others as possible.

IF YOU PICKED Bs: You may have a preference for *Introversion* (I). This means you get your energy from reflecting and thinking through things yourself—so you may enjoy your own company.

Es are sociable and may be frustrated that Is want to spend time alone rather than come out to play. Likewise, Is may be irritated if Es interrupt their thoughts, because Es typically like to talk through their ideas.

IF YOU PICKED As: You may have a preference for *Sensing* (S). You may prefer your homework to have clear specific instructions. You may enjoy remembering details and facts.

IF YOU PICKED Bs: You may have a preference for *Intuition* (N). You may prefer to see an example of what the homework should look like. You may enjoy daydreaming and using your imagination.

Ss can generally remember lots of details, which may surprise Ns. Ns typically reveal some surprising ideas, so that Ss ask, "Where did that thought come from?" It can be good for Ss and Ns to work together, because then they'll notice all the details and use the information imaginatively.

IF YOU PICKED As: You may have a preference for *Thinking* (T). This means you prefer to make decisions using logic.

IF YOU PICKED Bs: You may have a preference for *Feeling* (F). This means you make decisions by considering other people's points of view.

Ts may be seen by others as the ones who typically ask good questions. Fs can often be seen as very thoughtful. When you work in a group to solve a problem or make a decision, it's good to have people with both types of preference.

IF YOU PICKED As: You may have a preference for *Organizing* (Z). You like to have things planned and well ordered.

IF YOU PICKED Bs: You may have a preference for *Adapting* (A). You are happy to go with the flow and adapt to the situation.

Zs generally prefer to make decisions as soon as possible, plan things in advance, and know all the information they need upfront. As usually like to leave their options open and decide what to do on the day. They are happy to consider new information as they get it.

JOB CHOICES

People with different preferences can be attracted to different careers. This doesn't mean that if you have one set of preferences, you can't work in a different career—all it shows is that people with certain preferences may enjoy particular jobs. The list below shows some of the jobs that may suit certain types, using the letters from the test as a key.

ISTA	Police officer, sports coach
ISFA	Therapist, dance instructor
INFA	Novelist, translator
INTA	University professor, psychologist
ESTA	Police detective, farmer
ESFA	Nurse, firefighter
ENFA	Social worker, writer
ENTA	Editor, vet
ESTZ	Military officer, manager
ESFZ	Dentist, teacher
ENFZ	Counselor, actor
ENTZ	Manager, consultant
ISTZ	Airline mechanic, financial analyst
ISFZ	Interior designer, speech therapist
INFZ	Museum curator, architect
INTZ	Pharmacist, college professor

Your brain:
The feeling **MIND**

We often think of the brain as an organ made for *intelligent things* like THINKING, but it's just as important for creating *feelings.* Whether you're feeling glad, sad, or bad, your brain is to blame. Feelings (*emotions*) well up from deep inside your brain all the time, coloring your *every moment*, even in your dreams, and affecting your WHOLE BODY. The most powerful emotions are basic instincts—drives that push us away from danger and toward the things we *want*.

Emotions

Emotions are intense feelings such as anger and joy that we feel welling up from deep inside us. They affect not just our brain but our whole body and how we act. This is because our most basic emotions are related to primitive survival instincts.

Limbic system

Where do our emotions come from?

Emotions are generated in the limbic system, a cluster of structures deep under the cortex. The limbic system works mostly below the level of consciousness, creating "drives" that push us away from danger and toward opportunities. Intense emotions affect the whole nervous system and feed through to other parts of the brain, making us aware of them, though we don't always know their cause. Emotions have a profound effect on our thinking, swaying decisions even when we're trying to be balanced and logical.

There are six main expressions of emotion and they are exactly the same all over the world. This universal language shows that these emotions are hard-wired into our neural circuits and programmed into us by genes. They happen automatically, and although we can't stop them, we can learn to control or even hide them as we grow older.

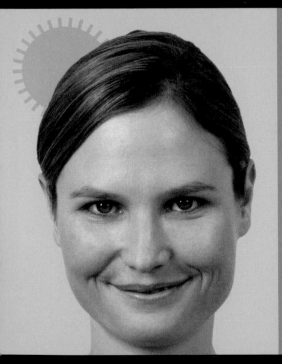

JOY

You can tell real joy from fake joy by looking for wrinkles by the eyes ("crow's feet"). The smile affects the whole face and makes the cheeks bulge.

SURPRISE

Surprise widens your eyes, raises your eyebrows, and wrinkles your forehead. Your jaw may also drop—hence the phrase "jaw-dropping."

DISGUST

A look of disgust involves a wrinkled nose, clenched nostrils, pulled-back lips, and narrowed eyes. The look can trigger a sense of disgust in others.

Moods

Emotions are usually short-lived and fade as the body and brain return to their normal state. But if an emotion lingers for hours or even days in the background, we call it a mood. Moods are more vague than emotions: you're either in a good or bad mood, never a "surprised mood" or a "disgusted mood." If a bad mood lasts for weeks or months, it can be a sign of a mental illness such as depression.

Complex emotions

Besides the six main emotions shown below, we experience dozens of more complex emotions such as suspicion, embarrassment, disappointment, guilt, pride, envy, and love. Most of these are concerned with the complexities of human society, and many of them help us to figure out instinctively whom we should trust or avoid.

Crying

Crying is a way of showing sadness and asking for help. Psychologists aren't sure why humans evolved the ability to cry, and as far as we know, we're the only species that does so. One possibility is that crying evolved because it's an honest signal—it's very difficult to shed tears without being genuinely upset or convincing yourself that you're upset.

Can you guess the emotions of the people around you right now?

ANGER

FEAR

An open mouth and raised eyebrows can mean surprise, but when you add enlarged pupils, a furrowed brow, and thin lips with a raised upper lip—you're scared!

SADNESS

The sadder a person gets, the smaller their pupils become. When you look at a sad person, your pupils shrink, too.

149

Inside teenage

The **teenage years** can be a *turbulent* time for the brain, as it slowly changes, bit-by-bit, from a **TANGLED MESH** of connections into an *efficient* network of information superhighways.

PRUNING THE TANGLED BRAIN

In early childhood, millions of new circuits form in your brain's gray matter as neurons connect together in a tangled web of connections. During later childhood and the teenage years, the gray matter thins as the neuronal pathways that aren't used and are no longer needed are "pruned" away.

Stage 1: Synaptic growth   Stage 2: Pruning

Use it or lose it

During what scientists see as a key "use it or lose it" stage, the activities learned as a teenager—be it playing sports or watching TV—reinforce specific neuronal pathways, while unused pathways are removed. You are left with an efficient brain with less gray matter and more white matter, full of fast neuron highways honed to the well-practiced tasks.

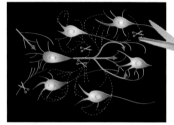

Gray matter

White matter

13 years old   15 years old   18 years old

The red areas show high gray matter volume, with blue and purple showing low gray matter volume.

Moody brain

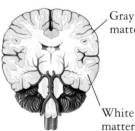
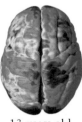

Teenagers can suffer from extreme mood swings and are prone to moments of rash or aggressive behavior. People often blame these on surging hormone levels, but brain development could be the main culprit. The parts of the brain develop at different speeds. The parts in charge of emotion, rather than thinking, mature first, and these are sometimes in control.

the BRAIN

SLOW RISER

Teenagers find it very hard to get up in the morning. The teenage brain not only needs about two hours more sleep than the adult brain, but also has a very different cycle of daily activity, being most active late in the day and sluggish in the mornings.

PREFRONTAL CORTEX
This area of the brain is in charge of planning, decision-making, and calming behavior. It is the last part of the brain to mature, and during the teenage years it is remodeled as neuron pathways are pruned.

CORPUS CALLOSUM
This bundle of nerves joins the left side to the right side of the brain. It thickens during your teens and is thought to be involved with creative thinking.

AMYGDALA
This is the emotional hub of the brain and is linked with primal feelings, such as fear and anger. It is one of the areas of the brain that makes teens impulsive.

BASAL GANGLIA
This region includes the brain's reward pathway (see page 152). It generates the "buzz" we experience during pleasure and excitement.

CEREBELLUM
In charge of body coordination, the cerebellum is also thought to play a role in regulating thoughts and learning.

Reckless youth

The age at which you take the most risks is 14. That could be because the 14-year-old basal ganglia are in full working order, giving you the thrill of excitement during risky behavior, but the prefrontal cortex (the part of the brain controlling decisions) is still maturing, so the brakes are missing. Lacking sound judgment, some teens take crazy risks.

Clumsy brain

The teenage body can seem hard to control at times, with legs and arms growing so fast that the cerebellum has to relearn how to coordinate them, making the body clumsy. Scientists also think the underdeveloped cerebellum can also make teenagers *mentally* clumsy, making them trip over words and causing moments of forgetfulness.

THE *rewarding* BRAIN

DEEP INSIDE the brain is a special network of neurons dedicated to creating the sensation of **PLEASURE**. These neurons form the brain's **reward system**, repaying behavior that promotes our survival with a *natural high*.

HOW WE GET A BUZZ

The reward system has certain goals, the most important being to help us survive and reproduce. When we satisfy the urge to eat, drink, or reproduce, we're rewarded with a buzz of pleasure. This encourages us to do the same thing again, reinforcing the behavior. The pleasure is triggered mainly by the chemical dopamine. Dopamine is a neurotransmitter— a chemical that jumps across the tiny gaps (synapses) between neurons to pass a signal on.

DOPAMINE ACTION

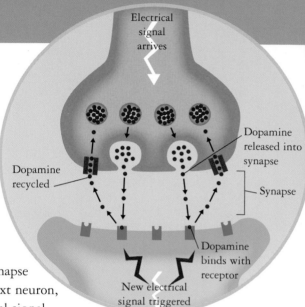

Electrical signal arrives

Dopamine released into synapse

Synapse

Dopamine recycled

Dopamine binds with receptor

New electrical signal triggered

Dopamine is released by a neuron into a synapse and stimulates the next neuron, triggering an electrical signal.

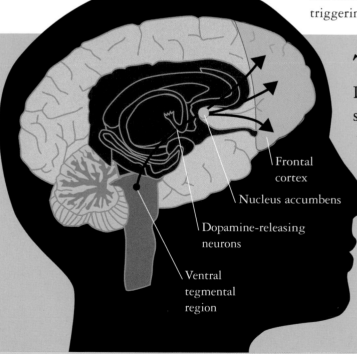

Frontal cortex

Nucleus accumbens

Dopamine-releasing neurons

Ventral tegmental region

THE PATH TO PLEASURE

Dopamine-secreting neurons are arranged in several major pathways inside the brain, one of which is shown here. The pathways start deep inside the brain, where the cell bodies of these neurons are clustered together in areas such as the ventral tegmental region. The neurons' axons (fibers) reach right across the brain, spreading out into the frontal cortex like a fountain to flood the higher brain with dopamine and create the wave of pleasure that we experience consciously.

Growing boring Older people don't seem as excitable as younger people. Scientists have found that during moments of new experience, older people produce less dopamine—which could be why they seek fewer thrills!

> If I can just press this button again
> I'll forget all my ratty woes...

Dopamine addict

In the 1950s, scientists studying the brain's reward system implanted electrodes into the brains of live rats, allowing the rats to trigger their dopamine pathways using a lever. The rats became so addicted to pressing the lever that they ignored food and continued pressing until they died of starvation. The research showed that the reward system is so good at reinforcing behavior that it can cause ADDICTION.

Addiction rituals

The brain starts releasing dopamine when we merely *anticipate* the experience of pleasure, and this anticipation can itself be addictive. Caffeine addicts can develop a fussy ritual over making coffee, from grinding special beans to brewing in a fancy machine. This ritual behavior triggers a dopamine hit even before the drinker has taken a sip.

Reward chemicals

Dopamine is not the only neurotransmitter that makes us feel good. Lots of other neurotransmitters play a role in how happy or excited we feel, among other functions.

Dopamine
- Pleasure
- Excitement
- Pain
- Nausea

Serotonin
- Happiness
- Sleepiness
- Fullness

Endorphin
- Reduced pain
- Relaxation

Noradrenaline
- Alertness
- Excitement
- Anxiety

Oxytocin
- Love

TOO MUCH OF A GOOD THING

One of the reasons illegal drugs are addictive is that they hack into the dopamine circuit in a similar way to an electrode implanted in a rat's brain (above). Moreover, repeatedly hacking the dopamine pathway causes its effect to fade, driving the addict to take ever-larger doses. A similar thing may happen with junk food. Scientists have found that rats given unlimited high-fat food become addicted to it and get increasingly greedy as the dopamine response in their brains fades. Obesity in humans could be caused by the same mechanism.

> Who you callin'
> a fatty ratty?

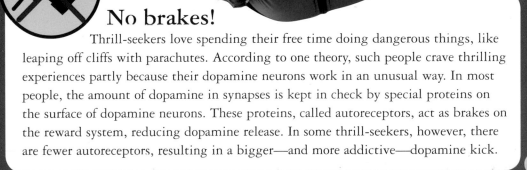

No brakes!

Thrill-seekers love spending their free time doing dangerous things, like leaping off cliffs with parachutes. According to one theory, such people crave thrilling experiences partly because their dopamine neurons work in an unusual way. In most people, the amount of dopamine in synapses is kept in check by special proteins on the surface of dopamine neurons. These proteins, called autoreceptors, act as brakes on the reward system, reducing dopamine release. In some thrill-seekers, however, there are fewer autoreceptors, resulting in a bigger—and more addictive—dopamine kick.

"What ARE you

You KNOW when your friends are *laughing*, but would you **recognize** laughter in a remote tribe on the other side of the WORLD? In fact you *would*. Unlike language, laughter is a form of communication that's UNIVERSAL. It's a **basic instinct** that *all people share.* Laughter also does wonders for your mood, increasing blood flow to the brain and releasing pain-killing ENDORPHINS that make you *feel great*.

The *laughing instinct* is programmed into our brains by our genes, but why did it evolve? One clue comes from the fact that we're 30 times more likely to laugh in social situations than when we're alone. Laughter is a form of communication—a way of sending a powerful positive signal to other people in our social group.

Animal crackers

It isn't only humans who laugh. A few other animals that live in social groups—including chimps, gorillas, and dogs—make panting sounds that are like laughter when play-fighting. Unlike humans, however, animals laugh in step with their breaths, whereas we laugh by chopping an outward breath into segments.

WORLD'S FUNNIEST JOKE

According to British pscychologist Richard Wiseman, who collected more than 40,000 jokes from around the world and surveyed their popularity, this is the world's funniest joke: ➡

WHAT'S SO FUNNY?

We all laugh at a good joke, and sometimes at a bad one, too. But what exactly is it that makes something funny? Psychologists have tried to dissect our sense of humor and find the funny bone. Here are their best theories about what gets us laughing...

THEORY 1: INCONGRUITY

I said to the gym instructor, "*Can you teach me to do the splits?*" He said: "How flexible are you?" I said: "*I can't make Tuesdays.*"

Most jokes involve something incongruous, which means out-of-place and unexpected. The typical joke sets up a situation that seems normal, but the punchline delivers surprising new information that overturns everything, creating a feeling of surprise that makes you laugh.

LaUgHiNg at?

Laughter and bonding

Laughter is a signal that strengthens social bonds. Most primates bond by grooming each other's fur, but humans are different—we use conversation and laughter. Studies have found that the most powerful person in a group often uses humor most, perhaps as a way of commanding loyalty. In tricky social situations, laughter may serve to ease tension, deflect anger, or just fill an awkward silence.

The dark side

Laughter is not without its dark sides. Although it's usually an expression of pleasure, laughter is often used to express aggression. Sharing a private joke about someone can be a way of plotting behind their back, and making a joke about someone in public is a way of ridiculing them and undermining their status.

Even darker—but thankfully very rare—is the potentially deadly effect of uncontrollable laughter, which has been known to trigger a fatal heart attack.

HE HAD THE LAST LAUGH!

Are you ticklish?

Try tickling yourself—it won't work. Tickling only makes you laugh if someone else is doing it. This is because tickling, like joking, is a form of social communication. Some scientists think tickling evolved from play-fighting, an activity that many mammal species engage in.

Two hunters are out in the woods when one of them collapses. He doesn't seem to be breathing and his eyes are glazed. The other guy whips out his phone and calls the emergency services. "I think my friend is dead!" he gasps. "What can I do?" The operator says, "Calm down—I can help. First, let's make sure he's dead." There's a silence, then a shot is heard. Back on the phone, the guy says, "OK, now what?"

THEORY 2: SUPERIORITY

A woman goes into a café with a duck. She puts the duck on a stool and sits next to it. The waiter comes over and says: *"Hey! That's the ugliest pig that I have ever seen."* The woman says, "It's a duck, not a pig." And the waiter says, *"I was talking to the duck."*

Many jokes work by making someone appear silly. Psychologists think we enjoy such jokes because we feel momentarily superior, and that feeling of superiority is so good it makes us laugh.

THEORY 3: RELIEF

You're watching a scary movie: a girl is alone in her room at night, slowly brushing her hair. It's so quiet you can hear everything—including the faint footsteps behind her. A hand reaches out, clasps her shoulder, and she shrieks—but it's her mom! According to the relief theory, we laugh after a dangerous moment has passed as a way of reassuring each other that there's nothing to be scared of.

BOO!

155

FAQ

Can money buy happiness?

The answer depends on whose research you believe. Economists figure that if everyone's income rises, so does their standard of living and so does happiness. But some research shows that rising wealth in the US has given no long-term boost to happiness. Some psychologists think that having more money than the people around you or more than you had previously can make you happier, if only for a brief while.

Where's the happiest country?

One psychologist conducted a survey involving thousands of people all over the world and used it to make a "world map of happiness." His research showed that wealthy countries tend to be happier, but happiness is more closely related to health than money, and good education is about as important as wealth. According to the UN World Happiness Report, the world's happiest country is Switzerland.

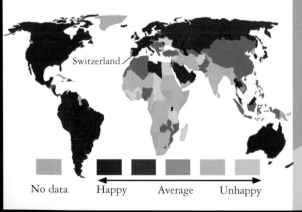

Switzerland

| No data | Happy | Average | Unhappy |

What MAKES

HAPPINESS is like a *sunrise* inside the brain, but how it happens still lies shrouded in a fog of mystery. Are we *born* happy because of our GENES? Does HAPPINESS depend on random circumstances? Or can we *choose* to make ourselves happy?

THE SCIENCE OF HAPPINESS

According to one study by psychologists, 50% of the variation in people's happiness can be explained by genes. This suggests that people can indeed be born happy—lucky for some! About 10% of the variation in happiness is due to life circumstances we have little control over, such as our age, where we live, who we share our home with, and the weather. The last 40% is the part we can control by making day-to-day decisions, such as how to spend our free time and how to treat other people.

How do we know happiness is largely genetic? Studies of identical twins adopted at birth and brought up apart reveal they have a similar level of happiness despite their different circumstances.

50% is INFLUENCED by our genes

Ten secrets of happiness

US psychologist and happiness expert Professor David Myers figures there are 10 simple ways to increase your happiness level.

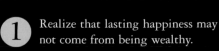

1 Realize that lasting happiness may not come from being wealthy.

2 Take control of your time.

3 Act happy—going through the motions may trigger the emotions.

4 Find the activity that puts you in "the flow" and do it.

us happy? :-)

BORN MISERABLE?

If some people are born happy or born miserable because of their genes, does that mean they're always going to be that way? Not at all. Genes don't *determine* our outlook on life, they simply *influence* it (though possibly by a lot). To put it another way, if you're born a grouch, you're not *certain* to stay a grouch, you're just *likely* to stay a grouch. And that's good news, so cheer up!

10% due to random CIRCUMSTANCE

40% IS OURS TO control

THINK A LITTLE

UK psychologist Richard Wiseman carried out a survey to see if simple strategies can boost our happiness. He randomly assigned 26,000 people to five groups and asked members of each group to perform a particular task each day. These were: smile; express gratitude for something good in life; perform an act of kindness; think about a pleasant event from the day before; or just think generally about the day before (the "control" group). The biggest rise in happiness was among people who thought about a pleasant event the day before. Performing an act of kindness actually made people less happy than the control group.

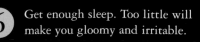

Go with the flow

When we're totally absorbed in an activity we enjoy, whether it's playing a guitar, surfing a wave, or solving a math problem, we find ourselves blissfully unaware of anything else. That's the theory of Hungarian psychologist Mihaly Csíkszentmihályi. The magical state, which he calls "flow," requires just the right combination of skill and difficulty:

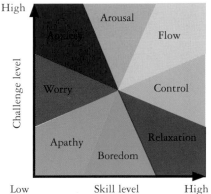

Is the mid-life crisis real?

Research suggests that we're happiest when we're young or old but least happy in middle age. This might be because people have to juggle the demands of stressful jobs and families during middle age. Or it might be that our careers become repetitive and less challenging after a number of years. At least there's a happy ending!

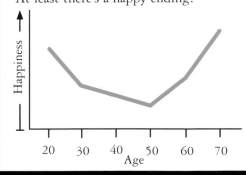

5 Be physically active. Exercise causes the brain to release chemicals that make you feel good.

6 Get enough sleep. Too little will make you gloomy and irritable.

7 Nurture relationships with people who care about you.

8 Focus on helping others, not just yourself.

9 Keep a diary of good things that happen to you.

10 Follow a religion. Religious people are reported to be happier.

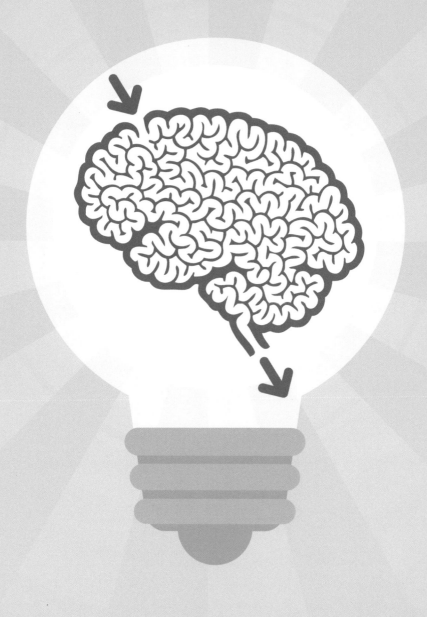

The human brain is a true *miracle*. More powerful than any computer (well... for the time being), it's capable of impressive feats that no animal brain can pull off, from transmitting thoughts by converting them into the coded sounds we call LANGUAGE to *inventing* spaceships, writing heartbreaking music, or figuring out how it came to exist. Your brain has ASTONISHING POWERS, whether you know it or not. You just have to learn to *harness* them.

Mind *your* LANGUAGE

The *human brain* is UNIQUE: its left hemisphere specializes in dealing with *language*— something only humans have.

> Goo goo, babble babble, aaahhh?

BABY TALK

Babies begin to respond to speech before they're born, and as soon as a baby is born it can distinguish its mother's voice from all other sounds. Babies start to babble from around 5 months old, using phonemes (the sounds that make up language). At this age, babies all over the world sound alike. This changes by 1 year old, when the baby's range of sounds has narrowed to only those used in its native language.

You don't understand!

Language requires several parts of the brain. Wernicke's area deals with meaning. It allows you to understand speech and it gives meaning to your words. To speak, you also need Broca's area, which generates the sequences of instructions to make speech sounds. Babies learn to understand speech before they can produce it, which can make them very frustrated when they can't express what they want to say.

Broca's area

Wernicke's area

PASSING ON THE MESSAGE

Speech is the most common form of communication, but there is a surprising variety of other ways of getting your point across.

Reading words on a page or computer screen that someone has *written* is a common way of learning.

Facial expressions and body language can reveal what a person really thinks.

Universal grammar

The American linguist Noam Chomsky developed the theory of "universal grammar." He noted that children everywhere pick up the complicated rules of language (grammar) once they are exposed to speech. Therefore, he claimed, we must be born with the patterns of language encoded in our genes.

It's easier to learn a second language as a child than as an adult. The "critical period" for learning language ends around 13–20 years old. Late learners may become fluent but probably won't ever master the accent.

Children who grow up hearing more than one language at home can become bilingual (use two languages) with little effort. They will also find it easier to learn additional languages in the future.

How many languages can you speak?

Brain-imaging shows that people who learn two languages at once use the same part of the brain to understand and speak those languages. People learning a second language later in life often learn it in a different way using different brain areas.

What on Earth is she saying?

I CAN'T UNDERSTAND EITHER OF YOU. I'M GOING TO SLEEP.

Use it or lose it

If parts of your brain are not used, their function may be lost forever. In the 1960s, an American girl named Genie grew up locked in a room by cruel parents, unable to speak to anyone. Genie was rescued when she was 13 but failed to learn to speak. She could hear and learn single words but couldn't speak in sentences. Although Genie may have had learning difficulties from the start, some scientists think she failed to learn language because it was too late for the unused parts of her brain to develop.

Braille is a system of raised dots that represent letters that blind people read with their fingers.

Sign language is used in conversation with deaf people, who might also **lip-read**.

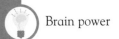

How does your *memory* work?

Memory holds everything we know and all we've ever done, whether we can recall it or not. It is highly *organized*: short-term memory briefly stores things we see, hear, or think about; and long-term memory stores the things that we never forget.

SHORT-TERM MEMORY

Short-term memories are made to be forgotten quickly, so they don't clutter our brains. One type of short-term memory, called "working memory," works like a notepad on which the brain stores information from the senses for only as long as we need it. A phone number, for instance, is held in working memory as an imagined sound. To keep it on the notepad, we repeat the sound of the numbers in our heads in sing-song fashion. As soon as we've dialed the number, the memory fades.

Very few people can remember

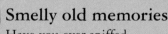

The magical number

Your long-term memory may be **vast**, but your short-term memory is tiny. Most people can briefly remember only **seven** "chunks" of information, making phone numbers longer than seven digits hard to recall. One way to boost short-term memory is to "chunk" information more efficiently. It's easier to remember "eighteen twelve eleven" (three chunks) than "181211" (six chunks).

Tip of your tongue

Sometimes we can't recall a word but feel as though we're just about to remember it, saying it's "on the tip of my tongue." One theory for why this happens is that links between the memory of the word and connected memories that help us recall it become damaged or blocked, like a road block in a city. With a bit of effort, we can usually "find a way around" and recall the word.

Smelly old memories

Have you ever sniffed something and suddenly recalled a place you'd forgotten? Smells can excite very powerful memories. The reason is that the parts of the brain that process **smells** are near the hippocampus, which is our memory gateway, and the amygdala, which handles emotions, so a smell can bring back memories and **emotions** at the same time.

LONG-TERM MEMORY

Remembering facts, people, and past events involves our long-term memory, which can last for life. We know this is separate from short-term memory thanks to studies of people with different kinds of *amnesia* (memory loss). Some people with amnesia can remember the distant past but have trouble recalling new things. Others have perfect short-term memory but struggle to recall the past.

What are memories made of?

Memory is a spider's web of connections between brain cells all across the brain. When you experience something, certain brain cells *fire* at the same time so that they learn to fire together and become LINKED. When you recall the experience, these same cells fire again, giving you back the sensation from when you first stored the memory.

The memory gate

Things you see, hear, or learn start off in your short-term memory and trickle into your long-term memory through a kind of gateway, called the **hippocampus**. We know this because of a famous medical patient named Henry Molaison (known as "H. M."). Molaison suffered from severe epilepsy, so he had brain surgery and his hippocampus was largely removed. His short-term memory was fine (he could still do crossword puzzles), as was his long-term memory (he could remember his childhood), but information could no longer move from short- to long-term memory and he couldn't remember new things or people, even if he saw them many times a day.

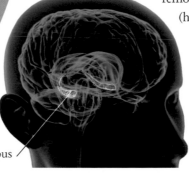

Hippocampus

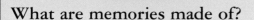

anything from before the age of three

Déjà vu and jamais vu

Emotions and memories are linked, so when you remember something it feels familiar. If something feels familiar but you don't remember it, that's *déjà vu*. It happens when our brains give us the familiarity alone, without the memory that goes with it. *Jamais vu* is when we remember things that don't feel familiar. If you say a word 30 times quickly, it will become unfamiliar, causing *jamais vu*.

Bad memories

People who go through horrible experiences such as war can get terrible flashbacks for years afterward. This is called post-traumatic stress disorder (PTSD). The brain protects us by blocking out these really bad memories. But a sudden shock (such as the sound of a car backfiring) will trigger both the memory (gunfire in a war) and the awful emotions that went with it.

Can you change your brain?

Our brains can improve with exercise. Scientists studied the hippocampus of taxi drivers and found that parts of it had grown larger. In addition to moving information between short- and long-term memory, the hippocampus helps us figure out maps and where things are, which cabbies do all day.

SUPER
memory

People often say their memory is *like a sieve*, but nothing could be further from the truth. If you live to the age of 80, you'll experience over 29,000 *different* days, yet you'll probably be able to REMEMBER many of them quite clearly and vividly. Most of us have super memories—and some people have really astonishing ones.

Memory champions

In 2006, a Japanese man, Akira Haraguchi, set an unofficial world record by correctly reciting the mathematical number pi (an infinite number, beginning with 3.141..., whose digits never repeat) to 100,000 digits. In the same year, an 11-year-old Indian boy, Nischal Narayanam (right), earned a place in the *Guinness Book of Records* by memorizing and recalling 225 random objects in only 12 minutes. Later, he earned himself another record by remembering a 132-digit number in just one minute.

Memory tricks

Memory champions make links between bits of random information so they can recall them later in the right order. "Mnemonics" are rhymes or phrases that link boring facts, such as spellings, into something more memorable. For instance, you can remember how to spell mnemonic with this mnemonic:

Monkcy **N**ut **E**ating **M**eans **O**ld **N**utshells **I**n **C**arpet

Another memory trick is to link objects to places. Imagine putting the objects at certain points along a *familiar walk*. Then you can recall them, in order, simply by retracing your steps in your mind.

Stephen Wiltshire

British artist Stephen Wiltshire has been drawing detailed panoramas of cities since he was eight. The amazing thing is that he works entirely from his "photographic memory." He can draw an accurate, 20-ft- (6-m-) long picture of a city after a single ride in a helicopter. Stephen has autism and did not speak fully until he was nine, but he has an exceptional memory. He became famous at 13 when he appeared on TV, and his paintings now sell for thousands of dollars.

Give yourself super memory

Ever worried you won't be able to remember everything for your school exams? *Don't panic.* There's an excellent technique that will boost your memory and make your exams a breeze. Research shows that when you learn something new from books or classes, you'll forget more than half of it within days. But if you spend a few minutes reviewing the information a week or so later, your ability to recall it is vastly improved. If you build weekly reviews into your study program when boning up for exams, your brain will commit the facts to long-term memory and you'll remember them for life. The technique works for learning everything from French verbs to the biology of plants.

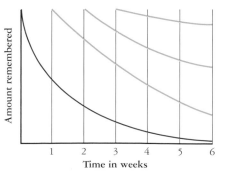

Green lines: amount remembered with weekly reviews.

Red line: amount remembered with no reviews.

Amount remembered

Time in weeks

TEST your *memory*

Try out these games to test the capacity of your short-term memory for storing **numbers, words,** and **visual** information. What will you remember best?

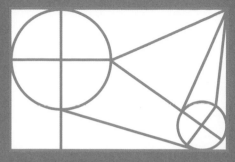

An artistic eye

STEP 1—To test your memory for visual detail, study the picture above for two minutes, then cover it up and try to draw it from memory. When you finish, give yourself a point for every line you got right.

Visual memory

How good is your memory for images? Study these 12 pictures for 30 seconds, then close the book, wait a minute, and write down as many as you can. How did you do?

You've done well if you remembered more than half of them, and more than 9 is excellent! Now test your memory for words in the game on the next page.

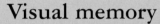

We hold **LONG** numbers in our heads by *remembering* their

NUMBER CRUNCHER

Numbers can be harder to remember than words or images. Give yourself 15 seconds to memorize the numbers on the right, then close the book, wait a minute, and see how many you can write down...

201290

STEP 2—Now do the same with the picture above, but this time look for familiar shapes in the lines. (Does it look like a picture of a kite with the Sun?) After two minutes cover up the picture and try to draw it from memory. Figure out your score again and compare it with your previous one.

You probably did better in the second test than the first because associating the lines with familiar shapes makes them easier to remember.

Did you know you have a photographic memory?

Get a friend to test you with some old photographs (40–50 is a good number). Ask them to keep five of the photos hidden to one side, noting what they are. Look through the main pile of photos quickly, spending a few seconds on each one. Ask your friend to shuffle the hidden five photos into the pile, then look through it again. Can you pick out the new photos?

You should be able to pick out the new photos quite easily. You'd struggle to describe what all the images were, but your brain must be storing information about each one of them or you wouldn't be able to tell the old photos from the new.

Carrot	Glass
Armpit	Elephant
Pillow	Trumpet	Flower
Nose	Chocolate
Turtle	
Moon	Stone

Word power

Study the 12 words above for 30 seconds. Close the book, wait a minute, and try to write them all down. Then check to see how well you did...

If you scored more than 8, good job! Most people remember words more easily than pictures by using the imagination to create memorable images.

SOUND

Most people can keep only 7 digits at a time in their memory. To help you remember more, try saying the numbers in pairs: 20, 12, 90, 99, 16.

9916

The creative mind

There's more to creativity than painting pictures or playing a musical instrument. The creative mind helps us solve problems and puzzles, and creative thinking has helped scientists to discover new ideas and invent new technologies. Creativity can help you in everyday life, too.

During a bit of creative bath-time thinking, Archimedes (257–212 BCE) discovered that you can measure the volume of a gold crown by seeing how much water it displaces.

Eureka moment

Greek scientist Archimedes was in the bathtub when the solution to a puzzle came to him. He leaped out of the water and ran naked down the street shouting *Eureka!* ("I found it!"). A "eureka moment"—when an idea pops into our head—can happen anywhere: in the bathtub, in bed, on a bus. Often a change of scenery or a relaxing setting is the trigger, allowing us to see a problem in a new light and hit upon the answer.

How to be creative

The brain works really hard behind the scenes when people are creative. To be inspired and come up with original ideas, the brain has to work through several stages.

WE HAVE A PROBLEM!
The first stage of creative thinking is to realize and understand the problem. In this case, how to cross the river.

BEHIND THE SCENES
You're not aware of the second stage happening. Your brain keeps mulling over the problem, even when you are thinking about other things.

LATERAL THINKING

The key to being creative is not to think *logically* but to think *laterally*—or sideways. Test your creative powers with these lateral-thinking puzzles.

1. It's spring. You see a carrot and two lumps of coal in somebody's garden. How did they get there?

They were part of a snowman, but when spring came the snow melted.

2. A dead man is lying on his back in a field. There are no footprints or tire tracks, and next to him is a backpack. How did he get there?

The backpack contains his parachute, which failed to open.

3. What's more powerful than God? To give you a clue: the rich need it, the poor have it, and if you eat it you will die.

The answer is the word "nothing."

WAVES OF CREATIVITY

Your brain is buzzing with electrical activity all the time, creating patterns that can be recorded by an EEG (electroencephalography) machine. The wavy lines these machines produce are called brain waves. Creative ideas are most likely to happen not when your brain is hard at work, producing "gamma waves," but when it's relaxed and producing more leisurely "alpha waves." A relaxed state opens up the mind to new possibilities, allowing unexpected thoughts and original ideas to come to the surface.

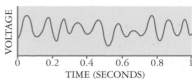

ALPHA WAVE

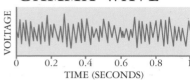

GAMMA WAVE

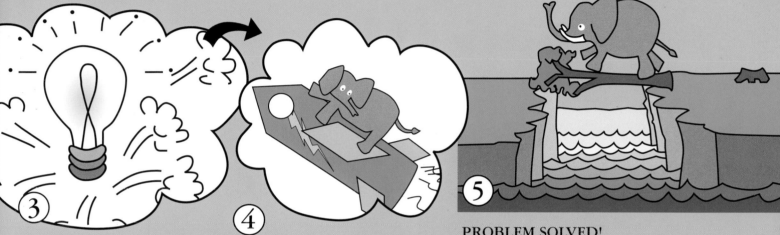

③ EUREKA!
This is the "light-bulb moment" when you hit on a great idea. Often the answer seems to come out of the blue, when you're thinking about something else.

④ MAYBE NOT...
Stage four is when you develop the idea. What at first looks like the best idea in the world may actually be useless. Great ideas are borne out of rejecting the junk and improving the good parts.

⑤ PROBLEM SOLVED!
The final stage is testing to see if the idea works. If you've gone through all the right stages, then this is when an idea really comes into its own. (Unless you're a very heavy elephant using a very weak tree...)

MAD GENIUS?

The highly creative mind shares some features with the mind of the mentally ill. A strong imagination, openness to new ideas, and lateral thinking are all helpful in creative thinking, but they are also common symptoms of mental disorders. So what's the difference? A sane person knows that their wild ideas are imaginary, but a person suffering from mental illness may confuse reality and imagination, resulting in delusions. A touch of mental illness can sometimes be a good thing though—some of the greatest thinkers and artists of history have suffered from mental illness.

ISAAC NEWTON

The brilliant scientist Isaac Newton (1642–1727) discovered the law of gravity and the laws of motion, yet he suffered from mental illness throughout his life. It is thought Newton may have had a condition called bipolar disorder, which causes swings of mood from severe depression to high excitement.

169

Test your *thinking* POWERS

WHAT'S IN A NAME?

Mary's mom has four children.
The first child is named April.
The second is named May.
The third is June.
What's the name of the
fourth child?

HOW LOGICAL ARE YOU?

You're given four cards, each of which
has a number on the front and a color
on the back. The visible faces show a
3, 8, red, and green. Suppose someone
tells you that if a card has an even
number on the front, the back is red.
Which cards do you need to turn over
to see if the rule is true?

Pretend you're going to bet $10
on the toss of a coin. First you
watch the coin being tossed five
times—it's heads every time.
Now it's your turn to bet.
Do you choose heads or tails?

DID YOU
GET THE
ANSWER
RIGHT?

Mary. It's a trick question!

The 8 and the green card. Very few people get this right. Most mistakenly turn over the red card, but it doesn't matter what's on the front of it. The rule says that if the front is an even number, the back is red—but it wouldn't be against the rule if the red card had an odd number. Instead of thinking purely logically (which the human brain isn't good at) we instinctively look for evidence to support the rule and so turn over the red card. But we should think like a scientist and try to disprove the rule. If the number on the front of green is even, the rule must be untrue. If the back of 8 is not red, the rule is untrue. The other cards cannot disprove the rule so don't matter.

We like to imagine we think things through LOGICALLY, but the truth is that our brains jump to conclusions. Even when we're *trying* to be logical, our subconscious mind and our *EMOTIONS* interfere with our thinking and trip us up. See if your thinking powers are good enough to solve these puzzles, but be warned: *they're tricky*!

THE SUNK COST FALLACY

You buy a movie ticket for $10 a day before going to see the film. When you arrive, you realize you've lost the ticket and the usher won't let you in. She offers to sell you another ticket for $10, but that will mean you've spent $20 on the movie. What do you decide to do: buy another ticket or walk away?

The rational answer is to buy a new ticket. The lost ticket should make no difference to your decision, just as losing a $10 bill the previous day should make no difference. If the movie was worth paying $10 to see yesterday, it still is today. This is an example of what economists call the "sunk costs fallacy." (A sunk cost is money that's already been spent.) Another example is watching a terrible movie all the way through "to get your money's worth" rather than walking out halfway. Walking out is the rational decision: the money has already been lost—don't waste time on top of it.

FALSE POSITIVES

TRUST ME, I'M A DOCTOR!

Imagine you go to the doctor and take a test for a rare illness that affects only 1 in 200 people. The doctor performs a blood test that works 98% of the time and tells you the result is positive, indicating you have the illness. What's the chance the test is wrong and you are, in fact, perfectly healthy?

It's 80% likely that the test is wrong. Does this feel unbelievable? The math proves it's true. Imagine 200 people take the test. Only one person is likely to have the illness, but the test will (on average) make four mistakes, most likely telling four healthy people they are sick. So there will be five positive results, but only one out of those five is a correct result.

THREE DOORS PROBLEM

Imagine you're on a TV game show. Hidden behind one of three doors is a sports car; pick the right door and you win it. You pick a door at random. The game show host, who knows where the car is, then opens another door and reveals an empty room. He gives you a chance to change your mind. Should you?

Yes. Your chance of winning if you change your mind rises from one-third to two-thirds. This can be hard to believe because it's counterintuitive (goes against your gut feeling)—it feels like the chance of winning if you switch should be 50:50, because there are two doors and the car could be behind either one. To see why the answer is two-thirds, work out your chance of losing if you always switch. You would only lose if you'd picked the car at first, so you have a one-third chance of losing if you always switch. Therefore, your chance of winning is 1 minus one-third, which is two-thirds.

STRANGE

When *injury* or *disease* strike the brain, the consequences can be strange. Like a computer program riddled with bugs, a damaged brain suffers from

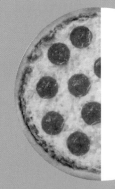

Lost in music

Clive Wearing was a brilliant musician until a virus attacked his brain and crippled his memory. Now he suffers from one of the worst cases of amnesia ever recorded: he constantly feels like he's woken from a long sleep and remembers nothing for more than 30 seconds. When his wife leaves the room then returns, he hugs her like a long-lost friend he's not seen for decades. When he meets someone, he'll shake their hand and ask, "Are you the king?" Because he can't remember them, he assumes they must be important. Despite his amnesia, he still knows how to play the piano and conduct an orchestra.

Two brains

People with severe epilepsy are sometimes treated with brain surgery that involves cutting their corpus callosum (a cable of nerve fibers between the two halves of the brain that helps them work together). After it's cut, people can behave as if they have two brains. They are able to draw different things at the same time with their two hands. Also, their "two brains" may fight for control, causing something called "alien hand" syndrome. One hand starts doing things the person can't control, like removing their clothes, or their left hand might lift a candy bar to the person's mouth while their right hand tries to snatch it away.

Taking sides

For people with spatial neglect, right or left suddenly ceases to exist. The right brain hemisphere helps us see things on the left side of space, and vice versa. If the top part of your right hemisphere gets damaged, you stop noticing things on the left, even though your eyes still work perfectly. If given food, you'll eat only food on the right side of the plate.

FACE OFF

Prosopagnosia is one of the weirdest disorders that can hit your brain. It means you suddenly stop being able to recognize people's faces, even though you can still see them perfectly well. People suffering from this disorder have to identify friends and family by their voice, smell, body language, or the clothes they wear. Prosopagnosia doesn't only affect human faces. One farmer with the disease could no longer recognize his cows, while another farmer couldn't recognize people's faces but could recognize his cows and dogs.

BRAINS

very specific *glitches*. These neural errors can shine light on what the various parts of the brain are for.

Scene from the film *The Diving Bell and the Butterfly* about Bauby's life.

Locked in

Following a massive stroke in the 1990s, French writer Jean-Dominique Bauby was left suffering from locked-in syndrome: his brain was conscious, but his body was paralyzed. All he could move was his left eyelid. He managed to write a book about his experience by dictating one letter at a time. It took two minutes to dictate each word and Bauby had to blink about 200,000 times to complete the book.

The strange case of the missing brain

About 30 years ago, a very bright math student in England was referred to a specialist to investigate the cause of a swollen head. The doctor conducted a brain scan and discovered, to his utter amazement, that the boy apparently had no brain. The boy's head was full of water and his cerebral (brain) tissue had been compressed into a thin layer just a millimeter or so thick that lined the inside of his skull. The student was suffering from hydrocephalus ("water on the brain"). Despite his condition, he had an IQ of 126, graduated summa cum laude, and went on to lead a perfectly normal life.

What can you see?

Nothing, I'm completely blind!

Well take a guess.

Um... then I guess horizontal red stripes??

Blindsight

In 1973, an English man underwent surgery to remove a tumor from the visual area in the back of his brain and was blinded as a result. But when doctors assessed his vision, they discovered he could correctly guess what he was looking at, despite being unaware of seeing it. The patient was just as astonished as his doctors. It was a fascinating discovery, since it suggested that the surgery had destroyed not vision but *consciousness of vision*. Some part of the brain was still processing images from the eyes and seeing.

Body doubles

Two creepy brain disorders are linked to prosopagnosia. People with Capgras Syndrome think their friends or family have been replaced by imposters. Cotard's Syndrome is even more bizarre. Sufferers see a stranger when they look in the mirror and think they don't exist, or they believe they're dead or dying. The two disorders are often caused by brain damage that disconnects the visual parts of the brain from the emotional parts.

Psychic

HAVE YOU EVER been thinking about an old friend just as they telephoned? Some people claim such experiences are caused by *psychic powers* such as

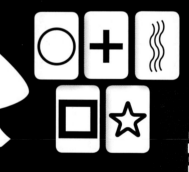

Telepathy

Clairvoyance

Telekinesis

Test your psychic powers

Try this with a friend. You need to:

1. Draw the five shapes (right) on identical pieces of card. These are called Zener cards after Karl Zener, who designed them to conduct scientific experiments on ESP.
2. Shuffle the cards and pick one at random, without showing anyone.
3. Concentrate hard on the pattern and try to beam it telepathically to a friend.
4. Do this 20 times, writing down a numbered list of the cards you've "sent"...

The science of ESP

If psychic phenomena really exist, it should be possible to detect them scientifically. This is what some scientists have tried to do in laboratories set up to investigate "parapsychology." In one typical experiment, scientists ask people to send images of Zener cards (above) telepathically. So far, there's no evidence that the person receiving the thought gets the right answer significantly more often than would happen by chance. One famous sceptic has even offered a prize of US$1 million to the first person to show ESP works under scientific conditions.

Will EVERYONE who *believes* in

powers

telepathy, but is there any scientific evidence that such things exist? Or are psychic phenomena just a matter of chance, coincidence, and trickery?

There's no doubt that people experience psychic phenomena. But is that because psychic powers are real, or could such experiences be more easily explained?

The power of coincidence

Some things do happen by chance, but because our brains are programmed to search for explanations and patterns, we have a tendency to over-interpret events. If you're thinking that a friend will call just as you're thinking about them, and the phone rings, you decide that you believe it was telepathy. But how many times did a friend call when you weren't thinking about them? We notice the coincidences and ignore the non-coincidences.

A miracle a month

British mathematician John Littlewood worked out that we experience an average of one miracle a month. Littlewood defined a miracle as a "one in a million" event. Assuming we're alert for 8 hours a day, we experience one million seconds each month, so the average number of miraculous seconds each month must be one. Next time you see Jesus on a slice of toast, put it down to the laws of chance.

Tricks of the trade

Psychics use a lot of trickery to read minds and tell fortunes. "Cold reading" involves looking for clues in a person's body language and appearance (a skill we all have). "Barnum statements" are seemingly personal insights that could apply to anyone, such as "I sense you're having problems with a close friend or relative..."

Confirmation bias

Visit a haunted house and you're *much* more likely to interpret spooky sounds as evidence of ghosts, especially if you already believe in the supernatural. We all have a natural tendency to notice evidence that supports our beliefs. Scientists call this tendency "confirmation bias" and try to avoid it by designing experiments that attempt to *disprove* (rather than prove) their theories.

... Your friend should write down each card, too. Add up the score at the end. By chance alone, your friend is 98% likely to get up to 7 cards right. The chance of guessing more than 10 is less than 1 in 300, and the chance of guessing all 20 is *1 in 100 trillion*. If you do get all 20, congratulations! You're both real psychics!

telekinesis please RAISE **MY** *hand*

WILL MACHINES BOOST OUR BRAINS?

Bionic bodies

People are already able to control artificial limbs using the power of thought. Nerves from the limb are connected to motors that make fingers or feet flex. Thinking about an action makes the limb respond.

Bionic brains

If we can replace parts of the body, why not parts of the brain, too? Scientists have already developed artificial retinas for blind people. They use tiny cameras, mounted on dark glasses, that send signals directly into the person's optic nerve, giving them a crude kind of replacement vision.

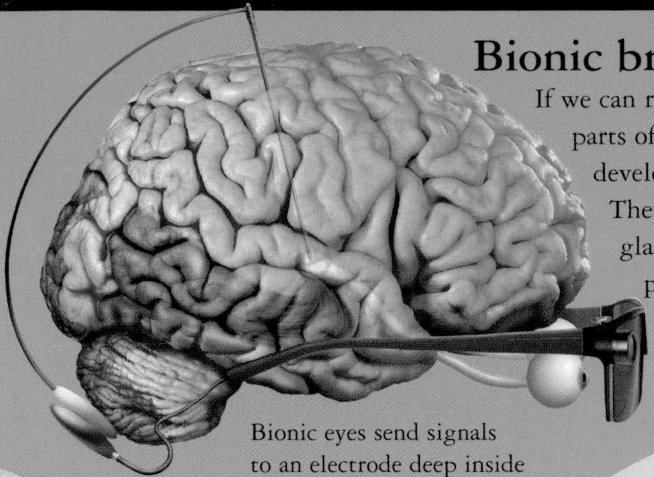

Bionic eyes send signals to an electrode deep inside the brain that stimulates the optic nerve.

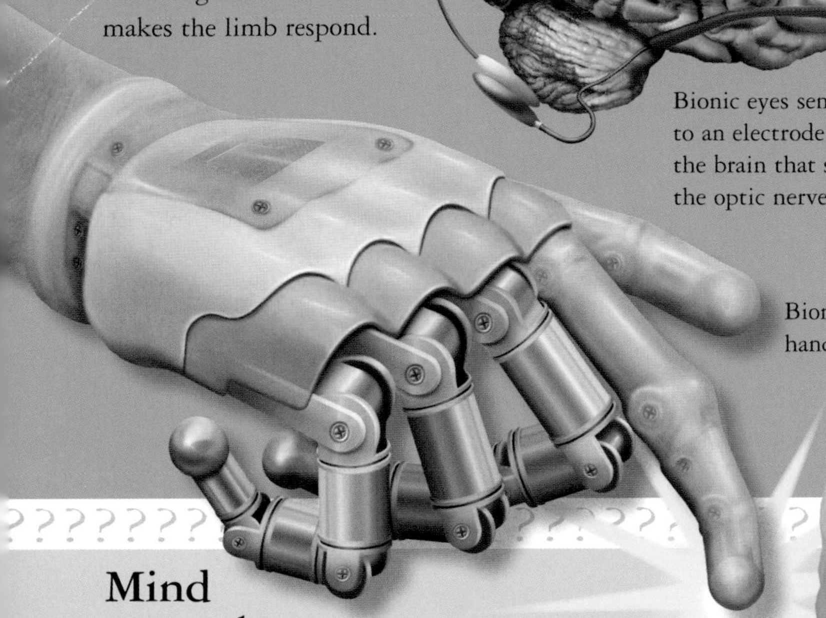

Bionic hand

Machine

The brain's been expanding and evolving for *millions* of years, but the story's **not** over yet. Some of the world's **SMARTEST** *human* brains are now

Mind control

If you hate typing messages into a computer keyboard or cell phone, you probably can't wait for a gadget that can read your mind. Scientists are testing brain-reading skullcaps and clip-on electrodes that detect brain activity, which may one day allow us to control cars, computers, games, and many other things simply by thinking about it.

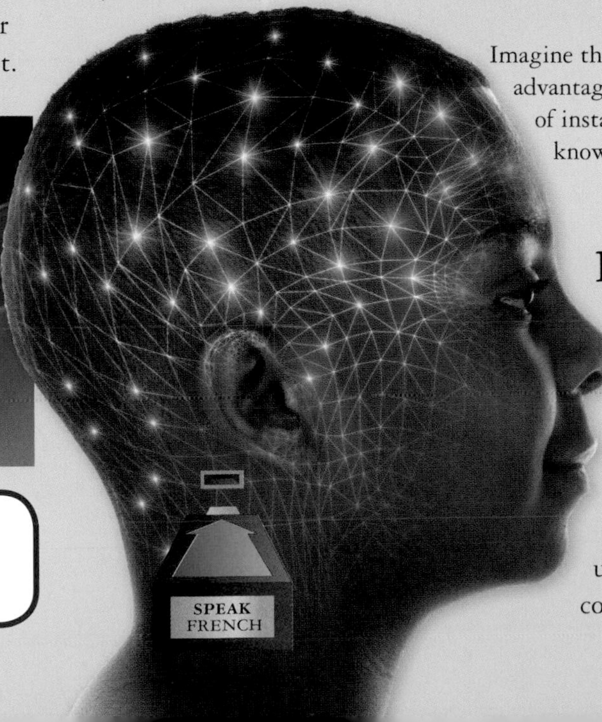

Imagine the advantages of instant knowledge.

I'm playing MINDBALL. If I **concentrate** *really* hard I can make the ball MOVE!

SPEAK FRENCH

Brainputers

Hate doing homework? What if someone could develop an electronic memory card for the brain that would enable you to learn a new language in seconds simply by plugging it in? In the future, brains and computers could merge together using implants inside your head and computers that work more like brains.

WILL MACHINES EVER THINK LIKE US?

Neural networks

One way to make computers more powerful is to build them more like brains. A neural network is a computerized model of a brain made up of artificial brain cells. If information is fed in, it slowly starts to recognize patterns and make connections, just like a human brain. If you show a neural network thousands of pictures of faces of people from France or China, then present it with an unknown face, it should be able to tell you whether it's French or Chinese without being told what to look for. That's very different from an ordinary computer, which has to be told exactly what to do.

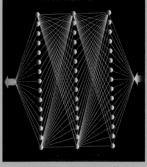

A neural network

A RAT flying a jet? Whatever next...

MINDS

developing AMAZING *artificial* ones, opening up astonishing new directions in which *brains* might evolve in the future.

Rat brain flies jet!

It takes a supercomputer the size of a warehouse to make a neural network as powerful as a mouse's brain, but it's much simpler to make an artificial brain from scratch. Scientists have done just that by taking 25,000 rat brain cells and forming them into a tiny neural network. They then wired the rat brain into a microchip and taught it to fly a jet fighter using a flight simulator program.

The "Interbrain"

Have you noticed how the Internet is turning our planet into a kind of giant brain? It already shows some brainlike behavior. It can store information and forget (delete) it. The Internet shows anger or excitement when lots of people discuss a hot topic in emails and blogs. It's almost as though the Internet has a mind of its own!

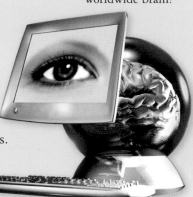

Are we creating a worldwide brain?

Turing test

Computers routinely beat people at chess, but no computer can walk, talk, think, or learn like a human—well, not yet. Scientists have been trying for decades to give computers artificial intelligence (making them think for themselves), but how will we know when they succeed? British mathematician Alan Turing suggested a simple but clever way of checking a computer's intelligence. You sit someone at a screen that's connected either to an "intelligent" computer or another person in a second room. Just by chatting and asking questions, the tester has to discover whether they're talking to a person or a computer. If they can't tell the difference, and it's actually a computer they're talking to, the computer can be regarded as intelligent.

One day, robots could react just like people.

177

Energy is everywhere. **Without it nothing would work.** The lights wouldn't come on in the morning, the shower wouldn't work, and don't even think about making toast.

To most of us, energy is what powers the gizmos and gadgets that make life easier. But it is also vital for life. Your body is a machine, and to live, move, and grow it needs energy.

Like fuel running a power plant, food gives you the energy to do stuff. But where did food get its energy?

In the following pages, we'll take a look at energy, where it comes from, and how the body uses it as a currency to get things done...

Body science: Energy

Life on EARTH in a YEAR

Humans have only been around for a blink of an eye. Scientists think the Earth is 4.6 billion years old and that life has only been around for about 4 billion years. All these billions of years can be confusing...

1 January

No life. Earth is a barren, lifeless chunk of space rock.

4.6 billion years ago...

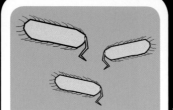

FEBRUARY 14

The earliest form of life appears—simple cells known as **prokaryotes**.

3.8 billion years ago...

MARCH 2

Cells start to use sunlight to make energy—a process called **photosynthesis**.

3.6 billion years ago...

MAY 30

More complex cells called **eukaryotes** start to appear.

2.7 billion years ago...

NOVEMBER 16

Primitive **invertebrates** scuttle along the ocean floor.

550 million years ago...

NOVEMBER 20

The large oceans start to house **fish and coral**.

500 million years ago...

NOVEMBER 25

The first mosslike **land plants** start to grow on the rocky surface.

430 million years ago...

NOVEMBER 28

Insects appear—first walking on land and then flying in the air.

410 million years ago...

DECEMBER 14

The first **mammals** start to roam the land.

210 million years ago...

DECEMBER 18

The skies are full of **birds** and **plants flower** for the first time.

150 million years ago...

DECEMBER 25

The **dinosaurs** bow out from the theater of life. Was it a meteor or disease?

65 million years ago...

DECEMBER 31

7:09 p.m. The first in the **genus of** *Homo* (early humans) walk on Earth.

2.5 million years ago...

... so let's take a look at the evolution of life as if it all happened in a year.

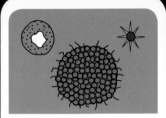

JULY 8

The first signs of **multicellular life** in the form of marine algae evolves.

1.7 million years ago...

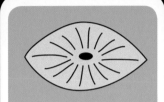

NOVEMBER 14

The first jelly-bodied **marine ancestors** of animals are born.

630 million years ago...

DECEMBER 3

Animals crawl from the sea and the **first amphibians** evolve.

360 million years ago...

DECEMBER 7

The first land-only **reptiles** are born.

290 million years ago...

DECEMBER 31

11:36 p.m. **Humans** start to look like we do today.

250,000 years ago...

DECEMBER 31

11:57 p.m. **Neanderthals**, the last of our early human relatives, die out.

25,000 years ago...

Science discoveries
COUNTDOWN

Wow! A lot has happened in a year. But it's not until the last 20 seconds that science really gets going. As the new year looms, here's a countdown of scientific discoveries!

20 seconds to go...

Anaximander thinks Earth is curved and floats in space (**550 BCE**)
Greek geeks consider the nature of matter (**450 BCE**)
Archimedes takes a bath and discovers water forces (**250 BCE**)
The Greeks measure the size of Earth using shadows (**240 BCEv**

10 seconds to go...

Persian scientist Alhazen writes the first book on optics (**1000 CE**)
The Chinese know the way and invent the compass (**1040**)
Grosseteste pioneers the value of scientific method (**1215**)

05 seconds to go...

Copernicus argues that Earth revolves around the Sun (**1543**)
Robert Boyle starts a discussion of chemical elements (**1661**)
Newton writes his laws of motion (**1687**)
Franklin uses a kite to prove lightning is electricity (**1752**)
Cavendish proves water isn't an element (**1784**)
Thomas Young enlightens us about light waves (**1803**)

01 second to go...

Darwin and Wallace write about the evolution of species (**1858**)
Pasteur proposes the germ theory of disease (**1861**)
Mendeleev draws up the periodic table (**1869**)
Lord Rayleigh explains why the sky is blue (**1871**)
Roentgen discovers X-rays (**1895**)
Landsteiner figures out basic blood groups (**1902**)
Albert Einstein publishes first paper on relativity (**1905**)
Tom Morgan discusses heredity and chromosomes (**1926**)
Lemaitre coins the Big Bang Theory (**1927**)
Programmable computers invented (**1943**)
The first nuclear bomb dropped on Hiroshima (**1945**)
DNA's double helix unraveled (**1953**)
One small step for man: first men on the Moon (**1969**)
Oh, Dolly! The first mammal (sheep) is cloned (**1996**)
The worldwide web moves into our homes (**1998**)
The human genome is deciphered (**2003**)

SOLAR POWER

The Sun is 93 million miles (150 million kilometers) away from Earth.

Solar power sounds like a recent invention, but it's not. It has been around since the dawn of time and almost every living thing on Earth is powered by it.

The Sun is a big ball of burning hydrogen gas. The temperature at the center of the Sun reaches over **18,000,000°F (10,000,000°C)!** This high temperature combined with the high pressure causes millions of nuclear reactions to take place.

SUNSHINE POWER PLANT

The Sun is the energy factory of Earth. Every second the Sun produces about 5 million tons of pure energy. This travels out into space as sunlight. Some of it reaches Earth and it is this sunlight energy that is trapped by plants and used as fuel. Humans are unable to convert sunlight energy directly. We aren't solar powered; instead, we need it changed into an energy we can use. A little like finding the right-shaped battery for your favorite toy, humans need the right type of energy to work—**chemical energy**.

The Earth's atmosphere reduces the intensity of the Sun's rays. The sunlight that gets through is ready to be converted into usable energy.

How is sunlight converted into chemical energy?

A brilliant process called **photosynthesis** allows plants to absorb the sunlight and change it into chemical energy, which is then used by the plants.

LIGHT ENERGY

CARBON DIOXIDE

A beneficial by-product of photosynthesis is oxygen.

OXYGEN

Plants suck up water from the soil and absorb carbon dioxide from the air to help change the sunlight energy into sugar (glucose).

Spare sugar is stored in seeds, roots, and fruits, ready for us to harvest.

WATER

water + carbon dioxide + sunlight = oxygen + chemical energy

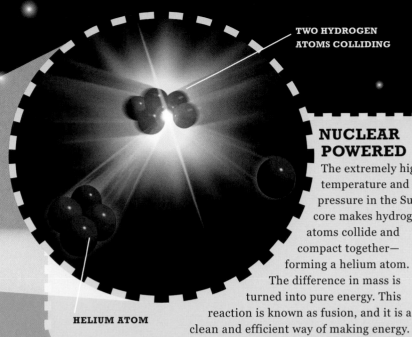

TWO HYDROGEN ATOMS COLLIDING

HELIUM ATOM

NUCLEAR POWERED

The extremely high temperature and pressure in the Sun's core makes hydrogen atoms collide and compact together— forming a helium atom. The difference in mass is turned into pure energy. This reaction is known as fusion, and it is a clean and efficient way of making energy.

HOME ENERGY Most of the electricity you use at home is made by the Sun. Large power plants are fueled by *fossil fuels*, which are the remains of plants that once, millions of years ago, trapped the Sun's energy.

RENEWABLE ENERGY Fossil fuels won't last forever and are polluting the atmosphere. So, scientists are spending more time looking for renewable sources of energy. Solar panels and wind turbines use the Sun's rays and its influence on our weather to make energy (and they are less polluting, too).

Sunlight takes 8½ minutes to reach Earth. It travels at the speed of light, 186,282 mile/s (299,792 km/s).

Humans have learned to combine different plants to make new foods, like bread, cakes, and candies. Eating plants isn't the only way humans absorb chemical energy. Humans are also meat eaters and we absorb the Sun's energy by eating animals that have eaten plants.

I spend a quarter of the day munching on grass and my four stomachs help me absorb the chemical energy.

Humans need energy to survive, from breathing and thinking, to moving and eating. We need oxygen to help turn stored chemical energy into movement (kinetic energy).

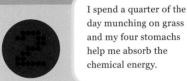

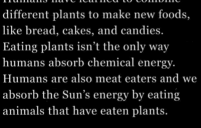

CHEMICAL ENERGY

KINETIC ENERGY

chemical energy + water = carbon dioxide + water + kinetic energy

ENERGY makes the body go round

Energy is used to get stuff done. The body wouldn't be able to do anything without it. So how does energy get work done? Well, the best way to see energy is as a currency. Like money makes the world go round, energy does the same to your body.

THE BODY BANK

Once you have eaten your energy, it gets stored around your body, like savings in a bank. Unless you release it, it just sits there and doesn't do anything. These savings are usually in the form of chemical energy.

Energy has the amazing talent of being indestructible. It never disappears, it just changes form, like money changing hands.

INVESTMENT
eating food stores chemical energy

The food we eat contains chemical energy and that is the perfect energy type to make our bodies work. By eating food we are *investing* energy into our bodies, like putting *savings* into the bank. Any chemical energy we don't use is stored for future activities, when it can be exchanged into different energy currencies.

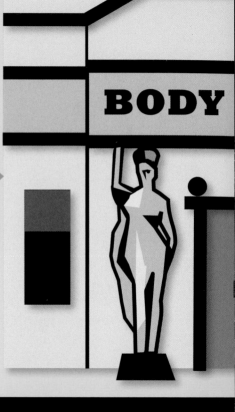

BODY

ENERGY CURRENCIES

There are different types of energy—similar to the different currencies you get around the world. You can change money from one currency to another when you need it for your vacations. Energy acts in the same way.

Electrical energy is a very fast and efficient type of energy. Our brain and nerves use a type of electrical energy to get messages around the body.

Heat energy is generated by particles moving. The faster they move the hotter they get. In the body heat is normally a by-product of energy conversion.

Kinetic energy is the energy of movement. The faster something moves the more kinetic energy it has. The body changes chemical energy into kinetic movement.

THE BODY BANK ACCOUNTS

There are two different energy bank accounts in your body. They both allow access to your invested energy, but offer different ways of getting your hands on it. Your body uses both energy bank accounts for different types of activities.

AEROBIC

The **aerobic** account is for the **patient** and **steady investor**. It has a slower release of energy and needs oxygen, but it gives you more for your money, allowing you to *keep going for longer*.

ANAEROBIC

The **anaerobic** account is for the **quick** and **explosive shopper**. They want their energy quickly, but unfortunately, it doesn't go very far and only supplies energy for *short periods of time*.

BANK

SPENDING
physical activity uses kinetic energy

The body has a lot of work to do. From the brain thinking, the lungs breathing, and to the heart pumping—they all need energy. Then on top of that there's all the physical activity we like to do. Luckily, we don't have to feed ourselves as we work; instead, the body draws on the chemical savings that have been invested and converts them into kinetic energy. The exchange isn't 100 percent perfect because some energy is changed into heat energy.

Chemical energy is the energy trapped in molecules. Most plants use photosynthesis to trap this energy. Food and gasoline are high in chemical energy.

Light energy is made in stars, like our Sun. It moves at amazing speeds and can travel vast distances. Unfortunately, the body can't process it directly.

Nuclear energy is made when minute particles, atoms, are split or fused. It produces lots of energy. The body doesn't use this form of energy.

CASH ENERGY The chemical investments stored in the body are used by the body's cells to do their work. For this, the cells need the chemical energy to be turned into a currency they can use. Instead of using a cash machine to take energy out as cash, they use *cellular respiration*, which converts stored chemical energy into ATP (adenosine triphosphate)—the raw energy used by every cell.

Body MATTER

Matter is all around you. Everything is made of it. Matter consists of three main states—**solid, liquid, and gas**. Each state of matter is influenced by energy and acts differently. These properties make them suited to different roles in the body.

The human body is made up of each state of matter—solid, liquid, and gas. They all work together to make the body run smoothly, like a finely tuned machine.

The particles in solids are packed closely together. They have little energy and this keeps them compact and strong.

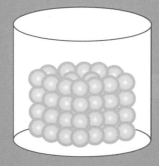

Liquid particles have more energy and flow easily over each other. Liquids take the shape of the container they are in.

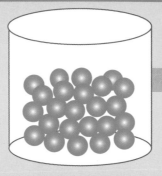

Gas particles have even more energy and are even farther apart. All they want to do is escape.

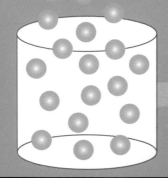

There is a 4th STATE OF MATTER...

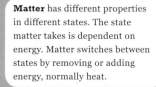

solid

Most solids are hard, like teeth and bone, though some can be soft, like the heart and brain. Solids have a fixed volume and can hold their shape without any support, but most can be chipped, snapped, or cut.

Matter has different properties in different states. The state matter takes is dependent on energy. Matter switches between states by removing or adding energy, normally heat.

When a liquid cools down its particles lose their energy and they slow down, becoming less fluid and more **solid**.

FREEZE

MELT

liquid

Liquids are fluid and want to flow away. Though liquids can change their shape, their volume remains the same. Some liquids flow more easily than others; this is known as viscosity. Blood, for example, is more viscous (thicker) than water.

When solids heat up, they gain more energy and their particles break their bonds and become **liquid**.

When gas loses energy it slows down and its particles stick together, becoming **liquid**.

CONDENSE

EVAPORATE

gas

Gases want to expand and drift away. Their shape and volume is constantly changing, depending on the space they are in. You breathe gases in and out of your lungs and they are carried around your body by the blood.

When a liquid heats up it gains energy and its particles start to move farther apart, until they are whizzing around as **gas particles**.

plasma

Plasma is a gas and is formed at extremely high temperatures. The Sun makes a natural plasma, but plasmas can also be created artificially for use in television screens and fluorescent light bulbs. Plasma gas acts differently to normal gases because it is influenced by electric and magnetic fields. Part of the blood is also called plasma, but it is not the same thing—it is a liquid.

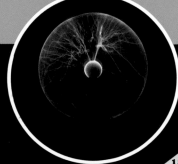

It's a GAS BUSINESS

Gas and energy go hand in hand. Without gas, humans would struggle to survive. This is because gas is what we breathe. And **breathing is vital to life**. But why is this? Well, believe it or not, most of the energy in our bodies is useless. It is chemical energy that we have absorbed from food. But this energy is trapped. To release it, we need oxygen, and we need it in our bloodstream NOW! Here's how it gets there.

It all happens in THE LUNG FACTORY
Swim with me to the factory. And then you'll see.

Your lungs' surface area is the size of a tennis court.

You breathe in and out around 20 times a minute.

A GOOD THING about gas is that it moves and diffuses at great speed. This means it positively races to your cells, where it helps make your body's energy. Just imagine if you breathed solids or liquids. Their slower particles would takes ages to reach the cells. This would make you very sluggish—unlike gas breathers who can run at high speed!

Air breathed measured in liters per minute

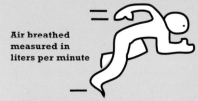

High intensity RUNNING—150 L/min

MARATHON RUNNING—90 L/min

SITTING— 6 L/min

Lungs are like a non-stop factory.

78% nitrogen 21% oxygen

Take a breath
The average person breathes in 6 liters of fresh air a minute. But not all of that is oxygen! The air we breathe is a mixture of gases. The main two are oxygen and nitrogen.

You breathe air
into your lungs through your nose and mouth.

CO₂

oxygen

Lungs

Capillaries

Alveoli

You have two lungs, one on each side of your chest. On the outside, they are pink and squishy, but inside they are packed with tiny airways, which branch out like trees.

WHERE THE GAS GOES
At the ends of the airways are around 600 million tiny air sacs (called alveoli), and these are covered in even tinier blood vessels (called capillaries). When you breathe in, the air sacs fill up with air. And when you breathe out, they empty out.

Blood O_2

CO_2 **Lungs**

GAS DIFFUSION
Once it's in the air sacs, oxygen (O2) pushes its way through the walls and into the bloodstream in a process called diffusion. At the same time carbon dioxide (CO2) diffuses back the other way—from the blood into the air sacs. You don't need the carbon dioxide, so you just breathe it out of your body!

THE GAS EXCHANGE
Gas can move from air to liquid (like oxygen from your lungs into your blood), or from liquid to gas (carbon dioxide traveling from your blood to your lungs). But how does this work? Well, when you breathe in, there is more oxygen in your lungs than in your blood. Oxygen doesn't seem to like this, so it travels into the blood in an effort to even things out. Carbon dioxide has the same sort of idea— there is more of it in the blood than the lungs, so it diffuses back into the lungs. It's a little like the carbon dioxide in a carbonated drink. There is far more carbon dioxide in the drink than in the air. So when you open the bottle, all the tiny bubbles of carbon dioxide race to get out!

A BODY OF WATER

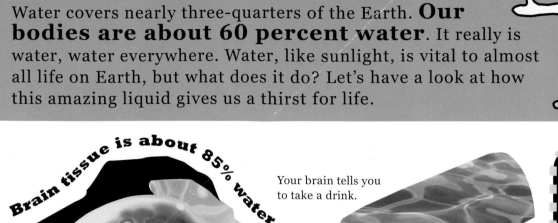

Water covers nearly three-quarters of the Earth. **Our bodies are about 60 percent water**. It really is water, water everywhere. Water, like sunlight, is vital to almost all life on Earth, but what does it do? Let's have a look at how this amazing liquid gives us a thirst for life.

Three-quarters of my body weight is due to water. That's heavy, man!

Brain tissue is about 85% water

The brain picks up the warning signals.

Your brain tells you to take a drink.

Your body tells the brain it needs water.

Water is drunk—it flows down into the stomach, where it passes into the rest of the body.

Brain fluid Your brain is key to your survival. Brain tissue is made from 85 percent water, and it is surrounded by a fluid that is also made largely of water.

KEEPING COOL
The average core body temperature is around 98.6°F (37°C). Exercise, illness, and even climate can increase the body's temperature, so it needs to cool down. The water released as sweat does that job. The body then uses heat energy to evaporate water, and so lower the core body temperature.

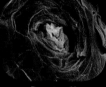

Sweat cell

THIRSTY WORK
You would survive less than a week without water, and only hours if you were in a hot desert without a drink. This vital need for water triggers an instinct in your brain, known as thirst, which kicks in when your body starts to dehydrate. The body steals water from less vital tissues and fluids, such as saliva; that makes your mouth feel dry. Sensors throughout the body keep a check on water levels and tell the brain when you need more water.

Lubrication Water is used by our joints to maintain cartilage and make synovial fluid. These supply much needed lubrication to the joints and allow smooth movement as well as longer-lasting joints.

Blood is made up of cells suspended in a fluid called plasma. Blood plasma makes up about 55 percent of blood and is mostly water. The body needs water to maintain a consistent volume of blood, around 5 liters (10½ pints).

Energy Water is vital in the production of the raw energy produced and used by the body's cells. Water is also needed to make the gastric juices that help break down food ready for energy production.

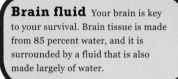

Rehydration

Replacing the water your body uses, especially after exercise, is very important. Many sports drinks also contain sodium and potassium salts, which are lost through sweating. These help your nerve cells to work as they should.

Isotonic

These are good for replacing fluids fast. They contain 20 percent fruit juice, which gives the body a sugar boost, replacing some of the energy that has been lost.

80% water
20% juice

Hypotonic

These offer fast fluid replacement and have a higher percentage of water. They don't give much of an energy boost and are best after exercise to prevent dehydration.

90% water
10% juice

Hypertonic

These offer more energy replacement, with nearly a third of their mix made from sugary juice. This type of drink is best drunk after exercise to replenish lost energy.

71% water
29% juice

Headaches When the body loses water, doing stuff becomes harder and you get tired. If your brain doesn't get enough water, it produces chemicals that cause pain, alerting you to the problem.

Sweating and breathing are two ways we lose water from the body. Exercise and hot weather make you sweat much faster.

Blood is mostly water, and when the amount of water in the blood drops, it affects the rest of your body. With less water present, the volume of blood decreases, and your heart has to work harder to pump it around the body. If the brain and other organs don't receive enough blood they can't work correctly, and you start to feel weak and confused.

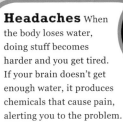

During vigorous exercise we sweat around 2 pints per hour.

The kidneys help regulate the levels of water in your body. As dehydration takes hold, your kidneys stop water from entering your bladder. This is only a short-term measure to save as much water as possible.

RUNNING ON EMPTY

All the water in the body has substances dissolved in it. Every living cell needs water, and the process by which water moves in and out of the cells is called osmosis. Water will move across a cell wall if there is less water on the other side, so as to keep the solution inside and outside the cell at the same concentration. If you start to dehydrate, water is drawn out of the cells to keep the amount of water in the blood at the right level. As little as a 2 percent drop in body water can lead to symptoms of dehydration.

Cramps If you are exercising hard you may start to get cramp in your muscles as they lose water and salts.

TOO MUCH WATER Even though it is important to keep hydrated, you can overdo it. Drinking too much plain water can upset the delicate balance between water and dissolved salts in the body. If the salts become too diluted, the brain starts to swell, which can be dangerous.

Our bodies might contain liquids and gases, but as a whole we are **solid beings**. Solids have many properties that make them ideal for certain roles in the body. Some of these properties are truly amazing, like superpowers. So, let's check out *solids* and your *inner superhero*.

SOLID PROPERTIES

Hardness
This is how resistant solids are to being dented or scratched.

Density
This is how much matter (atoms or molecules) is packed into the object's volume.

Elasticity
This is the ability to return to an original state after being stretched.

Strength
This is the ability to cope with force and stress...

Mild-mannered SKELETON
Superman uses Clark Kent, Batman has Bruce Wayne, and Wonder Woman is Diana Prince. So who is the alter ego of your solid superhero? Well, it's the skeleton. The skeleton is a collection of solids, most notably the bones. On the surface it doesn't look like much, but there's more to it than meets the eye socket...

Bones are **tough** and **provide protection** to major organs—most importantly the brain.

Bones are **lightweight and strong** and are **ideal for moving**. Imagine trying to walk with heavy bones!

Bones have a small amount of elasticity and absorb some of the impact from moving.

vertebrae

The skeleton offers a solid framework for muscles to attach.

The spine is made up of 33 small bones called vertebrae. They sit on top of each other, separated by cushioning disks. The spine provides amazing flexibility and strength.

spongy bone

The outside layer of bone is tough and compact. Inside is what is known as spongy bone, which is a mix of bone and air. This gives spongy bone a low density, making it light but also very strong.

The human adult body contains 206 bones. As a child you have nearly 300 bones, but some join together as you grow.

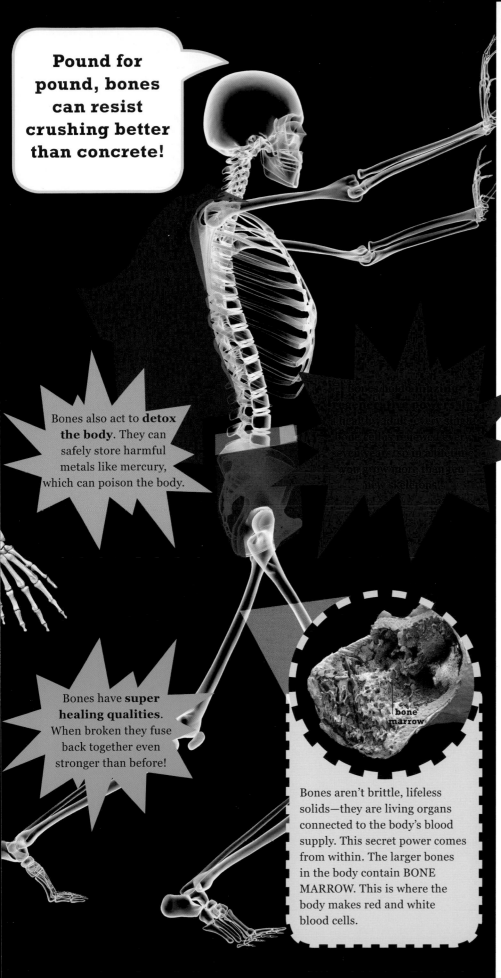

Pound for pound, bones can resist crushing better than concrete!

Bones also act to **detox the body**. They can safely store harmful metals like mercury, which can poison the body.

Bones have **super healing qualities**. When broken they fuse back together even stronger than before!

bone marrow

Bones aren't brittle, lifeless solids—they are living organs connected to the body's blood supply. This secret power comes from within. The larger bones in the body contain BONE MARROW. This is where the body makes red and white blood cells.

All good superheroes have a SIDEKICK

The skeleton can't perform all the solid roles the body demands. It is given a helping hand from some other dynamic solids.

Teeth

Their hard edges help to mash and cut food—vital for taking in the energy we need to survive.

Nails

Your fingernails might look useless, but think again. Try untying a knot without them!

Ligaments, cartilage, muscles

These tissues all attach, support, and move the skeleton. Their properties make them perfect sidekicks. Their main power is in their high elasticity, which helps absorb, stabilize, and control impact and movement.

Skin tights and underpants

Your skin is the body's largest organ. It protects and guards the body from the outside world and stretches over your unique body shape. On top of its protective qualities, skin is waterproof, helps to maintain body temperature, makes vitamin D from the Sun's rays, and gives us the ability to feel and touch. The skin can also mend itself—when broken or cut, it heals by forming a protective cap, known as a scab. A true super suit!

Little bits of Body

Making a body isn't as simple as pouring the right measurements of elements into a mixer and spinning everything around. The architecture of our bodies is fantastically complex, from systems, organs, and cells, right down to the tiniest building blocks of all—atoms.

ATOMS

These are generally considered the smallest building blocks, but atoms themselves are made from even smaller parts, called subatomic particles, meaning smaller than an atom. An atom has a nucleus made of protons (red, below) and neutrons (green). Protons have a positive electrical charge, and neutrons are neutral. The third subatomic particle is the electron (yellow). Electrons are little balls of negatively charged energy that orbit the central nucleus. Atoms of a particular element (or basic type) always have the same number of protons. This number gives an element its unique atomic number.

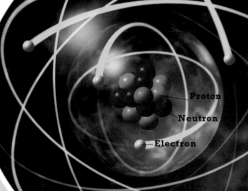

Proton
Neutron
Electron

SIZE MATTERS
If an atom is minuscule, how small is its nucleus? Well, if you think of the nucleus as the size of a golf ball, then the atom itself would be the size of the Eiffel Tower!

EACH CHEMICAL element is made up of its own type of atom. Millions of these tiny particles join together to make the element. So, calcium is only made from calcium atoms and hydrogen is only made from hydrogen atoms.

TYPES OF CELLS in the human body

BLOOD CELLS make up nearly half the cells in your body. Red blood cells carry oxygen to the body's tissues and carry away waste (carbon dioxide). White blood cells fight infection.

EYE CELLS include rod cells and cone cells at the back of the eye, which help you see color and tones. Lens cells (shown here), help to focus light on the back of the eye to make clear images.

NERVE CELLS are called neurons, and their job is to carry messages to and from your brain. The messages travel as electrical signals and tell your heart to beat, legs to walk, and fingers to feel.

FAT CELLS mostly occur just under our skin. They look a little like oil-filled bubbles and are where our bodies store excess energy from the food we eat. Fat cells increase in number as we get fatter.

BRAIN CELLS include neurons and glial cells. There are 100 billion neurons in the brain and even more glial cells. Glial cells are support cells—their job is to help neurons work effectively.

SKIN CELLS form under the surface of your skin, then move up over the next month. Around 30,000 skins cells flake off every day—and these make up most of the dust in your home!

ATOMS make ELEMENTS, which make our BODY CELLS!

ORGANS

The main players in the business of the body are the organs. Here are a few of the key members.

HEART This is the body's blood pump. It sends blood to the lungs, and pumps it around the whole body.

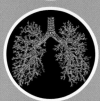

LUNGS These are where oxygen passes into the blood, and carbon dioxide passes out of it. Lungs fill with gas (and empty out) about 20 times a minute.

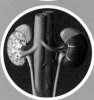

KIDNEYS These two organs are the cleaners of the body. They filter out waste chemicals and excess liquid, and turn them into urine.

BRAIN This is the nerve center of the body. It controls actions like breathing and allows us to think. The brain is as soft as pudding, so is protected by the hard bone of the skull.

SKIN The largest organ in the body, the skin acts as a protective barrier against the outside world. It is packed with nerves and senses touch or pain.

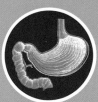

STOMACH This is where your food goes when you swallow it. Your stomach partially digests your food, churning it into a thick liquid called chyme.

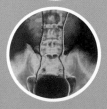

BLADDER The body produces a lot of liquid waste, and this is the holding area. When it's full of urine, you need to go!

CELLS join together to make ORGANS

BODY SYSTEMS

Organs work in teams, known as systems. There are seven major body systems with seven different functions, all make one working human.

ENDOCRINE SYSTEM This sends chemical messages, called hormones, around the body to control sleep, temperature, growth, and reproduction.

RESPIRATORY SYSTEM The most important part of this system is the lungs. They take in air, so oxygen can pass into the blood system. And they remove waste carbon dioxide.

DIGESTIVE SYSTEM This is pretty much one long tube from your mouth to your you-know-what! Everything you eat passes through here.

CIRCULATORY SYSTEM This is your heart and blood vessels. Blood carries oxygen and nutrients around the body, and carries away carbon dioxide.

NERVOUS SYSTEM This, the body's information network, comprises the brain and nerves. It works at lightning speeds—signals zip along nerves at 250 mph (400 km/h).

MUSCLES There are two kinds— voluntary muscles that you use when you turn your head, and involuntary muscles that work without you thinking about them, such as when your heart beats.

BONES These give your body shape and hold it upright. Bones are living tissue, with spaces for blood vessels and nerves. If you cut them, they bleed, and if you break them, they grow back together again.

Hormones are produced in glands. The pituitary gland (at the base of the brain), kick-starts puberty, and the thyroid (in the neck) controls your energy levels.

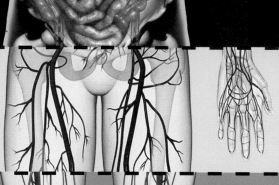

Chemical CREATION

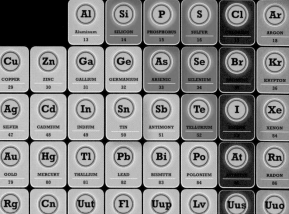

So we know that matter makes up everything around us, and that it has different states, making our bodies work efficiently. *But what is matter?* Matter is a general name for all the substances in the universe. **Wood**, **air**, **metal**, even your skin and bones, can be broken down into simpler substances called **ELEMENTS**.

H HYDROGEN 1																	**He** HELIUM 2
Li LITHIUM 3	**Be** BERYLLIUM 4											**B** BORON 5	**C** CARBON 6	**N** NITROGEN 7	**O** OXYGEN 8	**F** FLUORINE 9	**Ne** NEON 10
Na SODIUM 11	**Mg** MAGNESIUM 12											**Al** Aluminum 13	**Si** SILICON 14	**P** PHOSPHORUS 15	**S** SULFUR 16	**Cl** CHLORINE 17	**Ar** ARGON 18
K POTASSIUM 19	**Ca** CALCIUM 20	**Sc** SCANDIUM 21	**Ti** TITANIUM 22	**V** VANADIUM 23	**Cr** CHROMIUM 24	**Mn** MANGANESE 25	**Fe** IRON 26	**Co** COBALT 27	**Ni** NICKEL 28	**Cu** COPPER 29	**Zn** ZINC 30	**Ga** GALLIUM 31	**Ge** GERMANIUM 32	**As** ARSENIC 33	**Se** SELENIUM 34	**Br** BROMINE 35	**Kr** KRYPTON 36
Rb RUBIDIUM 37	**Sr** STRONTIUM 38	**Y** YTTRIUM 39	**Zr** ZIRCONIUM 40	**Nb** NIOBIUM 41	**Mo** MOLYBDENUM 42	**Tc** TECHNETIUM 43	**Ru** RUTHENIUM 44	**Rh** RHODIUM 45	**Pd** PALLADIUM 46	**Ag** SILVER 47	**Cd** CADMIUM 48	**In** INDIUM 49	**Sn** TIN 50	**Sb** ANTIMONY 51	**Te** TELLURIUM 52	**I** IODINE 53	**Xe** XENON 54
Cs Cesium 55	**Ba** BARIUM 56	LANTHANIDES or RARE-EARTH METALS 57—71	**Hf** HAFNIUM 72	**Ta** TANTALUM 73	**W** TUNGSTEN 74	**Re** RHENIUM 75	**Os** OSMIUM 76	**Ir** IRIDIUM 77	**Pt** PLATINUM 78	**Au** GOLD 79	**Hg** MERCURY 80	**Tl** THALLIUM 81	**Pb** LEAD 82	**Bi** BISMUTH 83	**Po** POLONIUM 84	**At** ASTATINE 85	**Rn** RADON 86
Fr FRANCIUM 87	**Ra** RADIUM 88	ACTINIDES or RARE-EARTH RADIOACTIVE METALS 89—103	**Rf** RUTHERFORDIUM 104	**Db** DUBNIUM 105	**Sg** SEABORGIUM 106	**Bh** BOHRIUM 107	**Hs** HASSIUM 108	**Mt** MEITNERIUM 109	**Ds** DARMSTADTIUM 110	**Rg** ROENTGENIUM 111	**Cn** COPERNICUM 112	**Uut** UNUNTRIUM 113	**Fl** FLEROVIUM 114	**Uup** UNUNPENTIUM 115	**Lv** LIVERMORIUM 116	**Uus** UNUNSEPTIUM 117	**Uuo** UNUNOCTIUM 118

La LANTHANUM 57	**Ce** CERIUM 58	**Pr** PRASEODYMIUM 59	**Nd** NEODYMIUM 60	**Pm** PROMETHIUM 61	**Sm** SAMARIUM 62	**Eu** EUROPIUM 63	**Gd** GADOLINIUM 64	**Tb** TERBIUM 65	**Dy** DYSPROSIUM 66	**Ho** HOLMIUM 67	**Er** ERBIUM 68	**Tm** THULIUM 69	**Yb** YTTERBIUM 70	**Lu** LUTETIUM 71
Ac ACTINIUM 89	**Th** THORIUM 90	**Pa** PROTACTINIUM 91	**U** URANIUM 92	**Np** NEPTUNIUM 93	**Pu** PLUTONIUM 94	**Am** AMERICIUM 95	**Cm** CURIUM 96	**Bk** BERKELIUM 97	**Cf** CALIFORNIUM 98	**Es** EINSTEINIUM 99	**Fm** FERMIUM 100	**Md** MENDELEVIUM 101	**No** NOBELIUM 102	**Lr** LAWRENCIUM 103

Each vertical column is called a GROUP, or family, of elements. Some groups have elements sharing very similar properties. Other groups have elements with less in common.

Dmitri Mendeleev was a Russian scientist who devised this version of the periodic table, which enabled other scientists to include new elements as they were discovered.

The periodic table

is a way of displaying the 111 known elements. All the elements are listed in order of increasing atomic number. Atomic numbers are based on the number of protons in the nucleus of an atom. The way they are arranged relates to the properties of the element. Scientists noted that some elements had similar properties according to the number and arrangement of the electrons in the atom's outer shell. This enabled them to put them into vertical columns called groups and horizontal rows, or periods. Elements in groups react in a similar manner and form compounds the same way.

Element types

Elements can be grouped into similar types. Every element has a name, a symbol of one or two letters, and an atomic number.

Kr — Symbol
KRYPTON — Name
36 — Atomic number

KEY:

Alkali metals: *These silvery metals are very reactive.*

Alkaline-earth metals: *These shiny, silvery-white metals are reactive.*

Transition metals: *Many are strong and have high boiling and melting points.*

Lanthanides: *Many are soft, shiny, and silvery-white metals.*

Actinides: *These are radioactive heavy elements.*

Poor metals: *Softer, weaker metals.*

Nonmetals: *Most are gases at room temperature and easily snap as solids.*

Halogens: *These nonmetals are highly reactive and harmful.*

Noble gases: *These nonmetals are the least reactive of all the elements.*

O
OXYGEN
8

Oxygen is the most abundant element in the body, mainly in the form of water, H_2O.

C
CARBON
6

Carbon forms the basis of the body's most complex molecules, such as proteins.

H
HYDROGEN
1

Hydrogen is found in water molecules but is also important in making ATP.

N
NITROGEN
7

Nitrogen occurs in proteins and other organic compounds, and is the main gas in the atmosphere.

P
PHOSPHORUS
15

Phosphorus is vital in the formation of teeth and bones, and also the energy chemical ATP.

K
POTASSIUM
19

Potassium is a key chemical in making nerve cells transmit electrical signals.

Cl
CHLORINE
17

Chlorine is usually combined with sodium as salt. It is used for respiration and kidney function.

Na
SODIUM
11

Sodium controls the flow of water in the body and works with potassium in firing nerve cells.

Mg
MAGNESIUM
12

Magnesium helps the immune system to work, as well as the muscles and nerves.

S
SULFUR
16

Sulfur is vital in proteins, helps the blood to clot, and also makes your hair curl.

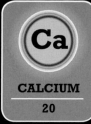

Ca
CALCIUM
20

Calcium makes the bones and teeth hard, and makes the heart and other muscles contract.

Fe
IRON
26

Iron is vital for carrying oxygen in the blood. It is found in meat and leafy vegetables.

I
IODINE
53

Iodine regulates many of the body's processes, such as digestion and hormones.

In addition to these 13, the body needs trace amounts of other elements, including copper, zinc, cobalt, lithium, fluorine, boron, chromium, and selenium.

10% hydrogen

65% oxygen (in H_2O)

18% carbon

0.15% chlorine

0.15% sodium

3% nitrogen

1% phosphorus

0.35% potassium

0.008% iron

1.6% calcium

0.25% sulfur

0.05% magnesium

0.00004% iodine

This is how much of each of the 13 ELEMENTS we're made of.

Not all of the elements are good for the body. Radioactive elements can kill cells.

There is a very strong acid in your body. Gastric juices contain hydrochloric acid, which breaks food down into smaller molecules during digestion.

The body also contains tiny amounts of poisonous elements, such as arsenic and mercury, but they are so small they don't cause any harm.

You are what YOU EAT

Your body is an amazing machine. But how does your body maintain and repair all its systems? Well, that's down to the fuel you put into your body. What you eat is vitally important because it has to contain everything that makes you you. Food doesn't just give you energy to do stuff, it also provides all the elements your body needs to grow and repair. To get the right elements **you have to eat a balanced diet containing the five main food groups**.

Carbohydrates

Carbo power

Carbohydrates are the body's main energy source. There are three main types—sugar, starch, and fiber. Carbohydrates are found in potatoes, rice, pasta, bread, and sugar. The body uses a sugar, called glucose, as fuel. Even though carbohydrates don't yield the most energy per gram, they are easy to access because they are stored in the blood, muscles, and liver.

 Fuel Fill up your tank with carbs so you have the energy to work.

 Digestion Fiber helps your body to digest and process food.

16 kJ **Energy** Carbo power only generates 16 kJ (3.8 kcal) per gram.

Fat

Fat at work

Too much fat isn't good for your body, but it does play a vital role. Fats help transport certain vitamins around the body in the bloodstream, like little taxis. They also help to build cell membranes and nerve cells. Fat does have the highest yield of energy per gram, however, it isn't used as a primary fuel source because the body is slower in turning it into usable energy.

 Transportation Vitamins hitch a ride around the body on fat carriers.

Builder Fat is a key building material in the body.

37 kJ **Energy** Fat power generates an amazing 37 kJ (8.8 kcal) per gram.

A MEASURE OF ENERGY

Energy is measured in two ways—**kilojoules (kJ) and kilocalories (kcal)**. A kilojoule consists of 1,000 joules (J). A joule is the amount of energy needed to lift one kg one meter in the air. Kilocalories are normally refered to as calories, but scientifically they consist of 1,000 calories. A scientific calorie is the measure of energy needed to heat one gram of water by one degree Celsius. Both kilojoules and calories are used, but when you look at food labels or talk to people about food energy, you will mainly hear calories.

(1 kcal = 4.2 kJ)

READY... SET... GO!

1 Resting can actually be exhausting. It can burn up to **60 calories an hour**—that's nearly half a packet of potato chips.

2 No one likes doing chores, but did you know a little light housework can burn over **120 calories an hour!**

BODY BASICS

The body needs a basic level of energy to work. This is known as the Basal Metabolic Rate (BMR). This rate changes as you grow up and your body changes. Men usually have a higher BMR than women because they have more muscle, which needs more energy. As we enter old age our BMR decreases as body mass decreases. Also, the more active you are the more energy you'll need to eat.

Children should try to eat about 1,500 calories (kcals) a day to help them grow.

Men have a BMR of about 2,500 calories (kcals) a day.

Women have a BMR of about 2,000 calories (kcals) a day.

Protein

Vitamins

Vitamins The body needs four main vitamins—A, B, C, and D. Vitamins play an important role in building, protecting, and helping the body make energy. The body can make Vitamin D in the skin from sunlight, but the rest need to be eaten.

Minerals

Minerals These are the inorganic elements you find in the body, like calcium and iron. Minerals play an important role in keeping the body systems working, and help to build bones and teeth.

Protein rescue

Proteins are the maintenance workers of the body. They help to build and repair your muscles and organs. This makes them a key component of any growing child's diet. Proteins are made from basic building blocks called amino acids. The body breaks down protein in food and turns it into amino acids, it can then change these into different proteins when they are needed.

Repair The body needs 22 amino acids to keep healthy and maintained.

Builder Proteins make blood, muscles, and boost your immune system.

17 kJ **Energy** Proteins are rarely used as energy, because of their building work.

Protect Vitamins A and C help the body protect itself from invaders.

Builder Skin, cartilage, tendons, organs, and bone all need vitamins.

Assistant Vitamin B helps the body release energy from chemical stores.

Repair Minerals help maintain cell chemical reactions and function.

Builder Bones and teeth get their strength from minerals.

Balance Water, nerves, and your heart need minerals to work.

The burning energy race...

3 A brisk walk to school every morning can keep you healthy—walking can burn **225 calories an hour!**

4 Jogging can be hard work. In this race it burns the most energy—over **500 calories an hour!** That's a third of what children should eat a day!

Tank full **and ready to go—well, nearly.** We have fuel and know where it comes from and how to use it. But how can we keep it under control?

Humans love control. Think about watching television. You want to change the channel—what do you do? Scramble for the remote control, of course. It's got to be here somewhere.

This need to control and the built-in desire for it to be convenient happens all over the human body. Your body is doing some amazing stuff without you even being aware of it.

In this chapter, we'll take a look into how your body controls energy. We look at the mastermind behind it all and the control agents it uses to keep a close eye on things.

Body science: Control

Brain POWER

The human brain is the most complex organ in the world. It not only houses everything that meaningfully makes you "you"—your conscious thoughts, your personality, your memories—but also processes sensory information, controls your body's movement, and handles millions of other operations at a purely subconscious level. And the best part? It can do all these things at the same time.

ELECTRIC ORGAN

Your brain is made of more than 100 billion neurons, which communicate through electrochemical signals. There are more potential connections between these neurons than there are atoms in the universe.

Most neurons cannot divide and multiply, so take good care of the ones you have!

THINK ABOUT IT

The brain is a pink, jellylike organ that is folded over on itself to maximize its surface area. Each part of the brain specializes in performing certain kinds of tasks.

FRONTAL LOBE—conscious thought, personality, and movement.

TEMPORAL LOBE—speech, language, and hearing.

CEREBRAL CORTEX—this is the wrinkled outer surface of the brain, where most of your thinking goes on.

PARIETAL LOBE—movement, sensation, and spacial awareness.

OCCIPITAL LOBE—processes information from the eyes.

CEREBELLUM—this fine-tunes muscle movement using feedback from the senses and keeps you balanced.

BRAIN STEM—this is the most basic, core part of the brain. It's responsible for many fundamental, life-preserving functions like breathing and heartbeat, and involuntary actions like blinking. It links the brain to the spine and the rest of the body. Some animals survive with only a brain stem, but they cannot process information in the complex way that higher animals do.

Man vs. machine

Writers have been comparing the brain to a computer for decades, but they aren't as similar as you might think. The most powerful computer ever built can run 1.026 quadrillion calculations a second, whereas the human brain can only manage 10 percent of that. But don't be fooled into thinking the human brain is second best. Unlike computers, the human brain is capable of learning and adapting. A computer may be able to beat a human at chess, but it can only perform the functions for which it was designed—a chess computer cannot cook an omelet!

RAPID RESPONSE

The brain isn't just versatile, it's also lightning-fast. Neurons send messages across the brain at around 100 meters per second (225 mph, or 365 km/h). That's nearly as fast as the Bugatti Veyron, the fastest commercial car in the world. But your body can react even faster to situations by bypassing your brain entirely. If you step on a thumbtack, you pick up your foot before you even think about it. This kind of reaction is a reflex triggered by nerves in your spinal cord.

DUAL CONTROLS

There are two types of control systems driving your body. Your conscious brain is constantly making decisions—for example, what to say, or where to walk. Simultaneously, your subconscious is making decisions such as how to keep your balance, or how to keep your body warm.

LEFT BRAIN, RIGHT BRAIN

The brain is split into two halves, which are called hemispheres. The left hemisphere controls the right side of the body, and vice versa. They each have different strengths: the left brain plays a crucial role in speech and language, whereas the right brain deals with abstract reasoning.

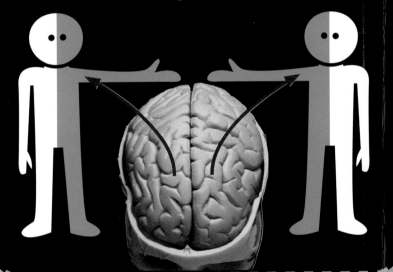

Here are just a few of the bodily functions your subconscious controls:

Breathing

Heart rate

Hormones

Blood pressure

Blinking

Digestion

The brain is only 2% of your body weight but it uses about 20% of the body's energy.

Are you thinking what I'm thinking?

PSYCHOLOGY

The human mind is a rich topic for scientific research. Using modern equipment like MRI scanners, scientists are able to watch different areas of the brain light up as patients think different thoughts. But the mind is still a long way from being fully understood—for example, scientists are still not able to explain the phenomenon of consciousness fully. It's an urban myth that we only use 10 percent of our brains. However, it's certainly true that much of the brain's activity is hidden from our conscious minds. Psychologists like Sigmund Freud have argued that the subconscious is hugely important in shaping our personalities.

GREEK GEEKS — The word ELECTRICITY comes from the ancient Greek word *elektron* (amber), which means "made by the Sun." When you rub amber with a cloth it creates a static electric charge.

DOWN THE WIRE

Electricity is a form of energy. It is carried through a wire by the movement of electrons from one atom to another along a closed loop called a circuit. The source of the electricity, such as a generator or battery, pushes electrons out of its negative terminal. Electrons have a negative charge. The electrons transfer to the next atom in their path, and so on, until they reach the positive terminal at the other end of the circuit.

Insulator

Conductor

STATIC ELECTRICITY

If you rub a balloon along your hair, your hair will stand on end. This happens because of static electricity. As you rub, your hair transfers some of its electrons to the balloon. This leaves your hair with a positive charge. Because like charges repel each other, each hair will try to get as far away from the next one as it can by standing up and moving away from your head.

Moving electrons

Materials with free electrons that can move around allow electricity to pass through them. These materials are called conductors. Materials with electrons that can't move are called insulators. Metals are good conductors, while plastics are good insulators, which is why they are used in electrical cables.

Electric AVENUES
Electricity is all around you. It's in your home, the sky, and even your body.

ALL-OR-NONE PRINCIPLE

Nerve cells are a perfect example of the all-or-none principle. When something stimulates a nerve cell, the cell either reacts or it doesn't, like turning on a switch. So, cutting your finger triggers the same impulse as someone stroking your finger. Instead, the strength of the reaction comes from how many impulses are traveling along the nerve per second.

The electrical impulse is passed from one

sprinter racing the 100 meters.

MAGNETISM and electricity are linked. When electrons move through a wire they create a magnetic field around the wire. Similarly, when a magnet is moved along a wire, the magnetic field makes the electrons in the wire move.

Electricity is a form of energy that can travel very quickly and efficiently. **Your body uses electrical impulses to send messages** to the parts it needs to reach. Your nervous system runs on electricity, but it's not the same as the electricity in your home. Your nerves might look like electrical wires, but there's a big difference.

A NEURON

Body

Axon

Axon terminal

Nerves

Dendrite

TYPES OF NERVE CELLS

There are several different types of nerve cells, or neurons, each with a specific purpose.

1. Sensory—these send information picked up by your senses to your central nervous system.

2. Motor—these send information from your central nervous system to your muscles.

3. Interneurons—These link the sensory and motor neurons.

DANGER! Water and electricity

Water and electricity are a dangerous mix. Water conducts electricity very easily. Humans are at great risk of electrocution because our bodies are 60 percent water.

ELECTRICITY IN THE BODY

Instead of flowing in a direct line from negative to positive, like electrical circuits, the body uses electricity and chemicals to produce a series of impulses that pass from one neuron to the next. When the neuron body is stimulated, it sends an electrical impulse along its axon to one of its terminals. Each terminal connects to a dendrite on the body of another neuron. Chemicals called neurotransmitters are released to help the impulse move across the tiny gap between neurons. These chemicals make the next neuron fire off a new impulse. This process continues along the chain until the signal reaches its destination.

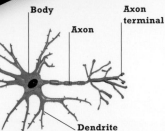

nerve cell to another, like a relay race.

Our sense of touch uses the largest organ in the body, the skin. Touch is how we detect physical sensations, such as pressure, temperature, pain, and vibration. Millions of tiny nerve endings are stimulated by the environment around us and send signals about it to the brain. The brain then interprets the signal and tells the body how to respond.

More than just feeling
The ability to feel things is important in keeping us warm, controlling our movements, and avoiding dangerous or harmful substances.

The sensory cortex, shown in red, is the part of the brain that processes signals from the nerve endings in the skin. If you make a slice through it, you can map which section will respond to a stimulus from a particular area of the body.

Cross-section of the sensory cortex

Each area of the sensory cortex connects with the corresponding number on this homunculus.

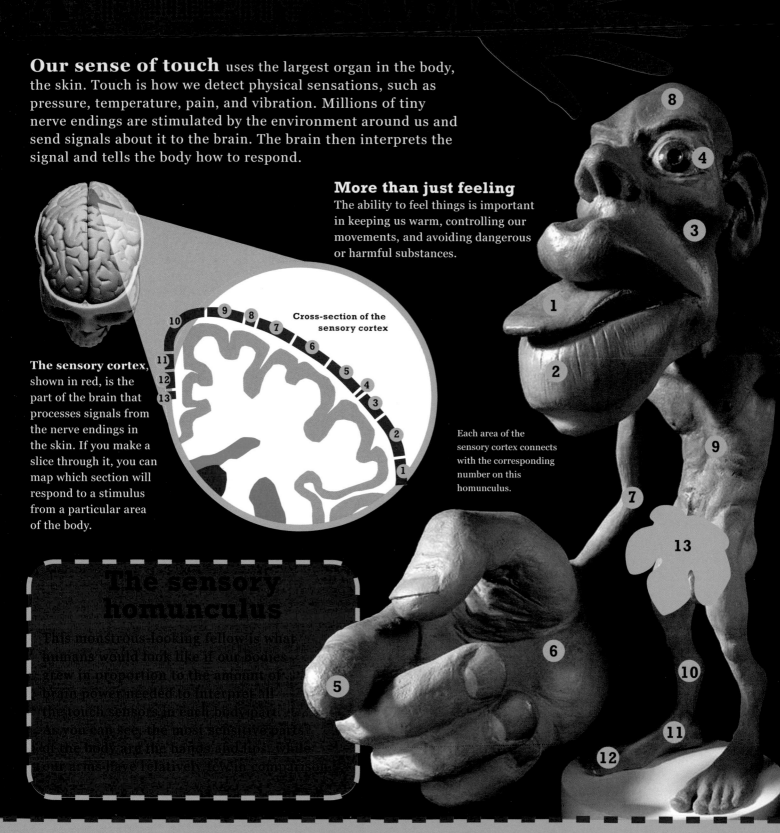

The sensory homunculus

This monstrous-looking fellow is what humans would look like if our bodies grew in proportion to the amount of brain power needed to interpret all the touch sensors in each body part. As you can see, the most sensitive parts of the body are the hands and lips, while our arms have relatively little sensation.

This is what we would look like if our bodies

UNDER YOUR SKIN

Our touch sensors are amazing. Not only do they react to pressure, but they also tell the brain whether the stimulus is hot or cold, hard or soft, rough or smooth, wet or dry, and moving or still. Most of our touch sensors are found in the skin. The skin is divided into three layers—the epidermis, or outer layer; the dermis, which contains most of the nerve endings; and the fatty hypodermis, which anchors the skin to the muscles.

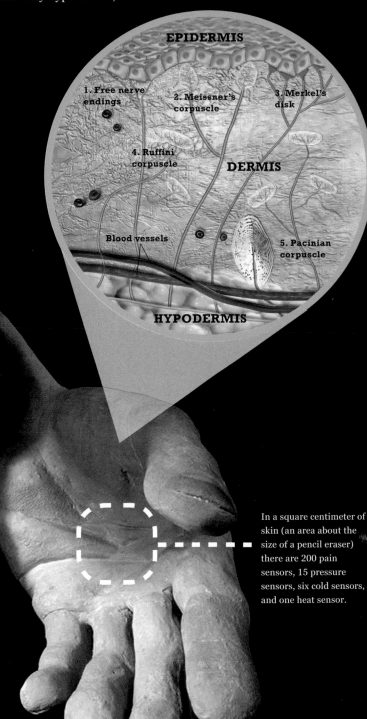

EPIDERMIS

1. Free nerve endings

2. Meissner's corpuscle

3. Merkel's disk

4. Ruffini corpuscle

DERMIS

Blood vessels

5. Pacinian corpuscle

HYPODERMIS

In a square centimeter of skin (an area about the size of a pencil eraser) there are 200 pain sensors, 15 pressure sensors, six cold sensors, and one heat sensor.

HOW DO YOU FEEL?
Well, there isn't just one type of sensory nerve ending—there are FIVE.

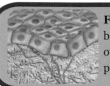

Free nerve endings—these branching nerve endings are found all over the body. They are sensitive to pain, light touch, and temperature.

1

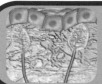

Meissner's corpuscles—found near the surface of the skin, mainly on the fingertips, feet, eyelids, and face. They respond to light pressure and tickling.

2

Merkel's disk—also known as junction nerves, they are found in the upper layers of the skin and sense continuous light pressure and textures.

3

Ruffini corpuscles—these oval-shaped cells are located deeper in the skin. They sense when the skin is stretched, and help you grip things.

4

Pacinian corpuscle—these are found deep in the skin near joints and muscles. They sense more sustained pressure and vibrations, such as when you exercise.

5

Internal sensors—Nerve endings also play a role inside the body. When your bladder is full, it stretches the nerve endings in the surrounding tissue, creating discomfort and an urgent need to run to the bathroom!

were in proportion to our touch sensors.

Secretion AGENTS

The brain is the control HQ of the body, and the nervous system is its speedy messenger service. But it can't run everything alone; it needs help from special secretion agents called HORMONES.

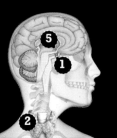

Hormones are chemicals made by the body that help control certain body systems, like metabolism, growth, and sexual reproduction. Hormones are water soluble and dissolve into the blood. Their special skill is that they target specific cells, effectively carrying out their mission objectives.

Hormones are made in the brain and other organs known as glands. They are part of the endocrine system and secrete their hormones directly into the blood.

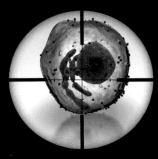

1 PITUITARY GLAND
This pea-sized gland is located in the brain and makes the growth hormone that controls your physical development.

2 THYROID GLAND
The thyroid gland is found in the neck and its hormones help with breathing, circulation, and energy conversion.

3 PANCREAS
The pancreas resides above the stomach and makes insulin, which helps the body use sugar (glucose) as its main energy.

4 OVARIES (women)/ TESTES (men)
The sex glands produce the sex hormones, estrogen (women) and testosterone (men). These help control puberty and fertility.

5 HYPOTHALAMUS
Controls the secretion of other glands and links the nervous system to the endocrine (hormone) system.

6 ADRENAL GLANDS
These sit on top of the kidneys and produce epinephrine (adrenaline), which acts to stimulate and protect the body from danger.

BRAIN—More oxygen and fuel (glucose) is transported to the brain. Now your brain is energized and ready for anything.

EYES—Epinephrine enlarges the pupils in your eyes. This allows more light in, and more light means more information and awareness of surroundings.

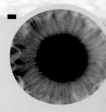

MOUTH—Epinephrine makes the smaller blood vessels in your mouth constrict. This reducesthe blood supply and makes your mouth feel dry.

SWEAT—Smell the fear. Epinephrine triggers your apocrine sweat glands. This type of sweat contains fatty oils, which react with bacteria, making you smell.

What makes us jump out of airplanes?

We must have a screw loose! Actually, we are fueled by the thrill hormone—epinephrine. Here's a lowdown on what happens to your body when it kicks in.

PAIN—An adrenaline rush is normally followed by an increase in endorphins (chemicals released by the brain that make you feel good). Endorphins also suppress pain—handy in moments of danger!

DIGESTION—In a state of emergency, digestion isn't at the top of your body's to-do list. Epinephrine suppresses nonvital systems, allowing oxygen and fuel to get to the places that need it.

MUSCLES—More oxygen and fuel (glucose) means more energy to help you move. Your muscles are ready to lift, fight, run, duck, dodge, or throw—basically anything!

HEART—Your stroke volume (how much blood is pumped) and heart rate increase. This helps to supply your body with more oxygen and fuel, as well as remove waste products.

BREATHING—Breathing can become more rapid to increase oxygen levels in the blood, as well as getting rid of built-up waste gases. Epinephrine also helps to expand your airways, so you breathe in more air with each breath.

FIGHT or FLIGHT

When the body is in danger or under stress, its survival instincts kick in. This is known as the fight-or-flight mechanism and epinephrine plays a major role. Epinephrine is released into the blood and is pumped around the body. Its main mission is to protect and ready the body for physical action, be it fighting back or running away.

TOP SECRET

What makes a hormone? Most hormones are proteins. Their long molecules are made from carbon, hydrogen, oxygen, and nitrogen. Some hormones also contain some of the body's trace elements, like sulfur and iodine.

Gamma rays

X-rays

Ultraviolet light

Visible light

Wavelength

ENERGY WAVES

Light is a form of energy. Like most energy, it travels in waves. Wavelength is the distance between wave peaks or troughs. It tells us how much energy waves carry. The shorter the wavelength, the higher the energy. Different wave types can be ordered on a spectrum, from dangerous high-energy gamma rays to safe low-energy radio waves. Visible light is only a small section of this spectrum.

SEEING WAVES
Natural light from the Sun looks white, but if you take a closer look it is actually a rainbow of colors. In 1665, Sir Isaac Newton discovered how to split light, using prisms and lenses. Each color of light travels at a different wavelength. The human eye can see from violet to red. But light energy doesn't end there—the other wavelengths are just invisible to the human eye.

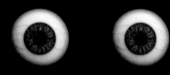

WHY DO HUMANS HAVE TWO EYES?
Our eyes are set apart and see slightly different images. The different views are then overlapped in the brain to create a 3-D image and help us judge distances.

Would you be surprised
to hear or read that your senses are all about energy? Seeing and hearing are two important senses we use all the time. They are also perfect examples of how our bodies make use of the different energy forms around us.

SEEING IS BELIEVING
The eye allows us to see by intercepting light waves and turning them into electrical impulses for the brain to interpret. Everything you see is actually a mental reconstruction of the light that has bounced off an object.

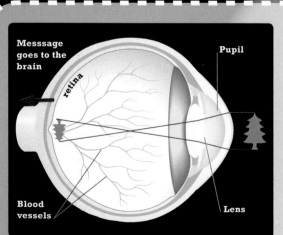

Messsage goes to the brain

retina

Pupil

Blood vessels

Lens

EYES SEE...
The eyeball is a spherical sac of fluid with an opening at one end and a nerve at the other. As light waves enter the eye, the lens focuses them onto the retina at the back of the eye. This turns the image upside down, but the brain flips it the right way up. There are two types of light-sensing cells in the retina, called *cones* and *rods*. Cone cells are sensitive to color and detail. There are far fewer rod cells, which are sensitive to low light conditions. Colors and detail are therefore easier to see in well-lit areas.

B
OD
YSC
IENCE
CAN YOU
READ THIS

Infrared light

Microwaves

Radio waves

SEEING THINGS

Light travels in straight lines. When light waves hit an object they bounce off. It is these bouncing waves that travel into the eye. When no light source is present, there are no light waves, so we don't see anything.

SOUND ENERGY

The sound energy we hear is different to the energy waves above. Audible sounds are transmitted by air molecules vibrating. When something vibrates, the air molecules around it are pushed together, leaving an empty gap behind them. With each vibration, groups of molecules are pulsed toward the ear, where they are collected for processing.

SENSES

Radio waves are at the slow end of the energy wave range. We can't hear them directly, since our bodies are unable to trap and interpret them. Instead, we use a radio receiver, which converts the radio wave energy into sound waves.

TINY BONES

The inner ear has the smallest bone in the human body—the stirrup. It is only 0.1 inch (2.5 mm) long!

GOOD VIBRATIONS

The ear collects and turns sound waves into recognizable noises. For this delicate job the body uses three tiny bones—the *hammer*, *anvil*, and *stirrup*. Vibrating air molecules channeled into the ear hit the eardrum. This makes the inner ear bones vibrate and transfers the energy into the fluid-filled tubes of the cochlea. The vibrations travel through the fluid, disturbing tiny hairlike cells, which convert the vibrations into signals that the brain can interpret.

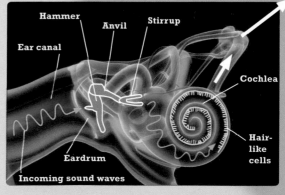

Messsage goes to the brain

Hammer

Anvil

Stirrup

Ear canal

Cochlea

Eardrum

Hair-like cells

Incoming sound waves

PERFECT VISION

The idea of 20/20 vision comes from being able to read an eye chart 20 ft (6 m) away. You can have better eyesight: 20/10 means you can read at 20 ft (6 m) what most people can read at 10 ft (3 m). A hawk, if it could read, would have 20/2 vision!

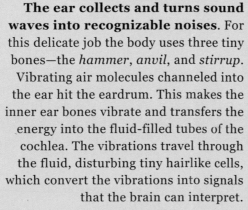

Chemical

Where seeing and hearing are about physics, **taste and smell are all about chemistry**. Smell and taste are linked—not only are the two systems

SMELL MOLECULES

What are smells? Actually, they are molecules that float around in the air, called *odorants*. We breathe in these molecules and our nose uses chemistry to detect the smell. An average person can recognize about 4,000 different smells, and someone with a well-trained nose can sniff out nearly 10,000! Smell is also linked to taste, and about 70 percent of what we think of as being a taste is actually detected by our nose.

Gone to your head
Both your smell and taste senses are connected by nerves directly to the brain.

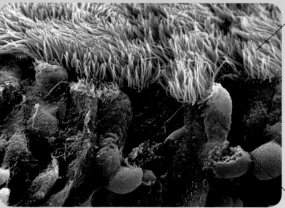

Cilia

The cells that line the nasal cavity are topped by tiny hairlike structures called cilia. The cilia sweep the mucus toward the back of the nasal cavity and down into the throat, taking dirt and other particles with it.

Cell

A NOSE FOR CHEMISTRY
Your nose is a finely tuned smelling machine. As air is drawn into the nostrils, it is warmed, and any dirt and dust is trapped by hairs and mucus. It then passes into the nasal cavity, which is covered in even more mucus. The odorants dissolve in the mucus and are detected by sensory cells. Each cell detects a specific type of chemical. These send signals to the brain, which figures out what the smell is.

Smelly dog
Dogs can be 10,000 times more sensitive to odors than humans. Yet a human smell sensor cell is just as sensitive as a dog's. So, what makes dogs such expert sniffers? Although their sensors are the same, they have many more of them (1 billion in dogs compared with only 10 million in humans).

Try holding your nose while you eat something. What happens to the taste? Why would a blocked nose have the same effect?

SENSES

physically close to each other in the head, but they both also interact to tell us as much as possible about the substances we eat and breathe into our bodies.

It's all in the mind!

TASTE MOLECULES

Tasting works in a very similar manner to the way you smell things. The key to taste lies on your tongue and in your saliva. Taste is linked to smell and sight, and both senses help trigger saliva production. Real mouth-watering stuff! As you eat, the chemicals that make up food dissolve into the saliva and are identified by the thousands of taste buds on your tongue. There are five main tastes: bitter, sour, salt, sweet, and umami, a savory flavor. Taste buds can detect all five, but are better with some tastes than others.

Most of your taste buds sit on your tongue, but you also have some on the roof of your mouth and in your throat.

Taste bud

Papillae

TONGUE ACTION

The surface of the tongue is covered by lots of tiny bumps, known as papillae. Between these bumps sit the taste buds. The taste buds are made up of lots of sensory cells, like segments in a orange. Tiny hairs on the top of these cells extend upward and it is here where the dissolved molecules lock on. The cells send signals to your brain, which adds in signals from the nose and tells you what the substance tastes like.

Acquired tastes
Our taste buds are more sensitive when we are younger, which explains why some children react strongly to some flavors that adults enjoy. As you get older, your taste buds lose their sensitivity and you even start liking vegetables!

Why do we need smell and taste?
There is a very good reason why we need to be able to taste and smell things—so we don't poison ourselves. Nasty tastes and smells are usually associated with toxic gases, decaying food, or poisonous plants, all of which could make us sick or even be fatal.

How many SENSES?

You can count the number of body senses on one hand? Wrong.

SENSING THE WORLD

Why are senses so sensible? Senses are important because they let us understand the physical and chemical world around us. This awareness of the environment is vital to our survival, from gathering food, avoiding danger, to finding other people. We communicate using our senses—we talk, listen, gesture, and touch. The extra senses follow the same mantra as our core five—they help us understand our surroundings. Here's a lowdown on these extra senses and how they help us survive the everyday as well as the extreme.

STRETCH Deep in your muscles are special receptors that allow your brain to know which muscle is moving and how hard it is working. Without these receptors the body wouldn't know what it was doing. So, even standing still would be tricky, let alone trekking through the cold Arctic wilderness.

6

Some people believe they have a sixth sense. Well, they do—we all do. We also have a seventh, eighth, ninth, and tenth sense. Our extra senses are all related to our main five, and are just as important when it comes to sensing the world around us.

7 **GRAVITY** Living on Earth means dealing with gravity. Small receptors in your inner ear called otoliths let you know which way is up and which is down.

MOTION Movement would be impossible without the motion sensors in your inner ear. If you spin around you can confuse your motion senses, making you dizzy. **8**

9 **HEAT** Heat receptors sense external temperatures, from icy weather to hot drinks. They are all over your body, with your lips and tongue being most sensitive. These senses even work at a distance.

10

PAIN There are pain receptors all over your body. Wouldn't life be more painless without pain receptors? Yes, but they do fulfill a very important job. They help limit damage and injury. When the body senses pain, it tells you not to use that area. So a bad leg makes you limp, protecting the injury—vital on long icy adventures.

ANIMAL SENSE

The ten human body senses help our bodies to work, but they are aren't the only senses in the natural world. Some animals use other senses to help them survive.

SHARK
In the nose of these marine predators are hundreds of electrosensors. Sharks use them to detect electrical signals let off by prey in distress.

BAT
Finding dinner in the dark isn't an easy job, unless you are a bat. They possess a kind of radar, called echolocation. This helps them lock onto flying insects.

BEE
Bees don't have a map to help them find their way—or do they? Bees have a ring of iron oxide inside their bodies and scientists believe it could act like a compass.

EARTHWORM
It doesn't look very tasty, but the earthworm is tastier than you think—its whole body is covered in chemoreceptors. So, it's like one big tongue.

MIXING Senses

We know that taste and smell are closely linked. But can your senses truly mix? Our senses are converted into signals for the brain to interpret. It is here where senses can overlap. People can develop a condition known as *synesthesia*, meaning their senses mix. This can make certain tasks seem easier. For example, some successful musicians hear musical notes as different colors, so when they write songs it's more like painting a picture.

A handy tool

Have you ever needed a helping hand? Well, you have an amazing tool on the end of each arm. Our hands have played a handy role in our survival as a species, as well as dealing with modern life. What is so amazing about the hand? It's all about control and movement. The hand can be precise and delicate—it can run thread throught the eye of a needle. But it can also be strong and powerful—it can crush, grip, and punch. This variety of action is down to four key handy components—bones, nerves, muscles, and tendons. The hand has 27 bones, 4 main nerves, and is controlled by 40 muscles and 40

tendons. Your hand also holds some fantastic attachments that make it a gripping machine. On your palm and fingertips are lots of tiny grooves that increase the force of friction and improve your grip. Also, on the end of each finger is a hard nail that allows you to pinch and pick very small items, like knots. On top of this is the mighty thumb. Our thumbs give us the upper hand. They are opposable, which means you can touch your little finger with your thumb. Without this special skill you would struggle to grip and hold. Try this at home—tape your thumb to your hand and try tying your shoelaces with just your fingers.

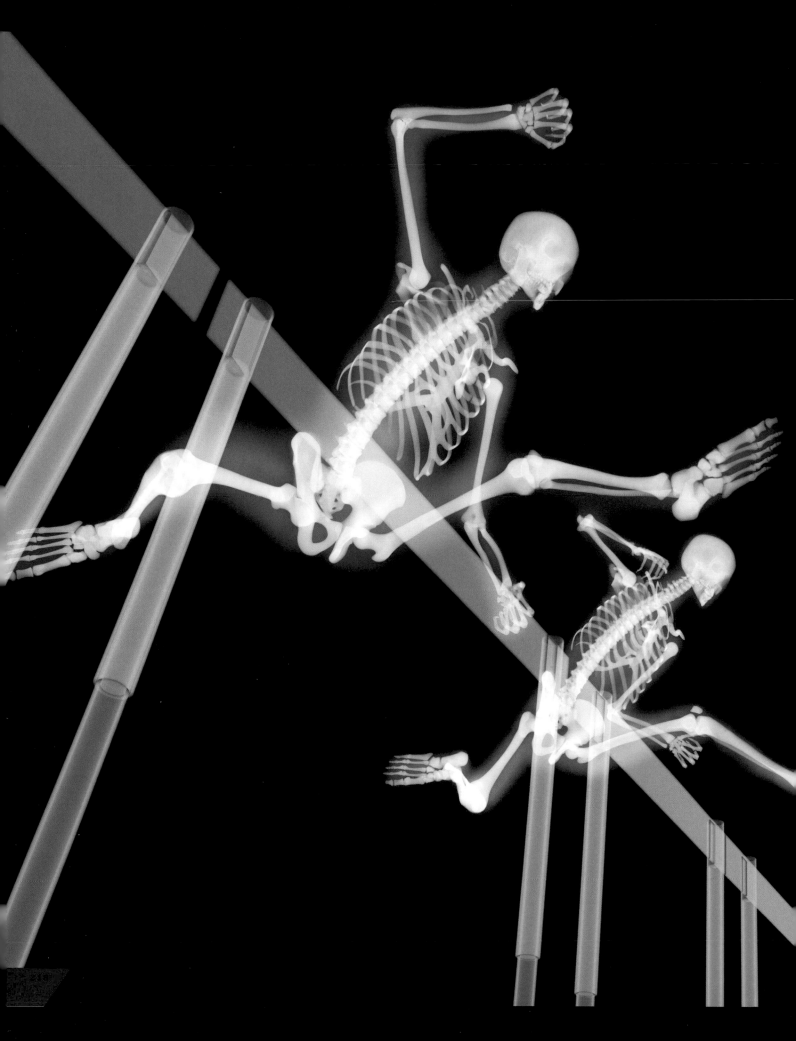

Done. You've got energy covered and know how to control it. The next big hurdle is movement. It seems simple enough, since you move around every day. True, but there's more to moving than just walking or standing.

Movement is all about laws; not the police, but laws discovered by a guy named Sir Isaac Newton. Forces make us move and stop. But where do these forces come from and what's the science behind them?

Movement isn't just limited to walking. Inside your body millions of little movements are happening every second. And how does where you are affect how you move?

In this chapter, we're going to be moving through the different types of forces, their impact on the body, and how the body reacts to them. So, let's get moving...

Body science: Movement

NEWTON'S laws

Movement is all about forces. Whether you are moving steadily, speeding up, or even just standing around, there are forces at work. In 1687, English scientist and mathematician Sir Isaac Newton figured out three laws that explain why and how things move.

Sir Isaac Newton (1643–1727) was responsible for many great scientific discoveries in optics, mechanics, and mathematics. While pondering why the Moon stayed in orbit around the Earth, he reputedly saw an apple fall from a tree. He realized that the same force, which he called gravity, was pulling both it and the Moon toward Earth. More usefully, it was helping him keep his wig on.

Law one

"An object that isn't **PUSHED** or *pulled* by a force either stays still or keeps moving in a straight line at a constant speed."

Law two

"Forces make things *accelerate*. The **BIGGER** the force, and the lighter the object, the greater the *acceleration*."

Law three

"Every **ACTION** has an equal and *opposite reaction*."

1

A force is simply a **PUSH** or a **PULL**. To make an object move, you need to apply a force. You will need another force to stop it.

It is easy to see how something standing still needs a force to get it moving, but why does it keep going? The perfect example for this law can be seen in space. Because there is so little matter in outer space, there is nothing to offer any resistance. If an astronaut pushes off, he will continue in a straight line, at the same speed, until another force stops him or speeds him up.

2

We can use this law to explain throwing a baseball a given distance. If you are trying to get a runner out, you need to get the ball to the base before he does. A baseball is light, but you have to throw it hard to make it accelerate faster than the runner. However, you would need even more force to make a bowling ball reach the base first.

To a scientist, acceleration means speeding up, slowing down, or changing direction.

An athlete running experiences the forces of friction, gravity, and air resistance acting against his forward movement.

3

When you push off from the block, the block pushes back at you equally hard.

This law is a little more complicated and looks at forces working in pairs. When you run, the force of your foot pushing on the ground sends your body forward. This also produces an opposite reaction, the ground moves away with an equal force. You are, in fact, making Earth turn under you by the teeniest amount. The thing to remember is that although the forces might be equal, their effects might not be.

Body FRICTION

Take a close look at your skin, and you'll see that it's covered in tiny grooves. Even at a microscopic level, its surface is rough and bumpy. Which is just as well, because it's the rough texture of your skin that creates friction, which enables you to pick things up. Friction may be most famous as the force that slows things down, but it's also essential to many of the functions our bodies perform.

Good Friction

"Somebody help me— I can't stop!"

GRIPPING—Without friction between your body and the world, you wouldn't be able to grip on to anything. Performing the simplest tasks would be like juggling wet soap. Getting from one place to another would also be a problem, since moving around would be like running on ice.

EATING—Your teeth use friction to tear food apart and to crush it up. Without friction you wouldn't be able to chew well at all.

Muscle fibers are like long cables.

MOVEMENT—Your muscles are made up of tiny fibers. When the muscle contracts, these fibers slide against each other and shorten. Friction between these fibers keeps the movement under control.

SENSES—Your sense of touch relies on friction. If your skin were perfectly smooth, things would slide quickly off it, leaving your nerves with little to sense.

Under a microscope, skin looks anything but smooth.

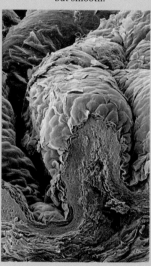

Harnessing friction
Friction can be a useful ally on the sports field. Take soccer cleats, for example. The cleats increase the friction between the playing surface and your feet, so you can get more grip for running, dribbling, and shooting!

Have you ever tried to start a fire by rubbing two sticks together? The friction between the sticks causes heat, which ignites the fuel. Matches also use friction to create a flame.

When a match head is scraped along a rough surface, the friction mixes flammable chemicals together.

Sliding friction

There are several different types of friction. Sliding friction slows down objects that are already moving. This is the kind of friction between moving skis and snow, or between your bike's tires and its brakes.

Static friction

Static friction is the resistance that has to be overcome before an object can START moving. It's much stronger than sliding friction. Imagine pushing a desk across the floor: it takes much more of a push to start it moving than it does to keep it going.

Oh, my poor aching joints!

JOINTS—Normally bones are protected from the constant wear and tear of friction by a protective, cushioning layer (see below). A disease called osteoarthritis can destroy this layer between bones. This can make joints swell up and become painful.

DRAG—As we move through air or water, we come up against a kind of friction called drag. It pushes back against our movements, which means we have to work harder to get anywhere.

BLISTERS—Blisters are one of the most common sports injuries. Blisters appear at friction hot spots—for example, where your sports shoe rubs against the back of your heel, or where an oar rubs against your palm. The friction makes layers of the skin separate from each other. Either the epidermis (the outer layer of skin) separates from the dermis, or the epidermis itself comes apart.

FRICTION BURNS—Friction produces heat, and friction between your skin and a rough surface can easily give you minor burns. If you've ever tripped and skidded across a rough surface like Astroturf, you'll know exactly what a friction burn feels like.

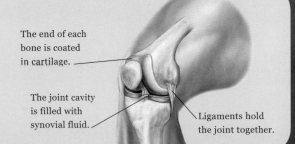

Fighting friction

To move smoothly, your body needs to overcome the friction between the parts that make it up. Your joints are protected by smooth cartilage, which covers the ends of bones and stops them from grinding against each other. Joints are also filled with a liquid called *synovial fluid*, which acts like the lubricating oil in a machine. Without these friction fighters, our bones would quickly get worn down.

The end of each bone is coated in cartilage.

The joint cavity is filled with synovial fluid.

Ligaments hold the joint together.

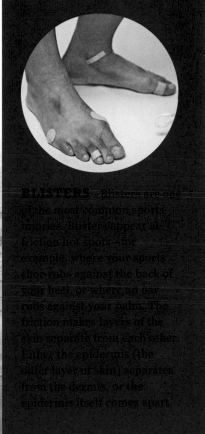

Muscle types

There are three main types of muscles in your body. Each has a different role.

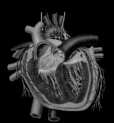

CARDIAC—This type of muscle is found only in the heart. The muscles act as a single unit and are involuntary, meaning they work without you having to think about it.

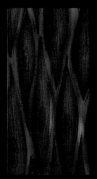

SMOOTH—Made up of long, thin cells, this type of muscle gets its name from its smooth appearance. Smooth muscle is also involuntary and is found in your internal organs, such as the arteries, stomach, and bowel.

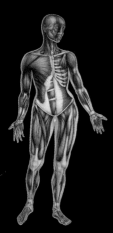

SKELETAL—These muscles are attached to your skeleton and help you move. These are voluntary muscles, so you tell them when to work. They are sometimes called striated muscle, because of their "striped" appearance under a microscope.

THE POWER OF MUSCLES

Skeletal muscles can produce an incredible amount of force. This strength comes from the shortening, or contraction, of the fibers that make up the muscle. When you think about moving, the brain sends a signal to the relevant muscle telling it to contract. The amount of force produced by the muscle depends on how much the brain tells it to contract.

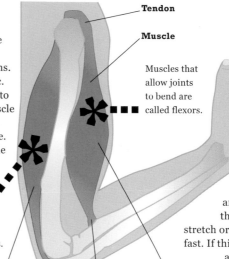

Tendon

Muscle

Muscles that allow joints to bend are called flexors.

Feel the force

Muscles are attached to the bones by strong pieces of fibrous tissue called tendons. Tendons are slightly elastic. They stretch across a joint to the next bone. When a muscle contracts, the tendons pull the bone toward the muscle. Tendons provide the muscle with extra leverage and increase the amount of force the muscle can supply.

Muscles that make joints straighten are called extensors.

When a muscle is relaxed, its fibers spread out.

Tendons

Full stretch

There are limits to how much a muscle can move. Special sensors in the muscles detect stress and tension, and ensure that the muscle does not stretch or contract too far or too fast. If this happens the muscles and tendons could tear.

When a muscle is contracted its fibers are close together.

INSIDE A MUSCLE

Muscles are bundles of fibers.

Myosin and actin microfilaments.

Inside each fiber are thinner fibers called myofibrils.

Each set of fibers is wrapped in a membrane.

Muscles are made of hundreds of tiny fibers. Inside these fibers are even thinner fibers, so the whole structure is like an electrical cable. At the very core are two microfilaments (really tiny fibers) called myosin and actin, which slide over and grip each other tightly. It is these actions that make muscles contract.

The heart is the hardest-working muscle in the body.

FAST AND SLOW

The fibers that make up muscles can be divided into two main groups, fast-twitch and slow-twitch muscles. Each muscle has a mixture of the two fiber types. In a healthy human there is usually a 50–50 split between fast- and slow-twitch fibers.

Catch me if you can!

FAST TWITCH
Fast-twitch muscles contract quickly and generate high levels of power. However, this means they tire very quickly and are better for short, sharp bursts of activity.

I think I'll stick to walking...

SLOW TWITCH
These are smaller than fast twitch and generate less power because they contract about 20 percent slower. However, they don't tire as easily and are good for low-level activities, like walking and long-distance running.

TEAMWORK

Forces work in opposite pairs and so do muscles. Everything about muscles is teamwork, from their tiny fibers locking together, to how they make joints move. But muscles can only pull, they cannot push.

SKELETAL MUSCLES

All the skeletal muscles work in pairs. When one muscle contracts, the partner muscle relaxes and lengthens. The contracting muscle is called the *prime mover*, while its relaxing partner is known as the *antagonist*. These roles can switch, depending on the movement of the joint.

I get a real kick out of doing this.

Antagonist

Prime mover

When you are about to kick a ball, the muscle at the back of your thigh (the prime mover) contracts to pull the lower leg backward.

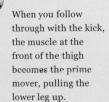

Antagonist **Prime mover**

When you follow through with the kick, the muscle at the front of the thigh becomes the prime mover, pulling the lower leg up.

Lifting weights can make muscles grow, which is why bodybuilders have bigger muscles than ordinary people.

There are more than 30 muscles in your face, which allows you to make different expressions.

You use your quadriceps muscles for running, jumping, and cycling.

The biggest muscles are in your bottom.

Made of muscle

There are more than 600 muscles in the human body. Muscles are what give your body its shape and provide 25 to 45 percent of its mass. Exercise helps keep the muscles in peak form. Some of the most powerful muscles are in the back, attached to the spine. These help you stand upright. They also provide the power to lift and push things. A number of muscles often act together to provide a complete range of movement, such as twisting or rotating.

It will beat about 2.5 billion times in a lifetime.

MOVE your body

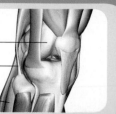

So far, we've looked at body movement in terms of generating energy, controlling it, and converting it into muscle power. But there are also **two types of movement—linear and angular**. Linear movement is getting from A to B, while angular movement is what your body does to make this happen. When it comes to movement, your joints play a vital role. There are several different types...

All your different joints work together to perform a variety of different movements, from jumping and running, to balancing and standing still.

Pivot joints (also called rotary joints) allow bones to move around each other. There are pivot joints in your neck and your forearms.

Ball-and-socket joints rotate—they move back and forth and around and around in every direction. Your hips and your shoulders are ball-and-socket joints.

Ellipsoidal joints can move from front to back and from side to side, but they can't rotate. Your wrists and your jaw are ellipsoidal joints.

Hinge joints—surprise, surprise—work just like hinges, allowing movement backward and forward. Your knees and your elbows are all examples of hinge joints.

Saddle joints allow for movement back and forth, and up and down, but not around and around like a ball-and-socket joint. There is a saddle joint at the base of your thumb.

TENDON power

Joints and muscles can't do anything without amazing strips of tissue called tendons. Muscles work hard, but they tear easily under strain. Tendons attach muscles to bones, but they are much stronger and more flexible than muscles. They have "elastic energy" (think of stretching a rubber band, then "pinging" it back). This allows them to withstand the force it takes to pull on bones and generate motion.

KNEE JOINT

Bone

Tendon

Muscle

MOTION

LINEAR MOTION is exactly as it sounds—movement forward or backward in a straight line. We can measure linear motion using certain variables: distance, displacement, speed, velocity, and acceleration.

Displacement and distance on face value sound very similar. But displacement is the shortest route in a straight line between start and finish, whereas distance measures the distance actually traveled.

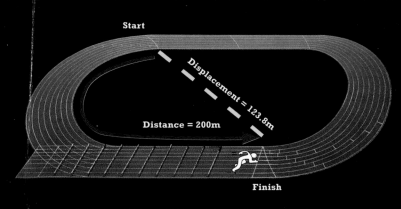

Start

Displacement = 123.8m

Distance = 200m

Finish

Speed and velocity also get mixed up. Speed is easy to figure out since you simply divide the distance by the time it takes to get there. Velocity is how fast you move in a particular direction. So, if you run at 12 mph (20 km/h), but in a circle, your speed will remain the same, but your velocity will be different because you are constantly changing direction.

Distance ÷ time = SPEED

Acceleration can be confusing. To accelerate doesn't just mean speeding up—it also means changing direction, or even slowing down! (But if we slow down we say acceleration is negative.)

The golfer swings at the ball—and the club *accelerates*.

Animal	SPEED mph	ACCELERATION ft/s²	
Human	28	11½	
Lion	50	31	
Gazelle	50	15	
Cheetah	65	33½	
Elephant	25	1¼	

Speed and acceleration

Here is some speed and acceleration data for humans—and some pretty fast animals, too! Speeds are measured in miles or kilometers per hour, and acceleration in feet or meters per second squared. So what you learn from this chart is that a human can only accelerate at around 11½ ft/s² (3.5 m/s²), whereas a lion and cheetah can pick up speed much more quickly. Not only that, but they also run much faster than you. Better to stay away!

EARTH forces

Gravity is one of the most important forces in the universe. It is also very important on Earth because it keeps us from floating away into space. As a force, gravity has affected how our bodies work. Our systems have adapted to its persistent force over the millennia of evolution. The circulation system, for example, uses muscles and valves in our veins so that blood can flow up as well as down. **Gravity also affects how we move**.

First, let's look at gravity and how it pulls on the body. Gravity is alway present—pulling you to Earth. Usually, the ground is in the way and you don't really notice it. So, the best way to show its effect is to take a dive off a high dive.

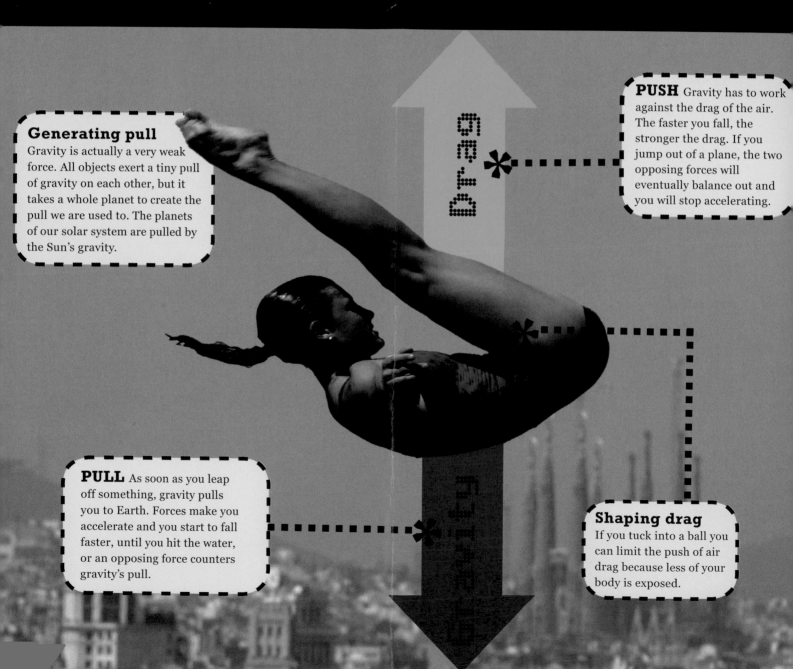

Generating pull

Gravity is actually a very weak force. All objects exert a tiny pull of gravity on each other, but it takes a whole planet to create the pull we are used to. The planets of our solar system are pulled by the Sun's gravity.

PUSH Gravity has to work against the drag of the air. The faster you fall, the stronger the drag. If you jump out of a plane, the two opposing forces will eventually balance out and you will stop accelerating.

PULL As soon as you leap off something, gravity pulls you to Earth. Forces make you accelerate and you start to fall faster, until you hit the water, or an opposing force counters gravity's pull.

Shaping drag

If you tuck into a ball you can limit the push of air drag because less of your body is exposed.

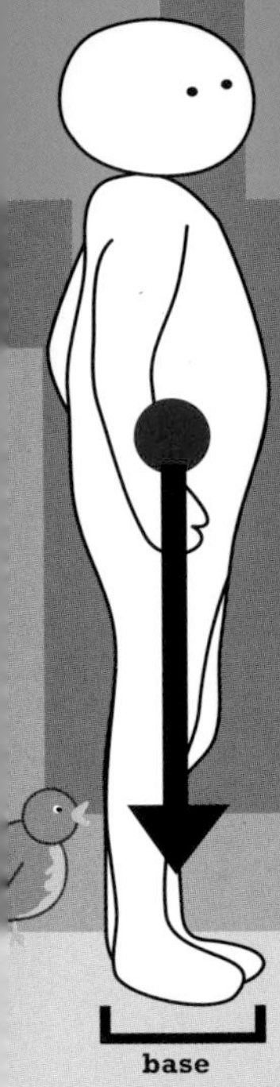

Standing still

The art of standing still is to make sure your COG stays between the limits of your stable base. You can improve your stable base by standing with your feet farther apart. But watch out, your COG can move left to right as well as forward and back, and having one foot too far in front of the other may make you fall sideways.

base

Running

All the motion in running, especially when changing direction, can alter your COG. Our skill of balancing while moving comes from our ability to bend and adapt. If we were rigid, like a car, and the COG moved outside our base, we would topple over. Being able to bend and counterbalance gives us a greater sense of balance and stability. Also, the COG, and therefore our weight, is slightly forward, helping us to move. Try this at home—run in a wide arc to your left; which way does your body bend?

base

= Center Of Gravity

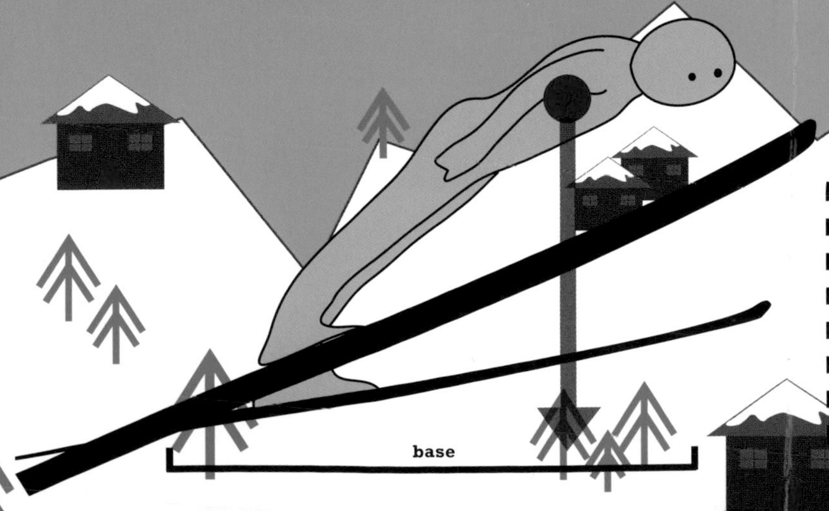

Ski jumper

Equipment can help stabilize the body. A ski jumper leans forward to accelerate down the slope. The long skis give him a long, stable base, so he can lean farther than if he were wearing normal shoes. As he lands, he keeps his feet slightly apart under his shoulders, giving him a long and wide stable base.

base

ARCHIMEDES' Principle

On his discovery Archimedes jumped out and ran down the street shouting EUREKA! (I have found it!)

What's scientific about bathtime?

As the great Greek mathematician Archimedes stepped into his bathtub, he noticed the water level rose. Archimedes discovered it is not only the weight of the object that affects if it floats or sinks, but also how much water it displaces. With this "eureka" moment, Archimedes had discovered the force of buoyancy.

WET forces at play

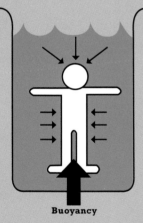

Buoyancy

Buoyancy

When an object is submerged the surrounding water exerts a force on the object from all directions. The overall effect is an upward force.

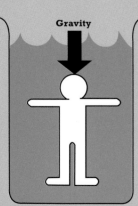

Gravity

Gravity

The mass of any object is affected by the downward pull of gravity. (Mass measures how much matter something contains.) The force produced by gravity acting on an object's mass is called weight.

WATER Forces

Water is denser than air and traveling through it is much harder. Also, gravity isn't the only force in play; there's another you have to deal with—buoyancy. To float or not to float isn't your choice. Instead, it comes down to a simple principle discovered over 2,000 years ago.

Floater or sinker

The interaction between the two forces of buoyancy and gravity decides if an object floats or sinks.

If the force of buoyancy is greater than the force of gravity, the object will float.

However, if the force of gravity is greater than the force of buoyancy, the object will sink. The heavier something is, the more likely it is to sink.

Not all heavy things sink. An oil tanker floats because it displaces lots of water and its weight is less than the weight of the displaced water. So, weight and volume are very important. If the oil tanker kept its weight, but was the size of a canoe, it would sink without a trace because it would be heavier than the volume of water displaced.

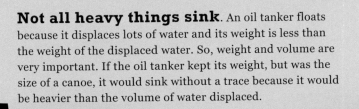

WATER resistance

Much like traveling through air, there is a similar resistance force at play in water. Water resistance can be a drag, so to move through water means generating enough force to overcome it. Try walking through knee-high water—not as easy as walking down the street!

The red areas show the parts of the body that experience the highest resistance as the swimmer travels through water. Dark blue shows areas of least resistance.

SHARK TECHNOLOGY

The shark is a master predator of the deep and can reach speeds of 68 mph (110 km/h). Swimwear manufacturers have examined sharkskin to find out how this speedy fish beats water resistance.

Tiny ridges in the shark's skin channel water, reducing resistance.

The fabric of the sharkskin inspired swimsuit copies the ridge effect.

SWIM LIKE A SHARK The new technology of the sharkskin inspired swimsuit reduces the water resistance by about 4 percent. It doesn't sound like much, but when Olympic swimmers dive into the pool, it could make the difference between a gold or silver medal.

Brace for IMPACT

Football players are big-framed, heavy guys, but they're not lumbering hulks—they can pound down the field at up to 20 mph (32 km/h). They know that the faster they move, the harder they hit, which is why they drive their bodies forward into tackles like muscular battering rams. When they collide, the impact force is determined by multiplying mass by acceleration. So that combination of weight and speed can result in some real bone-crushing, eye-watering power.

The AVERAGE LINEMAN charges his victim

1 newton = The force necessary to accelerate a mass of

160 kg (350 lb) ACCELERATING at 6 m/s²

=

F = ma

force = mass x acceleration

(the BIGGER and

The more momentum a player has, the harder he is to stop. When a defender tackles or blocks, he's trying to change his opponent's momentum, by applying a force in the opposite direction. Enough force will make them both grind to a halt.

AT A FORCE OF 960 newtons

1 kg at a rate of 1 m per second per second

as much force as having a BABY ELEPHANT dropped on you!

faster you are, the harder you hit)

Taking the STRAIN

The streets are no longer just for pedestrians, cars, and pigeons. A new mover-and-shaker has claimed rights to the block. **Free running** is a modern version of *parkour*, which started in urban France during the 1990s. It is a form of street gymnastics, in which participants use walls, stairs, benches, and balconies as apparatus to perform jumps, somersaults, and balances in a continuous, flowing style.

Strains and sprains happen when you are not fully warmed up or make movements that overstretch the muscles.

Repeated exertion can damage the body's shock absorbers and lead to arthritis and other problems.

The body's ability to generate, handle, and counter force is amazing. One modern sport that takes the body to its limits is **free running**. With all the running, jumping, and somersaults involved, the body takes a pounding. Just landing after a running jump exerts a force of ten times your body weight. But **where does this force and its energy go?**

SHOCK, RATTLE, AND ROLL

The force created by landing on concrete can be truly shocking. However, the body can take the pressure using its own built-in, high-performance shock absorbers—the knees. The amount of force they have to cope with depends on whether the knees are bent, the softness and slope of the landing surface, and the forward motion of the jumper. Jumping exerts 900 pounds (400 kg) of force on each knee joint.

cross-section

Shock absorbers in cars are pumps filled with gas that absorb energy from a spring and transfer it to a piston. The piston pushes against the gas, which slows it down and turns the energy into heat.

Femur

BONES AND MUSCLES

The knee is the largest joint in the human body. It has four bones, of which the thigh bone (femur) is the biggest bone in the body. Bones are very good at resisting crushing and absorb some of the impact energy. The muscles attached to the bones also help absorb energy. The thigh bone has two large muscle groups, the quadriceps and the hamstrings, on the front and back of the leg.

LIGAMENTS

For the bones to work at their best, they need to be stable. This is where ligaments come into play. These tough bands of tissue are made of dense fibers and hold the bones together. Ligaments are surprisingly tough—twice as strong as nylon rope—and keep the joint in place no matter what the movement or impact.

Simply bending your knees for climbing creates a force of 300 pounds (135 kg) on your knee joints.

CARTILAGE

When bone hits bone it can really grate, especially when friction is involved. This is where cartilage comes in. This tough, smooth tissue covers the ends of the bones, allowing them to slide over each other, and stops them from wearing away. It is also used to join tendons and ligaments to bones. Cartilage can endure up to 7 tons of force before it snaps, perfect for protecting the bones. It is also flexible and cushions most of any impact.

CAPSULE

The knee joint is known as a synovial joint. A capsule of thick, stringy fluid surrounds the joint, offering further protection. The fluid nourishes the joint, keeping it fit and healthy, ready for the next impact. Wearing correctly designed footwear can reduce the impact of landing by up to 20 percent—so if you are planning to go street running it's better for your knees if you wear cushioned sneakers instead of your school shoes!

OUTER SPACE

Beyond the Earth's atmosphere is outer space. Space is a weightless environment, and there is little gravity. Removing this important everyday force means your body's everyday systems, bones, and muscles work differently. You can't move your arms and legs as you would do on Earth, so they lose density and weaken. So, when you return to Earth, you get light-headed and need a helping hand as you come out of the shuttle.

Floating around space in a hi-tech, modern spacesuit looks like fun, especially compared to the extreme harshness of space. But it isn't as cozy as it looks. Living inside a spacesuit is actually like being at the top of a very high mountain, and living up there isn't easy...

SICK OF ALTITUDE

As you climb a mountain the air pressure decreases, which can lead to altitude sickness. This starts with a headache and can gradually worsen if exposed for too long, with some cases causing death. The cure is to walk back down the mountain, stopping at intervals to allow the body to get used to normal air pressure.

The highest mountain on Earth is Mount Everest. Its summit towers 29,028 ft (8,848 m) above sea level. No one lives there but many have climbed its treacherous slopes. In this extreme environment the forces the body deals with every day at sea level change dramatically. It all has to do with pressure, or more precisely, air pressure.

SEA DEEP

Deep below the waves there is a truly alien environment. Little light penetrates the deep, and, with all the weight of the water above pressing down on you, you begin to feel its effects. High pressure causes matter, especially gas, to compress, making it compact into a denser form. As you come back up, the gases in your body begin to expand again. So, divers swimming back to the surface have to swim slowly and stop at intervals. Swim too quickly and the diver would suffer from decompression sickness (the bends), which can be fatal.

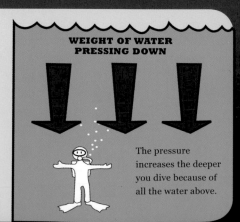

WEIGHT OF WATER PRESSING DOWN

The pressure increases the deeper you dive because of all the water above.

The human body can survive in space without a suit, though only for 15 seconds. The dangers are the low pressure, extreme temperatures, and radiation. Also, don't hold your breath—it will make your lungs explode!

UPSIDE-DOWN BLOOD

Gravity usually pulls our blood in one direction: toward the body. On Earth our bodies have to work against gravity, especially when pumping blood to our brains. In space there is no gravity to work against, but our circulation system doesn't know this, and too much blood is sent to the brain and less goes to the legs. This gives astronauts big puffy heads and skinny legs.

GRAVITY — NO GRAVITY
ON EARTH — IN SPACE

When you leave the safety of sea level, pressure on the body changes. But how does the body react?

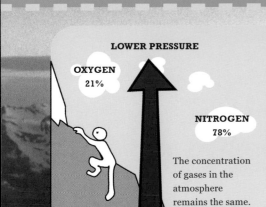

LOWER PRESSURE

OXYGEN 21%

NITROGEN 78%

The concentration of gases in the atmosphere remains the same.

SEA LEVEL

MOUNTAIN HIGH

As you climb up a mountain people say the air is getting "thinner." Actually there is the same concentration of oxygen at the top of Mount Everest as there is at sea level. The difference is AIR PRESSURE. In our lungs, oxygen moves into our blood because of the pressure difference between our blood and the air outside. The greater the difference in pressure, the easier oxygen diffuses. On top of a mountain the pressure difference isn't as high as it is at sea level, so with each mountaintop breath less oxygen enters our blood. With less oxygen to fuel your body, simple activities prove to be a challenge—even standing up can be tricky.

Our bodies are made mainly of water, which means even at extreme depths the water pressure will never crush us. However, solids and gases are affected and it is dangerous to dive deeper than 330 ft (100 m), although with special breathing equipment I could dive to 1,050 ft (320 m).

AROUND THE BENDS

What are the bends? Having dived deep underwater, the high pressure compresses gases in the body. As the diver swims back to the surface these compressed gases, mainly nitrogen, expand as the pressure reduces. This causes bubbles to form in the blood, tissues, and organs. Depending on the location of the bubbles, the symptoms can be anything from headaches and dizziness, to extreme limb pain and lung failure. If left untreated it can be deadly.

Physical UPGRADE

Do you want to be stronger, faster, or more flexible? Think of your body as a blank canvas that can be customized to your own design. It's fine-tuned to the kind of activity you put it through—whether that's deep-sea diving, weightlifting, or channel surfing.

No pain, no gain

When a body builder has a tough workout, he's making tiny tears in his muscle fiber—which is every bit as painful as it sounds. Those microtears make muscles feel sore a day or two after exercise. You'll know the feeling if you've ever been on a long run.

As a result of damage to the muscle tissue, chemical signals are sent through the body. These instructions tell your muscles to create new tissue as they recover.

Body builders must strike the right balance between putting stress on muscles, and letting them recuperate. Recovery time is crucial, since this is when the new muscle tissue actually forms.

Ultimate lungs Free divers can boost their lung capacity to 10 liters or more—they can breathe in a third more air than most people. They build up their lungs using a technique called packing, where they breathe in then breathe in again, compressing all the air into their lungs.

Bending over backward Olympic gymnasts need to be incredibly flexible as well as strong. They use exercises like splits, high kicks, and backbends to stretch their tendons and muscles, and to increase their range of motion.

This strongman has built up his muscles enough to move a 8.6 ton truck single-handedly.

Use it or lose it
Astronauts barely have to use their muscles at all to move around in low gravity, but they exercise for more than two hours a day. If they didn't, their muscles would gradually waste away.

What's the point of exercise?
Regular exercise isn't just about shedding fat. It can transform your whole body.

Muscle strength It makes you lean and mean.

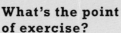
Bone density It helps build strong bones.

Joint mobility It helps you twist and flex without effort.

Heart strength It keeps you healthy and energetic.

Immune system It helps you fight off infection.

Brain function It helps you concentrate better and respond faster.

Coordination It makes your brain and body work better together.

Body at WAR

Your body is constantly under siege from tiny but ferocious alien invaders, called germs or pathogens. But your body is protected by a whole host of defensive measures, including strong outer walls, chemical alarm systems, and stalwart defenders in the form of white blood cells like macrophages.

Your body's surface is crawling with millions of germs, but these marauders need to get inside to cause infection. The dead outer layer of your skin acts as a solid barrier to keep them out.

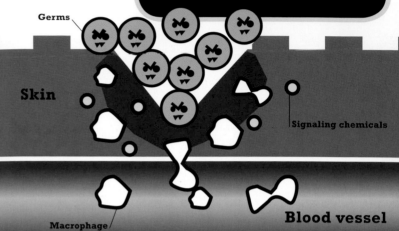

Germs

Skin

Signaling chemicals

Macrophage

Blood vessel

1

Macrophage

When germs enter your body through a cut, specialized skin cells release signaling chemicals to summon macrophages to the area. Macrophages engulf some germs and carry them away.

2

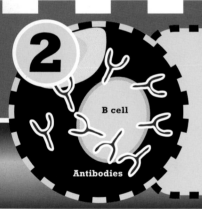

B cell

Antibodies

The germs rapidly multiply inside your body. Meanwhile, the macrophages carry germs to B cells. These are factories for making antibodies—biological weapons designed to attack that specific germ.

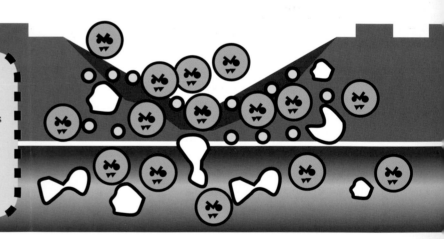

3

Phagocyte

Antibodies travel through the blood to the infected area and fix on to the germs. They send out signals to macrophages and other germ-engulfing cells called phagocytes, which digest the germs.

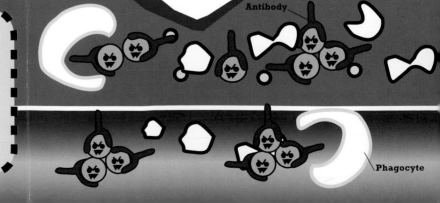

Antibody

Phagocyte

Body invaders

Germs leach our bodies' nutrients, and may also produce toxins. There are three main families of germs: bacteria, viruses, and protists.

Bacteria are single-cell organisms that can be helpful or harmful to people.

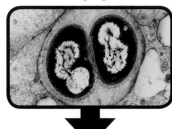

Viruses are tiny particles that take over cells and use them to reproduce themselves.

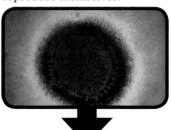

Protists are moisture-loving single-cell organisms. They cause diseases like malaria.

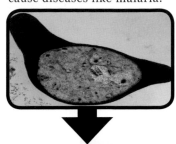

Body defenders

All white blood cells are produced in the bone marrow. When germs attack, your body responds by flooding the infected area with white-blood-cell-rich blood. That's why your skin turns red and swells up.

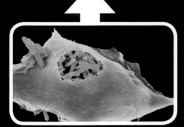

Macrophages are a kind of phagocyte that engulf germs and that carry them to B and T cells.

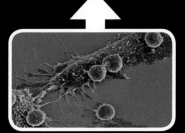

B & T cells (also called B and T lymphocytes) make antibodies and give orders to other white blood cells.

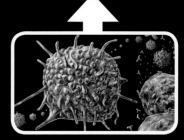

Antibodies have specialized projections that can fasten on to one particular kind of germ and disable it.

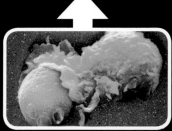

Phagocytes are white blood cells that fold their outer membranes around germs, then digest them.

INNER ARMOR

The lymphatic system is your body's infection-fighting rapid-response system. This network of channels runs through your entire body and connects together immune command centers called lymph nodes. These nodes produce B cells and T cells, which coordinate your body's response to infection. White blood cells can easily move between blood vessels and lymph vessels.

The thymus, spleen, and parts of the lower intestine are connected to the lymphatic system, and each plays an important role in your immune response.

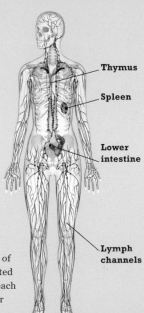

Thymus

Spleen

Lower intestine

Lymph channels

Extra protection Your body uses several other mechanisms to protect you from infection. You can add a further barrier by washing your hands.

Strong acid in your stomach kills the germs in your food.

Saliva, tears, sweat, and urine wash germs out of your body.

Mucus traps germs, and coughing or sneezing propels them away.

What makes you you?

Why is it that some people are as quick as a gazelle and as agile as a cat, while others seem to have two left feet? With practice and dedication, you can train your body to acquire amazing physical skills, but there are limits to what you can achieve. Those limits are set by the genes you inherited from your parents. It's your genes that really make you you.

DNA

Genes are stored as a four-letter code running along the middle of the DNA molecule. DNA (deoxyribonucleic acid) is shaped like a ladder that's been twisted around. It's "rungs" come in four different types, and these form the four letters of the genetic code: A, C, G, and T. The genetic code needed to build a human body is 3 billion letters long, which is enough to fill 90 volumes of the Encyclopedia Britannica with text or one CD with data.

GENES

A gene is a stretch of DNA that does a particular job. It might contain the code needed to build a particular protein, for instance, or it might be a length of DNA that switches other genes on or off. There are only about 20,000 genes within your DNA. Between these genes are great lengths of DNA that don't code for anything—we call this noncoding DNA "junk DNA," and no one is sure what it's for. It might simply be a kind of virus that hitches a ride in our bodies.

CHROMOSOMES

Each cell in your body contains a complete copy of your entire genetic code. That means that an awful lot of DNA has to fit into a tiny space, so your DNA is cleverly packaged. It's coiled into a thread, the thread is coiled into a rope, and the rope is coiled again and again to form chunky, X-shaped structures—your chromosomes. You have exactly 46 chromosomes: 23 from your mother and 23 from your father.

CELLS

Your body is made of 100 trillion cells. Each one (with a few exceptions) contains a full set of 46 chromosomes. When a cell divides as you grow, all that DNA has to be unwound, duplicated, and then packaged up again into the two new cells.

You share 98.5% of your genetic code with chimpanzees and about 50% with bananas!

Blame your parents

Do you have curly hair? Freckles? Skinny legs? Blame your parents—all your physical characteristics are set by the genes they gave you. You've actually got two whole sets of genes: one set is on the 23 chromosomes you inherited from your mother, and the second set is on the 23 chromosomes from your father. If there's anything you don't like about your body, it's your parents' fault. Or your grandparents'.

I've got the X-FACTOR!

Among the 46 chromosomes that everyone has are two special ones: the sex chromosomes. These are shaped like the letters X and Y. Your mother has two X-chromosomes, but your father has one X and one Y.

BOY OR GIRL?

Your gender is set by your two sex chromosomes. You get one of these from your mother and one from your father. Your mother can only pass on X-chromosomes, but your father can pass on either an X or a Y. If you get an X from your father, you're a girl. If you get a Y, you're a boy. It's the luck of the draw.

Nature ▼ vs. Nurture

Your genes set many of your characteristics, from the color of your eyes to your height. But they don't have absolute control. You can change your body by how you eat and exercise. You can also program yourself to learn new skills like swimming or skiing. Genes have a major influence on mental characteristics such as intelligence and personality, but scientists are undecided as to whether genes (nature) or experience (nurture) has the greatest effect.

You're UNIQUE

The chromosomes you inherited from your parents aren't simply copies of theirs. Each of yours contains reshuffled bits and pieces from your grandparents' chromosomes, giving you a totally unique combination of genes (unless you have an identical twin). You can see your uniqueness in things like your fingerprints and iris pattern.

The iris is a ring of colored muscle fibers around the pupil.

I see it in your eyes

The colored parts of your eyes—your irises—are as unique as fingerprints, thanks to their distinctive pattern of stripes and gaps. An iris scanner can read this pattern like a barcode and confirm your identify. But criminals can fool the system with printed contact lenses.

Biting an apple isn't a crime. Biting a person is.

Bite prints

Your teeth and the bite marks they leave are unique to you. Forensic scientists sometimes use "bite prints" to identify criminals, but the technique is not 100% reliable.

Fingerprints

Police have been using fingerprints to catch criminals for more than a century. Recently, fingerprint scanners have become a feature of laptop computers. With some ingenuity, these scanners can be fooled by fake prints glued on to your fingers.

Fantastic. You can energize yourself, control it, and move on up in life. The world is your oyster. So, what's left in life? Well, there's one horizon still out of reach—the future.

Science has given us so much, we know how to build a body, how to control forces, and how we became who we are. So what does the science of the future promise?

Modern science is progressing quickly. The microchip, nanotechnology, and genetics are opening doors and even windows to new possibilities.

In the following pages, we're going to have a peek into the future and see what science is working on today and what it predicts for tomorrow. From rebuilding the body, to choosing genes, and unearthing mysteries. So, let's enter the time machine...

Body science: Future

Dead body SCIENCE

When a dead body is found and the cause of death looks suspicious, the police call in forensic scientists to search for every tiny clue. Forensic scientists can tell a lot from a dead body, no matter how rotten and decayed it is. And if the cause of death is murder, the evidence scientists collect can track down the killer.

The crime scene

The first stage of investigation is to seal off the crime scene so that the evidence can't be disturbed. The body is photographed before being removed, and its outline is drawn on the ground in chalk. The positions of the limbs may reveal whether the victim fell violently, was dumped, or lay down before dying. Forensic scientists comb the entire crime scene for the tinest clues: hairs, spots of blood, fibers from clothes, fingerprints, footprints, and any dropped objects, from bullet casings to shards of glass. Every speck of evidence is bagged, labeled, and taken back to the lab.

POSTMORTEM

After a suspicious death, a specially trained doctor called a pathologist performs a kind of operation called a postmortem. The naked body is examined for injuries or signs of a struggle (such as damaged fingernails). Next it is cut open and each organ is inspected for signs of damage or disease that might reveal the cause of death. If the body has decomposed, an insect expert identifies the maggots and beetles that have infested the flesh. These can reveal how long the body was left to decay.

Clue 2

Clue 4

Footprints that don't match the victim's shoes may have been left by the killer. In addition to revealing what kind of shoes the killer wears, the prints are clues to the killer's sex, height, and weight.

A dropped wallet is sure to contain fingerprints. If items are missing, the killer may have been a thief or may have faked robbery to hide their true motive for murder.

POLICE LI

Clue 3

The direction and shape of blood splatters can reveal the path of a bullet or the type of injury a victim suffered.

FACIAL RECONSTRUCTION

When a person dies, their body decomposes (rots). Soft, fleshy parts such as the eyes, skin, and muscles rot and disappear quickly, but bones and teeth last much longer. When bones and teeth are all that remain, a forensic scientist can still tell a lot about the person's age, sex, build, and ethnic background. A forensic artist can even re-create the shape and appearance of a person's face by using a model of the skull to rebuild facial muscles. This technique, called facial reconstruction, has helped police solve murders committed decades ago. It has even been applied to ancient Egyptian mummies to reveal what the Egyptians looked like thousands of years ago.

FINGERPRINTS

Look carefully at your fingertips. The skin is covered with swirling grooves that improve your grip just as the tread of a boot or a tire improves grip. Along the tiny ridges of skin are microscopic glands that secrete grease and sweat for even better grip. When you touch anything, your fingers leave an almost invisible print made of grease from these glands. Forensic scientists can reveal the prints with a sprinkling of dust and then record them with adhesive tape or a photograph. If the prints match those of a suspect, then the police have proof that the suspect was present at the crime scene.

Clue 1

Fingerprints can identify who the criminal is. No two people on Earth have the same fingerprints—not even identical twins.

DNA FINGERPRINTING

Just as everyone's fingerprints are unique to them, so is everyone's DNA—the molecule that carries genes. After a murder, investigators search both the crime scene and the victim's body for traces of the criminal's body fluids in order to obtain a sample of DNA. DNA can even be extracted from hairs. To make the DNA "fingerprint," forensic scientists break down the DNA into chemical fragments and then make these spread out through a sheet of jelly to form a pattern of stripes that's unique to every person (except for identical twins). The chance of an accidental match with a suspect's DNA is less than one in a million.

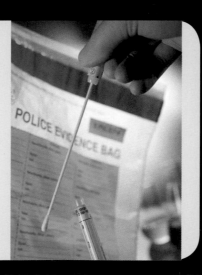

Thanks to DNA fingerprinting I'm more than just a brilliant detective—I'm a gene-ius!

DO NOT CROSS

REENGINEERING the body

When a car needs to be repaired after a crash or a breakdown, ordering spare parts is easy. Not so for the human body. You only have one heart, one liver, one stomach, or just a pair of many other organs. If disease or injury damages your organs beyond repair, your life could be cut short. In years to come,

Harvesting stem cells

Stem cells can be harvested from various parts of the human body. These "adult stem cells" can regenerate only a limited range of body tissue.

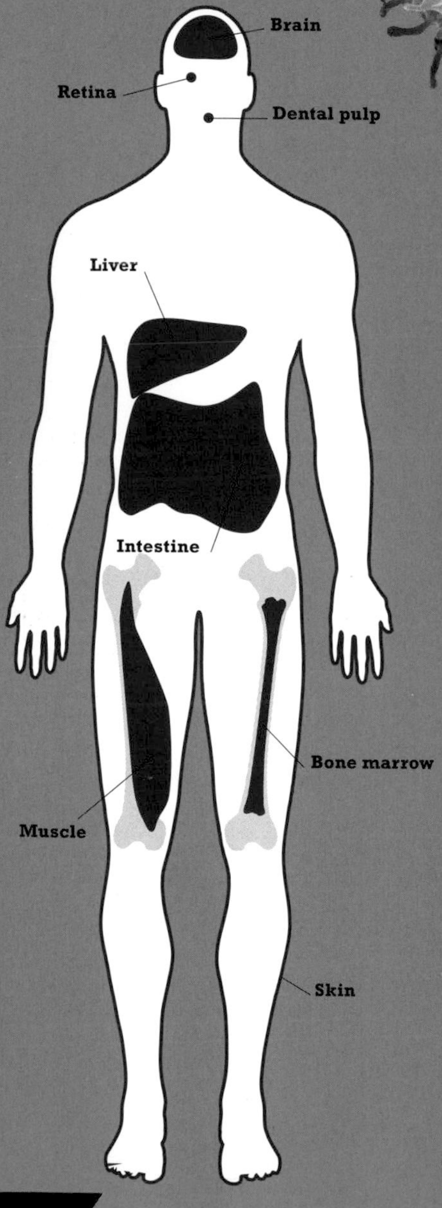

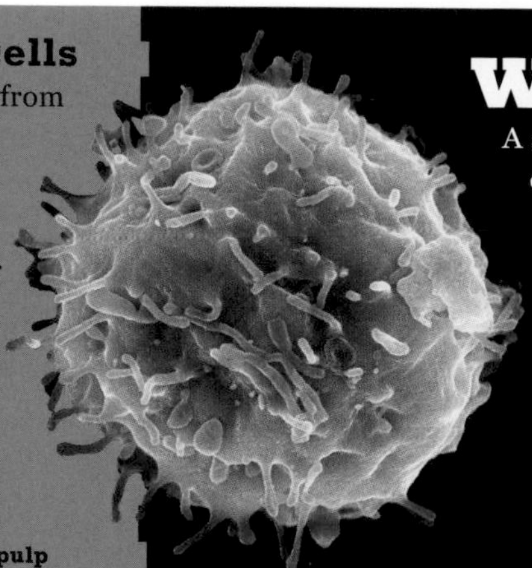

Brain

Retina

Dental pulp

Liver

Intestine

Muscle

Bone marrow

Skin

A stem cell from a baby's umbilical cord (above) can regenerate a wide range of body tissues.

What is a stem cell?

A stem cell is a kind of blank cell that has the ability to multiply and develop into many other types of cell. They occur naturally in the body and serve as a built-in repair system. Scientists hope to harness this ability and use stem cells to regrow whole organs to replace body parts damaged by disease. But so far only very simple tissues have been grown using stem cells. The stem cells with the most potential are found in embryos, but there are also useful stem cells in a baby's umbilical cord and in parts of the adult human body.

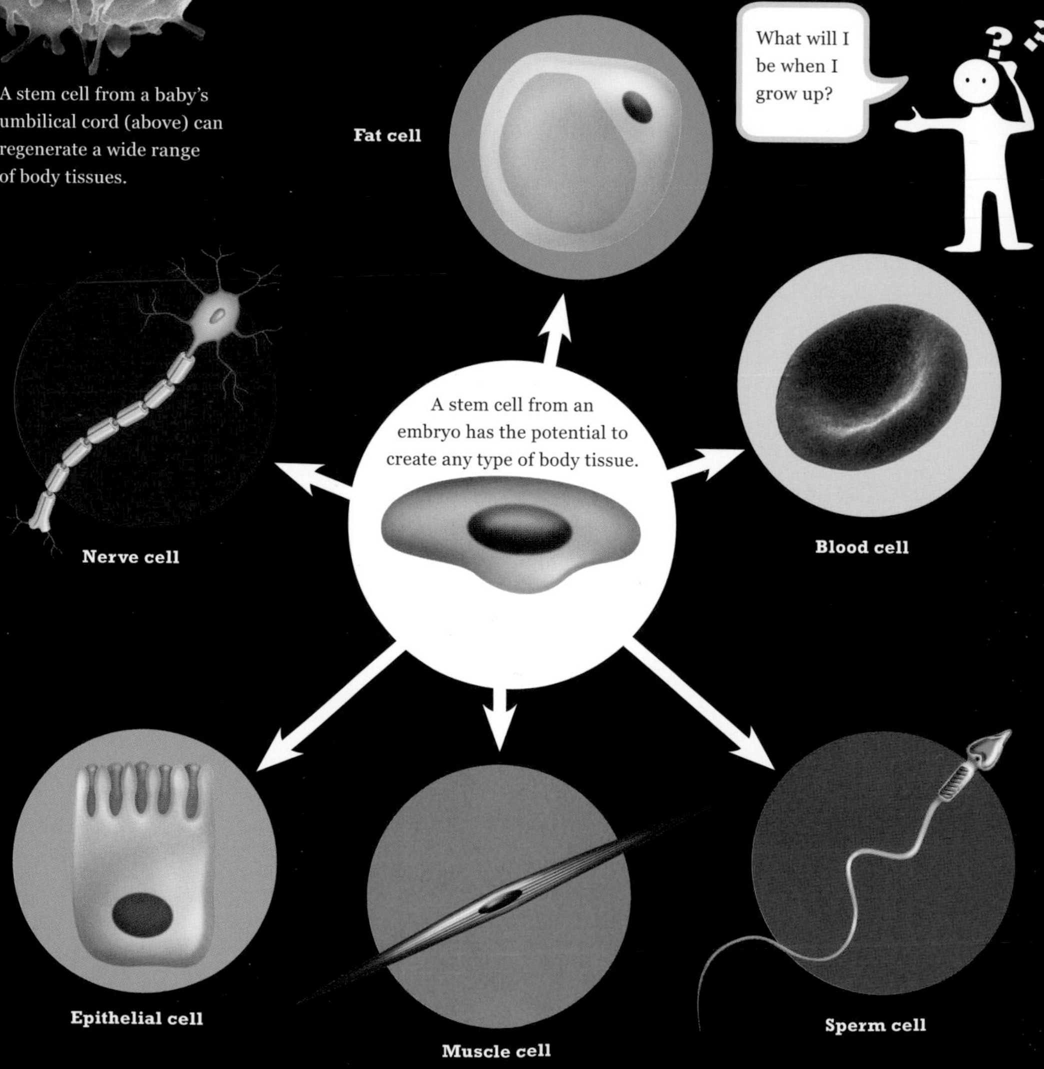

Fat cell

What will I be when I grow up?

Nerve cell

A stem cell from an embryo has the potential to create any type of body tissue.

Blood cell

Epithelial cell

Muscle cell

Sperm cell

however, scientists might find a way of regrowing spare parts of your body. **Research** into stem cells, cloning, and genetic engineering could lead to an **amazing range of new treatments** that can keep your body in tiptop shape throughout your life. But such research is presenting some **difficult questions**.

Genetically engineered humans are still science fiction, but genetically engineered crops are a reality.

Genetics was pioneered by an Austrian monk, Gregor Mendel in the 1850s. Although today, the science of genetic engineering arouses resistance from many religious corners.

Skin graft

Even without using stem cells, scientists can regrow some parts of the body. Thin sheets of skin can be grown from live skin cells and then grafted over wounds such as burns to repair them.

Designer babies

Some people think that genetic technology will one day allow us to choose the genes our children get, enabling us to create custom-made "designer babies" who grow up to be highly intelligent, good-looking, and so on. But this technology may never be truly possible, since many of our genes interact in complex ways.

PRO

Scientists conduct research into genetics and stem cells not to enhance the human body but to fight disease. Such research could lead to the discovery of life-saving drugs and new ways to replace damaged organs.

CON

However, many people say it's wrong to experiment with embryos that have the potential to become individual human beings. Some people also think it's wrong to "play God" and interfere with nature by altering genes.

Dolly the sheep was created by cloning. She was the world's most famous sheep.

Cloning

Cloning is nothing new. Identical twins are natural clones that form when an embryo splits in two, and many plants and animals can produce offspring by cloning themselves. In recent years, scientists have figured out how to make artificial clones by taking the nucleus out of a normal body cell, inserting it into an egg cell, and then zapping it with electricity to activate it so it can develop into an embryo. Cloning can already by used to create genetically identical copies of animals. The real benefit, however, might come in the future when scientists have figured out how to use embryonic stem cells to regrow whole organs. When this becomes possible, doctors will be able to take any cell from your body, turn it into a cloned embryo, and then use the embryonic stem cells to regrow your organs and cure you of disease.

We have the same DNA.

Surgery SCIENCE

We're lucky to be living through a medical revolution.

Modern science is constantly finding new ways to repair and transform bodies: failing organs can be replaced and shattered bones can be repaired. Surgeons can remodel faces and bodies to make people look more normal, or to help them stand out from the crowd—or even to turn them into a work of art.

Keyhole surgery

A very small cut is made in the patient's body, through which a camera and tiny instruments are inserted. The surgeon watches on a screen as he performs the operation.

BODY MECHANICS

Surgeons are the service engineers of the human body. They use tools to cut into and physically repair or reshape the bodies of patients. Surgery is at the cutting edge of modern science. It is already common for robots to help perform complex operations in the least invasive way. In the near future, it may be possible to clone replacement organs from a patient's own cells.

> It can be a little tricky, but brain surgery is hardly rocket science!

Anesthesia

There are two kinds of anesthetics. Local anesthetics make one part of your body feel numb, whereas general anesthetics make you lose consciousness completely.

Sterilization

Surgical staff must protect patients from infection. Before starting an operation they "scrub up" by washing thoroughly and putting on disinfected gowns and masks. Surgical instruments are cleaned with ultrasound, heat, and disinfectant chemicals.

Brain fixers

During brain surgery, a piece of the skull is removed to give surgeons access to the body's most complex organ. Some brain operations are performed with only local anesthetic, so that surgeons can see how the patient's reactions are affected.

Organ transplants

If an organ starts to fail, a replacement can be transplanted from a living or very recently deceased donor. The organ is packed in ice during transportation, and the recipient is given drugs to stop her immune system from attacking the new organ.

Surgical timeline

 Earliest known form of surgery is trepanation (drilling holes in the skull).
Neolithic period

 Napoleonic wars—first modern surgery performed by barber surgeons.
1796–1815 CE

B James Blundell performs first successful blood transfusion.
1818

 Modern anesthetics like chloroform begin to be used in surgery.
1840s

Plastic fantastic

Plastic surgery can make a dramatic difference to the lives of people who have been horribly disfigured by injuries or disease. Isabelle Dinoire lost her lips, chin, and most of her nose when she was mauled by her own labrador. She could barely speak or eat. But in November 2005 she was given the world's first partial face transplant.

Scar tissue was removed before the transplant.

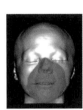

Blood vessels were connected to the new face.

Five months later, Isabelle could feel with her new mouth.

Plastic extreme

Some people have taken the idea of body transformation to its outer limits. As far as they're concerned, the more people stare in the street, the better. Native American Stalking Cat has had a series of operations on his body to turn him into his totem animal, the tiger.

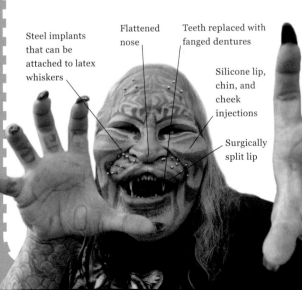

Steel implants that can be attached to latex whiskers

Flattened nose

Teeth replaced with fanged dentures

Silicone lip, chin, and cheek injections

Surgically split lip

BODY BEAUTIFUL?

Many people have something they dislike about their bodies, and today an increasing number of people are opting to have these "imperfections" reworked under the knife of a cosmetic surgeon.

Face lift (rhytidectomy)

By tightening the skin on the forehead, surgeons can make wrinkles disappear. They cut a line along the hairline, detach the skin from the face, then pull everything up before letting it heal.

I want to look like Brad Pitt...

Eyelid surgery (blepharoplasty)

Eyelid reshaping is the most common form of cosmetic plastic surgery in East Asia. Half of people there don't have a double-crease in their eyelid, and some feel it's more attractive to have one.

Nose reshaping (rhinoplasty)

Large noses can make people very self-conscious. Surgeons can change the shape of a nose by making small incisions inside the nostrils, then remodeling the bone and cartilage.

Fat removal (liposuction)

In this operation, a small hole is made in the skin of the abdomen through which a narrow tube is inserted. This tube is moved around to break up fat, which is then sucked up the tube.

The body REBUILT

When the human body fails, technology can rebuild it.

BLADE RUNNER

Richard Whitehead is an athlete who blurs the boundary between disability and super-ability. A double-leg amputee since birth, Richard has been running on prosthetic legs and collecting world records in marathons and sprints. These legs, the *Ossur Cheetah Flex-Feet*, are used by many Paralympic sprinters. Some athletes have made a bid to compete in able-bodied athletics meetings. This has created a debate amongst fellow competitors. The *Flex-Feet* give Richard the ability to run stride-for-stride with able-bodied sprinters, but do they also give him an unfair advantage? Are they better running machines than normal, flesh-and-blood legs? Let's take a closer look at this technology.

As the *Flex-Foot* hits the track, its J-shaped curve acts like a spring, compressing and storing potential energy. When the athlete moves forward, the curve returns to its original shape and releases its stored energy as a forward push.

Prosthetic timeline

	Golden artificial eye (found in Shahr-i Sokhta, Iran)	Artificial toe (found on Egyptian mummy)	Bronze artificial leg (discovered in Capua, Italy)	First dentures	First artificial heart implant
	Circa 2900–2800 BCE	1295–664 BCE	300 BCE	1700s CE	1982

The human body is a complex and powerful machine. But for all its wonder it is also fragile and can easily be damaged beyond biological repair. Using pioneering science and technology, we're increasingly finding ways to rebuild the body, swapping muscles for motors, and nerve fibers for microchips.

There's no simple answer to the question of whether *Flex-Feet* offer an advantage over conventional limbs. On the plus side, the prosthetic allows the the athlete to run using about 25 percent less energy. However, the spring effect of the *Flex-Feet*, which return 90 percent of the energy put into them, is much weaker than the push of real feet.

The *Flex-Foot* is made from carbon fiber. This lightweight material has superior strength, durability, and flexibility.

The *Flex-Foot* also acts as a shock absorber, reducing impact on the knee, hip, and lower back. This means that athletes can train for longer.

Heart of steel In extreme circumstances, it's possible for the human heart to be removed and replaced with a mechanical pump, which uses hydraulic force to push blood around the body. During the seven-hour operation, the patient is kept alive by an external heart–lung machine. The artificial heart is powered by internal and external batteries.

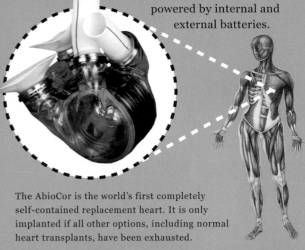

The AbioCor is the world's first completely self-contained replacement heart. It is only implanted if all other options, including normal heart transplants, have been exhausted.

Eye spy Ocular prosthetics are often called glass eyes, though most are actually made of acrylic. While they may look like a real eye, they don't provide sight. However, they do help to smooth social interactions, in which eye contact can play an important part.

Custom-made ocular prosthetics have hand-painted pupils, which are a perfect match for the patient's working eye.

Bionic arm Former US marine Claudia Mitchell lost her arm in a motocycle accident. Now she's become the world's first real-life bionic woman, after an operation that connected nerve endings in her chest to an artificial arm. She can operate the three motors in the mechanical arm with her thoughts. The arm also sends signals to the brain through her nerve endings, which allow her to feel with it.

 First mind-controlled bionic arm

 First face transplant operation

 First bionic eye operation

2003 **2005** **2008**

Future SENSES

Plug my new senses in!

Senses help us see, feel, hear, taste, and smell the world around us.
But, sometimes our senses go a little haywire, perhaps breaking down completely or deteriorating with age. Don't worry, we are resourceful beings and have long helped our failing sight and hearing with external devices like glasses and hearing aids. But these can be crude and old fashioned; surely science has more to offer? Let's see what's in store for our future senses.

FIXING Sight

Sight is an energy sense; it is all about trapping light waves and converting them into electrochemical signals, which are then interpreted by the brain. However, sometimes the body doesn't trap the light waves correctly, or the optic nerve fails to relay the correct message.

Glasses act as an external lens to help bend the energy waves onto the correct area of the retina, allowing you to see clearly. There are two common ailments that require glasses—nearsightedness and farsightedness. You are nearsighted when your lens is too curved and it focuses the light waves in front of the retina. Farsighted is the opposite: the lens is too flat and focuses the light waves beyond the retina. Both form a blurred image.

Contact lenses offer an alternative to glasses, providing a more subtle sight fix. However, because they sit on the eye there is a limit to how thick or curved they can be, so in extreme cases glasses are the only option.

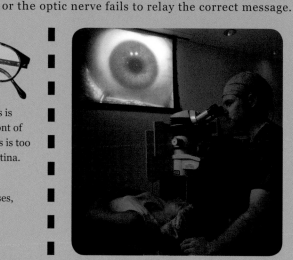

Laser surgery
Recent scientific advances have given us laser refractive surgery. The procedure uses a laser to reshape the lens so it correctly focuses the incoming light waves onto the retina. The procedure isn't permanent and several treatments might be necessary. Also, the operation takes place while the patients are awake! But don't worry, they are given local anesthetic.

FUTURE Sight

As we learn more about the brain we can start to help our senses. How? Well, it all comes down to interpreting external energy waves. If we can plug adaptations into our brain we can even cure blindness.

Video glasses
The future of glasses is already here. The Dobelle Artificial Eye is a video camera mounted on a pair of glasses and connected to electrodes implanted into the brain. The device allows patients to see outlines of shapes, large letters, and numbers on contrasting color backgrounds.

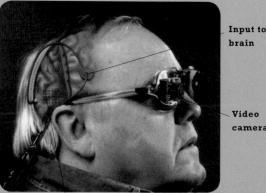

Input to brain

Video camera

Electrodes

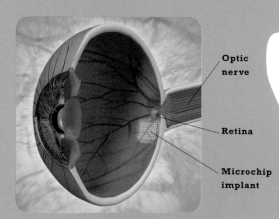

Optic nerve

Retina

Microchip implant

Chip and see
If you don't want to walk around with a pair of bulky video glasses, then the retina implant might be for you. Still being developed, it acts in the same way as the light-sensitive cells in the retina, reading the incoming light waves and sending signals to the brain via the optic nerve.

Pardon?

Sight makes sense now, but what about sound? Hearing is also an energy sense, which makes it easier to combat any ailments. Injury, illness, and old age can all affect your body's ability to read and transfer sound vibrations. Don't worry, we've heard there are some solutions.

The air-conducting hearing aid sits on top of the ear and feeds a small, thin plastic tube into the ear. The hearing aid captures and amplifies sound vibrations. It has been around for a while and works in a similar way to the old-fashioned ear trumpet, by focusing sounds onto the eardrum.

In-ear hearing aids offer a more discreet and less bulky alternative. They work along the same principles, of translating and amplifying sound waves. They can also be finely tuned to the wearer's individual needs, as some people struggle with certain sound frequenices.

Sound waves

Microphone transmitter

Receiver

Cochlea

Bionic ear

The bionic ear is actually a cochlear implant. It works differently than a regular hearing aid. Instead of amplifying sound waves it transmits to and stimulates functioning sound cells and nerves in the cochlea. An external microphone sends electrical impulses straight to the cochlea. It can help deaf people to hear sounds and clearly pick out speech in quiet rooms.

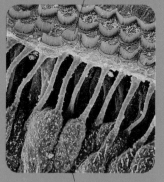

The external transmitter is attached to the internal receiver by a magnet.

Sounding old

As you enter old age, the cells in your inner ear that sense sound, known as hair cells, deteriorate and die off. This leads to partial or even complete deafness. Without these cells the link between your ear and brain is broken.

Fine "hairs" that detect sound

hair cell

Virtual reality

The holy grail of all sensory futures is the virtual reality machine. The early promises of a complete gaming experience with surround sound, sight, smell, and even touch, have long faded from computer companies' lips. But is virtual reality a forgotten dream? In an online world, consumers are bypassing long lines and shopping more online, so computer companies are leaving gaming behind and looking into "virtual touch" devices to help customers "feel" what they are buying. The emergency services and armed forces already use virtual reality simulators to train staff in extreme situations like terrorist attacks and natural disasters.

Virtual reality gaming has been in the pipeline for decades, but no devices have yet reached the stores.

Air traffic control towers could use virtual reality to help controllers visualize incoming airplane trajectories.

MICRO medicine

The medicine of the future

will involve less exploratory surgery and more therapies that target individual cells. Using nanomaterials and microtechnologies, many injuries and illnesses will be dealt with from inside the body.

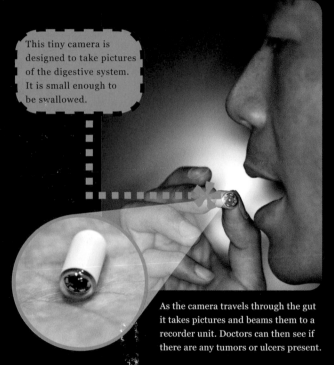

This tiny camera is designed to take pictures of the digestive system. It is small enough to be swallowed.

As the camera travels through the gut it takes pictures and beams them to a recorder unit. Doctors can then see if there are any tumors or ulcers present.

Nanoshells are tiny spheres coated with gold that can be engineered to respond to infrared light. Scientists have been using them to kill tumors. The nanoshells collect in the cancer cells. When an infrared light is switched on, the shells heat up and kill the cancer, leaving healthy cells undamaged.

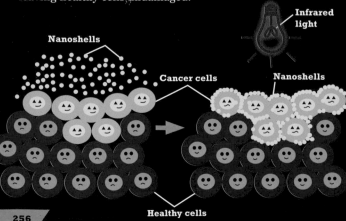

Nanoshells

Cancer cells

Infrared light

Nanoshells

Healthy cells

Red blood cell

White blood cell

Nanorobots are tiny machines. One day they could be used inside the body to destroy blood clots or maintain blood vessels. Equipped with tiny lasers and instruments, they could repair cells and organs that humans are too clumsy to manage with their hands.

Under the skin

Micro- and nano-technologies are too small to be seen with the naked eye, but that makes them perfect for dealing with cells and molecules in the body.

This microchip is being tested with human cells to see if they react. Chips like this could be used to control implantable devices in parts of the body, such as the brain or eye, to restore function.

Stem cells are being grown on nanowires that relay electrical signals. The signals tell the stem cells how to develop, so that they grow into neurons, heart cells, or other specialized cells that are needed to repair damaged organs.

Silver nanoparticles are being used in wound dressings to help injuries to heal. Silver has an antibacterial effect, and tiny particles can penetrate the wound to stop it becoming badly infected.

Sun screens and other cosmetics often use nanoparticles that can penetrate the top layers of the skin. Some scientists are becoming concerned that they could also enter the bloodstream, which could lead to tissue damage.

Nanorobot

Skeletal system

Try and imagine your body without a skeleton. You would be a baggy and shapeless mess! The skeleton, or skeletal system, acts as the framework that shapes and supports your body. Consisting of 206 bones, the skeletal system also protects vital organs such as your heart and brain. When bones meet they form a joint that enables flexibility and movement.

Front

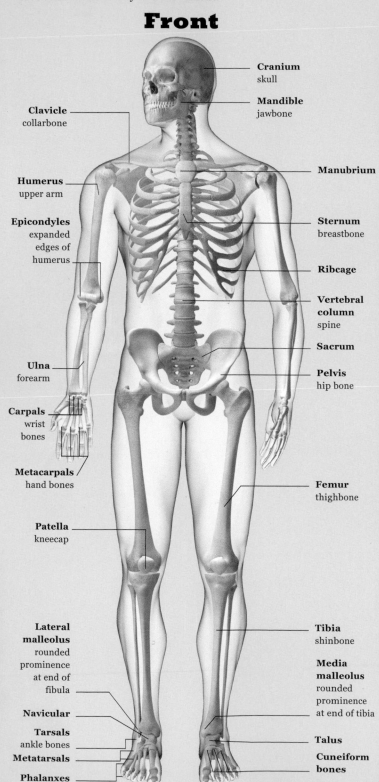

Cranium
skull

Mandible
jawbone

Clavicle
collarbone

Manubrium

Humerus
upper arm

Sternum
breastbone

Epicondyles
expanded edges of humerus

Ribcage

Vertebral column
spine

Sacrum

Ulna
forearm

Pelvis
hip bone

Carpals
wrist bones

Metacarpals
hand bones

Femur
thighbone

Patella
kneecap

Lateral malleolus
rounded prominence at end of fibula

Tibia
shinbone

Media malleolus
rounded prominence at end of tibia

Navicular

Tarsals
ankle bones

Talus

Metatarsals

Cuneiform bones

Phalanxes

Back

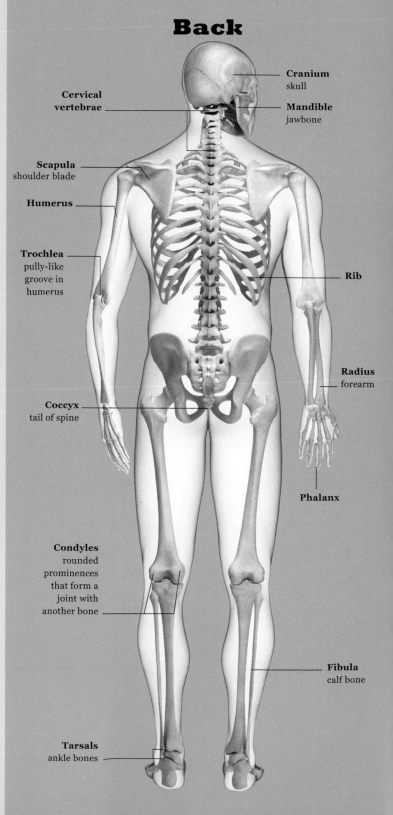

Cranium
skull

Cervical vertebrae

Mandible
jawbone

Scapula
shoulder blade

Humerus

Trochlea
pully-like groove in humerus

Rib

Radius
forearm

Coccyx
tail of spine

Phalanx

Condyles
rounded prominences that form a joint with another bone

Fibula
calf bone

Tarsals
ankle bones

Muscular system

The muscular system includes more than 650 skeletal muscles and accounts for up to half your body weight. It is responsible for generating every movement you make. Muscles are made up of fibers that contract, or shorten, to make your heart pump blood, your lungs breathe in and out, and different parts of your body move.

Front

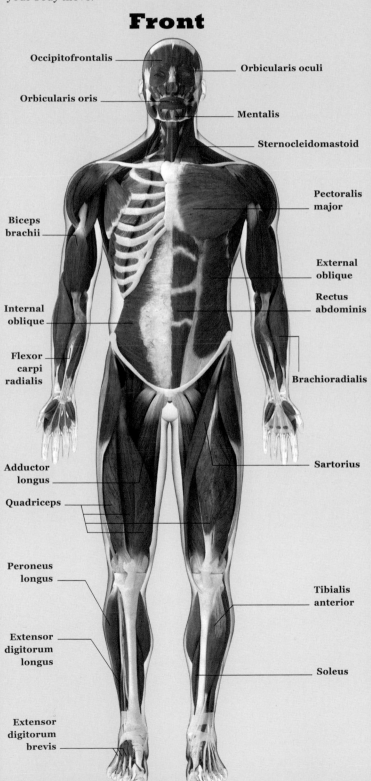

Occipitofrontalis

Orbicularis oris

Biceps brachii

Internal oblique

Flexor carpi radialis

Adductor longus

Quadriceps

Peroneus longus

Extensor digitorum longus

Extensor digitorum brevis

Orbicularis oculi

Mentalis

Sternocleidomastoid

Pectoralis major

External oblique

Rectus abdominis

Brachioradialis

Sartorius

Tibialis anterior

Soleus

Back

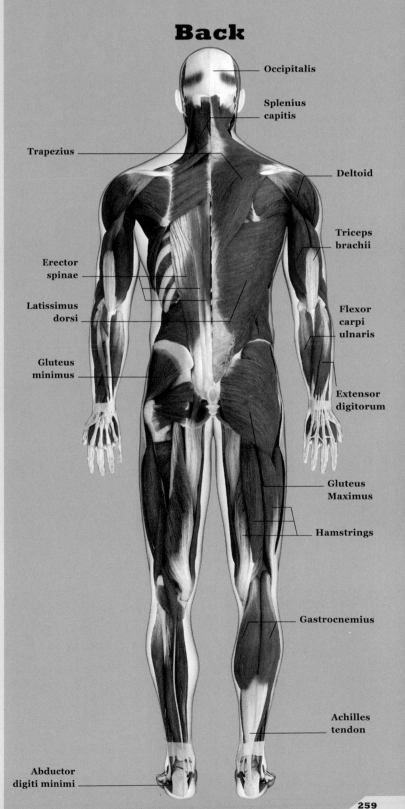

Occipitalis

Splenius capitis

Trapezius

Deltoid

Erector spinae

Triceps brachii

Latissimus dorsi

Flexor carpi ulnaris

Gluteus minimus

Extensor digitorum

Gluteus Maximus

Hamstrings

Gastrocnemius

Achilles tendon

Abductor digiti minimi

Respiratory system

Because your body needs a continual supply of oxygen, you breathe around 20,000 times a day. The respiratory system draws this oxygen into your bloodstream across the lungs' inner surfaces; carbon dioxide is released as a waste product. Your lungs and air passages make up the respiratory system.

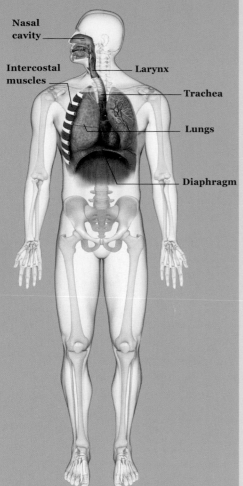

Nasal cavity

Intercostal muscles

Larynx

Trachea

Lungs

Diaphragm

Components checklist

- Nasal cavity
- Larynx
- Trachea
- Lungs
- Diaphragm

Cardiovasular system

To fight off infection and to stay alive, your cardiovascular system works hard to supply food and oxygen to your cells as well as removing waste matter. It does this by transporting substances, such as oxygen, in your blood along the network of tubes known as blood vessels. Arteries are shown in red, veins in blue.

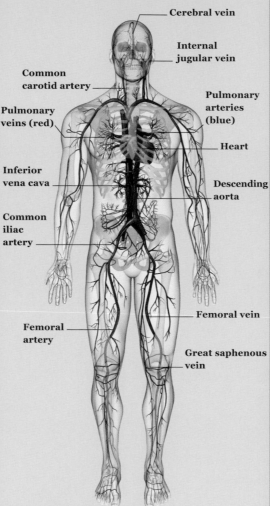

Cerebral vein

Internal jugular vein

Common carotid artery

Pulmonary arteries (blue)

Pulmonary veins (red)

Heart

Inferior vena cava

Descending aorta

Common iliac artery

Femoral vein

Femoral artery

Great saphenous vein

Components checklist

- Cerebral vein
- Common carotid artery
- Internal jugular vein
- Heart
- Pulmonary arteries and veins
- Inferior vena cava
- Descending aorta
- Common iliac artery
- Femoral artery and vein
- Great saphenous vein
- Blood

Nervous system

The nervous system configures your entire body's control structure. Consisting of the brain, spinal cord, and nerves, the nervous system carries high-speed electrical signals, called nerve impulses, around your body. These ensure you keep breathing and carry out hundreds of other essential tasks without even realizing it.

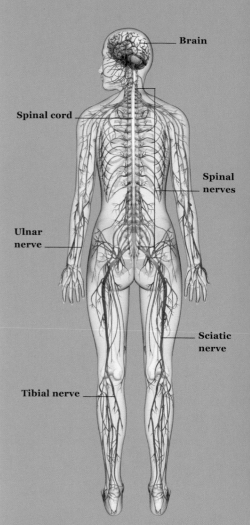

Brain

Spinal cord

Spinal nerves

Ulnar nerve

Sciatic nerve

Tibial nerve

Components checklist

- Brain
- Spinal cord
- Spinal nerves
- Ulnar nerve
- Sciatic nerve
- Tibial nerve

Endocrine system

The endocrine, or hormonal, system works as a slower control network. Made up of endocrine glands, messages are released, as chemicals called hormones, into your bloodstream. They target specific cells and tissues to alter their activity. Growth and reproduction are controlled by hormones.

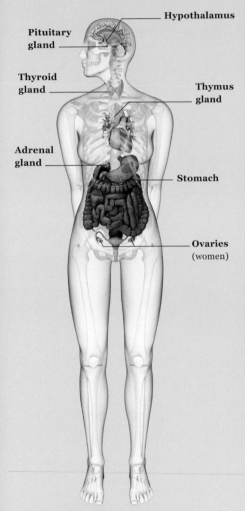

Hypothalamus

Pituitary gland

Thyroid gland

Thymus gland

Adrenal gland

Stomach

Ovaries (women)

Components checklist

- Hypothalamus
- Pituitary gland
- Thyroid gland
- Thymus gland
- Adrenal gland
- Stomach
- Ovaries (women)
- Testes (men)

Digestive system

Food is the key to supplying your cells with energy and the essential materials for your body's repair and growth. Before your cells can utilize food it has to be processed into simpler substances. That is done by your digestive system. It breaks food down into sugars, fats, and other simple chemicals that can be absorbed into your blood.

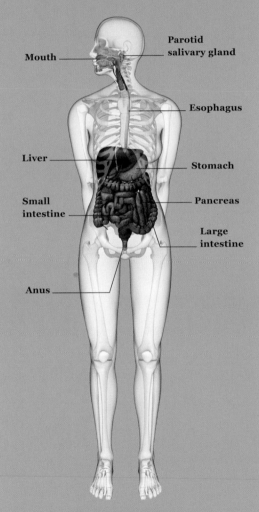

Mouth

Parotid salivary gland

Esophagus

Liver

Stomach

Small intestine

Pancreas

Large intestine

Anus

Components checklist

- Mouth
- Parotid salivary gland
- Esophagus
- Liver
- Stomach
- Pancreas
- Small intestine
- Large intestine
- Anus

Lymphatic & immune system

The lymphatic and immune system work together to help your body fight off infection. They identify, target, and destroy specific germs that would otherwise make you ill. In addition, the lymphatic system collects any excess fluid that has moved into your cell tissues and returns it to your bloodstream.

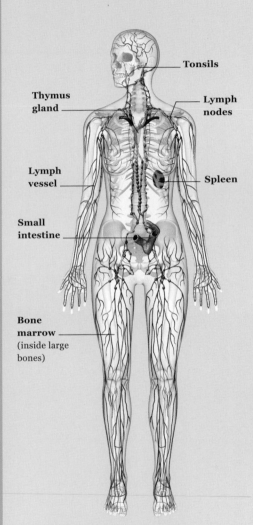

Tonsils

Thymus gland

Lymph nodes

Lymph vessel

Spleen

Small intestine

Bone marrow (inside large bones)

Components checklist

- Tonsils
- Lymph nodes
- Thymus gland
- Spleen
- Bone marrow
- Lymph vessel
- Blood (white blood cells)

GLOSSARY

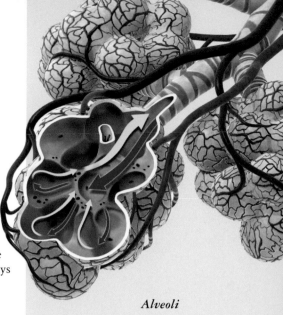

Alveoli

3-D seeing an object in three dimensions means you see its length, width, and height. A cube is 3-D, but a square is 2-D, because it has only length and width.

Acceleration a change in velocity. Acceleration happens when things speed up, slow down, or move in a different direction.

Actin one of the building blocks of muscle fibers that plays a key role in contraction.

Adolescence the period of life between childhood and adulthood.

Adrenal glands glands located on top of the kidneys that make the hormone epinephrine (adrenaline).

Aerobic describes a chemical process that requires oxygen to generate energy.

Air pressure the weight of the air pushing down on Earth. The more air pushing down, the higher the pressure.

Algae tiny plantlike organisms that make food by the process of photosynthesis.

Allergen a harmless protein (or protein-carbohydrate complex) that can trigger the immune system, causing an allergy. Pollen is a common allergen.

Allergy abnormal reaction of the immune system to a harmless substance, such as pollen or dust.

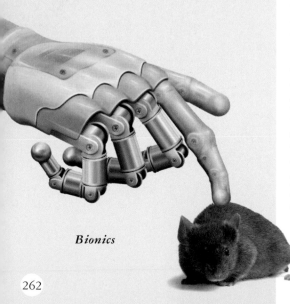

Bionics

Alveoli tiny sacs in the lungs through which oxygen and carbon dioxide pass to and from the bloodstream.

Amino acids the basic building blocks that make all proteins.

Amygdala an almond-shaped structure in the limbic system of the brain. It plays an important role in emotion.

Anaerobic describes a chemical process that does not require oxygen to make energy.

Antagonist term describes the muscle that relaxes and stretches during movement of a joint.

Antibody a protein made by certain types of white blood cells in the immune system. Each type of antibody has a specific shape that enables it to locate and bind to specific germs.

Artery a thick-walled blood vessel that carries oxygen-rich blood away from the heart.

Atom a tiny particle of matter that cannot be divided (except in a nuclear explosion).

ATP (adenosine triphosphate) the chemical molecule used by cells to make energy.

Axon a long fiber that extends from a nerve cell (neuron). It conducts nerve signals away from the cell.

Bacteria single-celled microorganisms that are common in all living or dead organic matter. Some bacteria cause disease.

Basal ganglia a region at the base of the front of the brain containing millions of nerves that deals with choosing and controlling movement.

Behaviorism a branch of psychology that is devoted to the study of animal and human behavior but disregards the internal workings of the brain that control behavior.

Bionics the application of technology to living systems—for example, artificial body parts.

Bipolar disorder a mental illness in which sufferers experience extreme highs (mania) and lows (depression).

Bladder the organ that collects and stores urine.

Body clock a natural time-keeping mechanism in the body that controls regular cycles such as daily sleeping.

Brain stem the part of the base of the brain that connects to the spinal cord. It controls functions such as breathing and heart beat.

Broca's area an area in the brain's frontal lobe that deals with speech and producing language.

Buoyancy the upward force exerted on an object submerged in a liquid.

Capillaries microscopic blood vessels that branch off from arteries and veins. They carry blood to all the body's cells.

Carbon one of the main elements in the human body. Carbon atoms link together to form long chains in organic molecules.

Carbon dioxide (CO2) a waste gas produced when we breathe.

Cell one of the microscopic building blocks that make up living organisms. Cells normally have a jellylike filling and an outer membrane.

Cell membranes thin fatty layers that surround cells.

Central nervous system the brain and spinal cord together make up the central nervous system.

Cerebellum a cauliflower-shaped structure at the base of the back of the brain that helps to coordinate body movements and balance.

Cerebral cortex the wrinkly, folded layer of tissue that forms the outer part of the brain. It's used for thinking, memory, movement, language, attention, and processing information from our senses.

Cerebral hemispheres the two halves of the cerebrum: left and right.

Cerebrum the main part of the brain, not including the brain stem and cerebellum.

Chromosome one of a set of microscopic structures inside cells that carry DNA.

Cilia tiny hairlike cells in the nasal cavity and lungs.

Clone an organism that has been grown from a body cell of another organism and is genetically identical to it. Identical twins are natural clones.

Cochlea a snail-shaped, fluid-filled organ of the inner ear that helps process sound waves.

Concentration (of solution) the strength of a mixture of substances.

Conscious awake and aware of the world.

Consciousness the state of being mentally aware.

Cramps painful muscle spasms.

Critical period a period of life in which the brain has a greater ability to learn new skills. The critical period for learning a second language is in childhood. After this time, it becomes much harder.

Dendrite a short fiber that extends from a nerve cell (neuron). It picks up signals from other nerve cells.

Density the degree to which particles of matter are closely packed.

Diffusion the movement of a substance from an area of high concentration to one of low concentration.

DNA (deoxyribonucleic acid) a very long, helical molecule that carries genes—the blueprints of life—as a chemical code.

DNA fingerprint a pattern of stripes obtained by breaking down someone's DNA and separating the fragments in gel. Police and forensic scientists use DNA fingerprints to identify people.

Dominant a gene that overpowers another gene is said to be dominant. Dominant can also refer to a person who acts in a bossy or overpowering way.

Egg cell a female sex cell.

Elasticity the ability of a substance to return to its original shape after being stretched.

Electrons negatively charged particles that revolve around the nucleus of an atom.

Element a chemical that cannot be broken down into simpler chemicals.

Embryo the earliest stage of development in a plant or animal.

Emotions inner feelings that affect both the brain and body, such as joy, fear, disgust, and anger.

Endorphin a kind of neurotransmitter that relieves pain when it is released in the brain.

Enzyme a protein that speeds up the rate of a particular chemical reaction. Digestive enzymes speed up chemical reactions that break down large organic molecules into smaller fragments.

Epilepsy a brain disorder that can cause violent physical seizures resulting from bursts of abnormal electrical activity in brain cells.

Epinephrine hormone released into the bloodstream in response to danger and stress.

ESP (extrasensory perception) Also known as psychic powers or a "sixth sense," a claimed ability to read minds, move objects with the power of thought, or see into the future.

Estrogen a female sex hormone.

Evolution the gradual development of living things over a long period of time.

Fertilization the fusion of a sperm cell and egg cell to create a new individual.

Force a push or a pull that makes an object move or stop.

Fossil fuels fuels formed over millions of years from the remains of animals and plants.

Frontal lobes two main divisions of the cerebral cortex. The frontal lobes are involved in higher mental functions, such as planning and making decisions.

Fuels substances that are used to produce energy.

Gastric juices fluids the stomach produces to break down food.

Gene an instruction carried by the DNA molecule. Genes are passed from parents to offspring during reproduction.

Genome the full set of genes in an organism.

Germ any microscopic organism that can cause disease, such as a bacterium or virus.

Gravity a force that pulls objects together. On Earth it keeps us stuck to the ground.

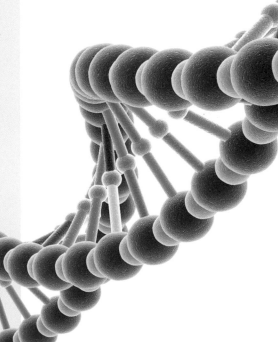

DNA
(deoxyribonucleic acid)

Gray matter darker brain tissue that contains nerve cell (neuron) bodies and dendrites.

Hemoglobin the oxygen-carrying protein in red blood cells. Hemoglobin contains iron and gives blood its color.

Hippocampus a seahorse-shaped structure in the brain that helps lay down long-term memories.

Histamine a chemical released by white blood cells that makes tissue become tender and inflamed. Histamine is released during allergic reactions or when germs or dirt enter the body.

Hormone messenger chemicals released into the blood that help control body functions such as growth and reproduction.

Immune system a complex system of tissues and cells that defend the body against invading germs, such as bacteria and viruses.

Instinct a behavior that is programmed into an animal from birth and does not need to be learned from scratch.

Intuition the use of a hunch or insight to figure something out quickly, without reasoning.

Invertebrates animals without a backbone.

IQ intelligence quotient, a measure of intelligence derived from a test of numerical, spatial, and verbal abilities.

Iris the ring of colored muscle in the eye. It controls the size of the pupil.

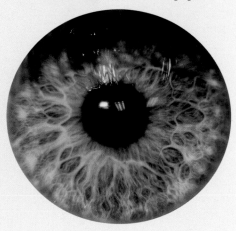

Iris

Joint the meeting point between two bones.

Laser a form of intense light on one wavelength.

Lateral thinking thinking creatively to solve a problem, using ideas that may not appear logical.

Lens the part of the eye that focuses light onto the retina.

Limbic system a collection of structures in the center of the brain that deal with emotions, memory, and the sense of smell. The amygdala and hippocampus are parts of the limbic system.

Lobe one of four main divisions of each cerebral hemisphere. Each hemisphere has four lobes: frontal, occipital, parietal, and temporal.

Lubrication reducing the friction between two surfaces.

Mammals warm-blooded animals that feed their young with milk.

Metabolism all the chemical reactions that take place inside your body.

Microchip the part of a computer made from silicon on which tiny electronic circuits are etched.

Mind the thoughts, feelings, beliefs, ideas, and sense of self that are generated by the brain make up what we call the mind.

Mirror neurons neurons in the brains of monkeys that become active when the monkey watches another monkey or a person doing something. Mirror neurons are also thought to exist in humans and may enable us to feel an echo of other people's sensations.

Molecule a group of chemically combined atoms. A water molecule, for example, is made of two hydrogen atoms and one oxygen atom (H_2O).

Momentum the product of an object's mass and velocity.

MRI magnetic resonance imaging makes it possible for medical body scanners to produce pictures of your insides using powerful magnets and radio waves.

Mucus a thick, sticky fluid produced by the inner lining of the mouth, nose, throat, and intestines.

Myosin one of the building blocks of muscle fibers that makes them contract.

Nerve a bundle of long nerve-cell fibers. Nerves carry electrical signals between the brain and the body.

Nerve cell *see neuron.*

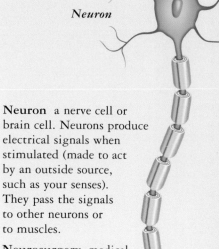

Neuron

Neuron a nerve cell or brain cell. Neurons produce electrical signals when stimulated (made to act by an outside source, such as your senses). They pass the signals to other neurons or to muscles.

Neurosurgery medical treatment of the brain involving an operation.

Neurotransmitter a chemical created by neurons that helps nerve signals move across the tiny gaps (synapses) between nerve cells.

Nuclear reactions reactions involving the nuclei of atoms.

Nucleus the dense center of an atom or a cell.

Nutrients substances your body needs to live and grow.

Occipital lobe the lobe at the back of the cerebral cortex. The occipital lobe processes vision.

Odorants molecules floating in the air that we detect as smells.

Organ a large body structure with a specific function, such as the heart, stomach, or brain.

Organ transplant an operation in which a surgeon replaces a diseased organ with a healthy organ taken from another person.

Osmosis movement of water through a membrane from an area of high concentration to an area of low concentration.

Oxygen the gas that blood absorbs from the air when we breathe. Our cells need oxygen to release energy from food.

Parietal lobe a lobe between the top and rear of each cerebral hemisphere. The parietal lobe receives nervous signals from all over the body and helps create the sense of touch.

Photosynthesis the process by which plants use sunlight to convert carbon dioxide and water into carbohydrates and oxygen.

Placenta the organ through which a developing baby absorbs oxygen and nutrients from its mother while it is still in the womb. The baby is linked to the placenta by an umbilical cord.

Plasma (blood) the colorless watery fluid in the blood that contains no cells.

Plasma (state of matter) the fourth state of matter in which a gas exists as charged particles.

Prefrontal cortex the outer layer of the front of the brain. It deals with conscious thought and planning.

Prime mover term describing the muscle that contracts and shortens during movement.

Proprioception a sense that keeps us aware of the position and motion of every part of the body.

Prosopagnosia a brain disorder that causes people to become unable to recognize faces.

Prosthetics the branch of medicine that deals with the manufacture of artificial body parts.

Protein a complex biological molecule made of a chain of units called amino acids. Muscle and hair are mostly protein. Protein molecules called enzymes control most of the chemical reactions in living organisms.

Protons positively charged particles that are found in the nuclei of all atoms.

Psychoanalyst someone who attempts to treat a patient by discussing their dreams, memories, and childhood family relationships. Sigmund Freud was the father of psychoanalysis.

Psychologist a scientist who studies the mind, behavior, and personality of people.

Psychology the scientific study of the mind.

Puberty the stage of development when the body becomes capable of sexual reproduction.

Pupil the black circle in the middle of the eye. The pupil is a hole that lets light enter the eye.

Radioactivity the process by which unstable atoms break apart, releasing energy in the process.

Recessive gene a gene that is overpowered by a dominant gene.

REM (rapid eye movement) sleep the lightest form of sleep, during which the eyes move rapidly under their lids. The most memorable dreams take place during REM sleep.

Retina a layer of light-sensitive neurons lining the back of each eye. The retina captures images and relays them to the brain as electrical signals.

Saccade the movement of the eye as it flicks from place to place.

Schizophrenia a mental illness in which hallucinations and delusions give the sufferer a false sense of reality.

Senses the five main senses are vision, hearing, smell, touch, and taste. Other senses include pain, proprioception, and sensitivity to heat or cold.

Sensory cortex the part of the brain that processes information coming in from the senses.

Spatial awareness a grasp of shape, distance, and space.

Sperm male sex cells, made by the testis.

Spinal cord a large bundle of nerves down the backbone, connecting the brain to nerve cells throughout the body.

Sterilization protecting against infection by cleaning and disinfecting.

Subatomic particles the particles that make up an atom.

Atom

Subconscious below the level of consciousness. Subconscious processes happen in the brain without your being aware of them.

Sympathetic nervous system one of the two main divisions of the involuntary part of the body's nervous system. The sympathetic nervous system prepares the body for action.

Synapse a tiny gap between two nerve cells (neurons).

Telepathy the claimed ability to read someone's thoughts through extrasensory perception (ESP).

Temperature how hot or cold something is.

Temporal lobe the side lobe of each cerebral hemisphere. The temporal lobe deals with hearing, language, and memory.

Tendon a very tough fibrous connection that ties a muscle to a bone.

Testosterone the male sex hormone. Testosterone triggers the development of male characteristics at puberty.

Thalamus an area near the base of the brain that assesses incoming information from the eyes and other sense organs.

Tissue a collection of cells of a similar type that work together to do the same job, such as skin, bone, or muscle.

Vein a thin-walled blood vessel containing blood flowing back to the heart.

Vertebrae small bones that make up the spine.

Virus a very simple type of organism consisting of a length of DNA, usually in a protein coat. Viruses reproduce by infecting cells, often causing disease.

Viscosity the thickness of a fluid.

Visual cortex a part of the occipital lobe at the back of the brain that processes vision.

Vitamin a complex organic compound needed by the body in very small quantities.

Wernicke's area a part of the temporal lobe that deals with understanding language. In most people it is in the left hemisphere.

White matter lighter-colored brain tissue mainly containing axons.

INDEX

Descartes, René 95
development 38–43
diarrhea 24, 25
digestive system 19, 25, 80, 190, 195, 256
dimples 34
diseases 181, 240–241, 248–249, 250–251
disgust 79, 148
dishonesty 87
dislikes 83
DNA (deoxyribonucleic acid) 29, 30–31, 181, 242–243, 247
    fingerprints 29
dog 96, 154
dominance 86
dominant 50–51
    eye 51
    foot 51
    gene 33, 35
dopamine 152, 153
dreaming 39, 76–77, 96, 133
dyslexia 89
earlobes 35
ears 13, 23, 211, 215, 254–255
education 156
egg cell 11, 32, 36, 38
electricity 104, 105, 181, 183, 184, 204–205, 249
electroencephalography (EEG) 97, 169
electrons 194, 204, 205
elements 7, 8–9, 181, 194, 196, 197, 198, 209
embryo 32, 36, 38, 248, 249
emotional intelligence 59

emotions 47, 52, 76, 78–81, 94, 148–149, 151, 162, 171
empathizing skills 72
endocrine system 195, 208–209
endorphins 89, 127, 153, 157, 208
energy 103, 179, 182–183, 184–185, 210–211
energy waves 210–211
environment 36, 58
enzymes 19
epilepsy 97, 98, 163, 172
epinephrine (adrenaline) 208–209
ESP 174–175
estrogen 208
evolution 180–181
exams 165
exercise 157
expressions 78–79, 84
extroversion 66, 68, 71
eyebrows 85
eye color 33
eye contact 85
eyelids 16, 85
eyes 13, 23, 28, 38, 39, 84, 111, 112–113, 118, 140, 194, 202, 208, 210, 211, 243, 247, 253, 254, 257
    cells 11
face recognition 114, 115, 117, 140, 172
faces, reading 84–85
facial expressions 84–85
families 32, 35
fat 10, 12
fathers 32, 38
fats 194, 198
fear 78, 80–81, 82,149

feelings diary 79
fingernails 193, 217, 246
fingerprints 28, 38, 243, 246, 247
fingers 16, 34, 35, 72
food 184, 185, 188, 193, 197, 198–199, 214, 222
forces 181, 219, 220–221, 222, 224, 228–229, 230–231, 232–233, 234–235, 236
forensic science 246–247
fovea 113, 115, 117
fraternal twins 36
freckles 34
free running 234–235
free will 139
Freud, Sigmund 96
friction 217, 222–223, 235
friends 41, 42–43, 70, 71
frontal lobe 101, 103, 133

GHI

Gage, Phineas 95
Gall, Franz Joseph 106
gamma rays 210
gas diffusion 189, 237
gases 186–187, 188–189
gender 73
genes 27, 30–33, 58, 69, 74–75, 143, 156, 161, 242–243, 245, 248–249
genius 59, 90
genome 31, 32, 38
germs 24, 25, 28

gestures 89
girls 33, 42
glands, *see endocrine system*
goblet cells 11
grammar 89
gravity 23, 221, 228–229, 230, 231, 236–237, 239
gray matter 105, 150
growth 38, 208
    spurt 42
hair 12, 21, 42
hairy toes 35
hand 50, 51, 216–217
happiness 90, 156–157
Haraguchi, Akira 164
Head, Henry 113
head 38, 40, 84
hearing 22–23, 39, 111, 214–215, 254–255
heart 13, 17, 38, 185, 187, 191, 194, 195, 197, 199, 209, 224, 239, 248, 252–253
heart attack 128, 155
Herophilus 94
hippocampus 52, 163
histamine 24
Hitzig, Eduard 96
Holmes, Gordon 97
honest muscles 84
hormones 42, 43, 100, 128, 129, 150, 195, 203, 208–209
hydrogen 8
identical twins 36, 37, 69
identity 41
illusions 120–121, 122–123
imagination 49, 59
immune system 9, 24–25, 28, 197, 199, 239, 240–241, 250

inner self 48
inner voice 49
insomnia 132
instinct 80, 101
intelligence 58–61, 90
interpersonal skill 90
intestines 13, 19
introverts 68, 70, 71
intuition 138–139
iodine 9
IQ 58, 59, 72
iris and iris scans 28
iron 9

JKL

jet lag 75
joints 15, 190, 223, 226, 235, 253
jokes 154–155
joy 78, 148
kidneys 12, 191, 195, 197
lactose-intolerant 33
language 40, 50, 88–89, 160–161
lateral intelligence and thinking 59, 62–63
laughing 154–155
laughter 89
learning 40, 41, 56, 57, 101, 151
left brain 50, 72
left-handed 50
ligaments 193, 223, 235
light 100, 111, 112, 114, 119, 129, 181, 185, 208, 210, 211, 236, 254
limbic system 47, 78, 81, 82, 103, 148
lips 23, 25
liquids 186–187, 190–191

ANSWERS

Page 51
LEFT OR RIGHT

You will almost certainly have gotten farther through the dots with one hand. This is your dominant hand and the one you use for writing. If you got equally far with both hands, consider yourself extremely unusual— almost everybody has a preference for one hand or the other.

Page 54
HOW'S YOUR MEMORY FOR WORDS?

If you scored more than 8, well done. Words are harder to remember than faces, but easier than numbers. You probably found unusual words (like "vomit") easier to remember than boring ones (like "salad"). That's because your brain is good at paying attention to anything unusual. You may have found that your visual memory helped on this test, especially if you joined words in odd combinations, like jam on a carpet or a pebble on a chair.

Page 55
HOW'S YOUR VISUAL MEMORY?

If you remembered more than half of the objects, well done. This test is harder than the word test because you can't use your imagination to create memorable images. The objects on the tray are uninteresting and unlikely to stay long in your short-term memory.

Page 55
NUMBER CRUNCHER

Most people can keep only 7 digits at a time in their short-term memory, so if you got more than this, well done. Numbers are much harder to remember than words or pictures because they are much less interesting. However, you can improve your memory of a long number by saying it so many times that your brain remembers the sound of the words. This works even if you say the words silently in your head without speaking them. If something distracts you while you're doing this, the number will quickly disappear from your short-term memory.

Pages 60–61
SPATIAL INTELLIGENCE

1e, 2b, 3b, 4e, 5d, 6a, 7d, 8b, 9b, 10e

Pages 60–61
VERBAL INTELLIGENCE

1c, 2d, 3a, 4d, 5e, 6c, 7e, 8d, 9a, 10c, 11d, 12c, 13e, 14a, 15b, 16b

Pages 62–63
NUMERICAL INTELLIGENCE

1e, 2e, 3a, 4d (each pair of numbers adds up to the next one in the sequence), 5b, 6a (the numbers show the position of each letter in the alphabet), 7e, 8d (be careful—it's a trick question!), 9d, 10c (another trick question!), 11d, 12a, 13b, 14b (all the numbers are squares), 15c

Pages 62–63
LATERAL INTELLIGENCE

1. A chick inside an egg.
2. They were part of a snowman's face in winter, but the snowman melted.
3. The backpack contains his parachute, which failed to open.
4. They are triplets.
5. A square utility cover can fall down the hole if you turn it, but a round one can't.
6. The punch contained ice cubes made from poisonous water. The ice melted after the man left.
7. Nothing.
8. Turn the first switch on and leave the second switch off. Turn the third switch on for two minutes and then turn it off. Run upstairs—one of the lights (switch 1) will be on and one of the other light bulbs (switch 3) will be warm. The cold light bulb is switch 2.
9. The man is a dwarf and can't reach higher than button 7 in the elevator. On rainy days he carries an umbrella and can use it to push the top button.

Page 75
OWL OR LARK

Score 4 points for each A, 3 points for each B, 2 points for each C, 1 point for each D.

6–11 points. You're an owl and you love staying up late. But you might be sleep-deprived, which could make you bad-tempered during the day and affect your schoolwork. Try going to bed a little earlier on weekdays if you think you need more sleep.

12–18 points. You're neither an owl nor a lark, and you probably have sensible sleep habits.

19–24 points. You're a lark and you love the mornings. Consider yourself lucky—most people hate getting up early.

Page 85
SPOT THE FAKE SMILE

1, 2, and 3 are fake; 4, 5, and 6 are real.

ACKNOWLEDGMENTS

Dorling Kindersley would like to thank the following people for help with this book: Janet Allis, Penny Arlon, Maree Carroll, Andy Crawford, Tory Gordon-Harris, Lorrie Mack, Pilar Morales for digital artwork, Laura Roberts, Cheryl Telfer, Martin Wilson.

Thanks also to Somso Modelle for use of their anatomical model (p. 16)

The publisher would like to thank Paul Yarker for helping to devise the personality test and Kathrin Cohen Kadosh for supplying the brain scans on page 107. The publisher would also like to thank the following for their kind permission to reproduce their images: Position key: a=above, b=below/bottom, c=center, l=left, r=right, t=top

YOUR BODY

Corbis: Bettmann 77cl; Cameron 57tr; Cheque 36-37b; L. Clarke 37tr; Robert Holmes 52cb; Richard Hutchings 22crb; Thom Lang 6tl, 13bcr, 14clb (brain); Lawrence Manning 35bl; John-Marshall Mantel 52ca; Reuters 28bc; ROB & SAS 33br; Royalty Free Images 29tc (mouth), 79c; Nancy A. Santullo 64bc, 70tl; Norbert Schaefer 36-37c; Strauss/Curtis 22l, 78r; Mark Tuschman 64clb, 78l; Larry Williams 34c; Elizabeth Young 34cl. DK Images: Commisioner for the City of London Police 73cr; Denoyer/Geppert Intl. 17clb, 19tr, 20tr; Eddie Lawrence 59tr; Judith Miller, Otford Antiques & Collectors Centre, Kent 64cb (bear), 67bl, 69clb; 16r; Jerry Young 62c. Dreamstime.com: Glowonconcept 89cb. Getty Images: Alistair Berg 26-27; Tipp Howell 49cra; Andreas Kuehn 64ca (face), 79r; Stuart McClymont 52c; Eric O'Connell 80-81b; Royalty Free/Alan Bailey 64br, 78c; Chip Simons 77r; Anna Summa 79l, 85bcl; Trujillo-Paumier 64tr, 76-77b; V.C.L. 36cl; David Zelick 34tr. Science Photo Library: 10l, 11tl, 11tr, 11l, 11r, 14crb (left jar), 14crb (right jar), 15cl, 18cl; Alex Bartel 39cr; Annabella Bluesky 22cra, 35br; Neil Bromhall 39cl; BSIP Ducloux 22cr; BSIP, Joubert 18cla; BSIP/Serconi 11tcl; BSIP VEM 18clb, 78bl; Scott Camazine 19bl; CNRI 6cr, 13bcl, 17clb, 20cla, 20bl; Dept. of Clinical Cytogenetics, Addenbrookes Hospital 33bc; John Dougherty 12bl; Eye of Science 19clb, 20cl; David Gifford 6, 22tr; Pascal Goetcheluck 28tcr; Nancy Kedersha 3cl, 44-45; Mehau Kulyk 11tc, 18r, 30clb; Francis Leroy, Biocosmos 38l; Dick Luria 21bl; David M. Martin, M.D. 19cl; Hank Morgan 29bc, 29tc (graphic), 47br, 81tr; Dr. G. Moscoso 38r; Prof. P. Motta, Dept. of Anatomy, University "La Sapienza," Rome 15cla; Profs. P.M. Motta & S. Makabe 38cr; Dr. Yorgos Nikas 38cl; David Parker 28tcl; Alfred Pasieka 29bl, 46-47c(brain); Prof. Aaron Polliack 10r, 14crb (middle jar); Victor De Schwanberg 12bcl, 13tr, 14clb (heart), 14clb (kidney); Volker Steger 58tl, 72-73; VVG 6tr, 21crb; Andrew Syred 6clb, 11tcr, 17cla, 21cl, 28tr, 30cl; Paul Taylor 12bcr; Tissuepix 39l; Geoff Tompkinson 46bl; 83 (car) National Motor Museum, Beaulieu, Somso Modelle 14tl.

YOUR BRAIN

Edward H. Adelson: 120c, 120cr; **Alamy Images:** ARCO Images GmbH 155tl; Art Directors and TRIP 155cl, 155cr; Richard Green / Commercial 4cl, 136cl; Interfoto 95c; Andrea Matone 118cr; Patti McConville 174cl; Medicalpicture 176cl, 176tr; David Price 150bl; StudioSource 125bl; Richard Wareham Fotografie 125cr; **The Bridgeman Art Library:** Tretyakov Gallery, Moscow, Russia 114b, 115b; (c) David Macdonald (**www.cambiguites.com**): 121bl; **Corbis:** Lucas Allen 103 (Book); Bettmann 95br, 95cl, 95tc, 106bl, 106cl, 117tl, 123tl; Bloomimage 136-137bc; Coleen Cahill / Design Pics 126c; Alan Copson 132-133tc; Leonard de Selva 95bl; DLILLC 154cl; Robert Dowling 155bl; EPA/ Toni Garriga 134c; Francis G. Mayer 117c; Frank Lukasseck 103cr; Frare / Davis Photography / Brand X 99bc; The Gallery Collection 94-95b, 117tr, 119tc; Etienne George 173cl; Michael Gore/FLPA 128bc; Sven Hagolani 113tr (TV), 123tr, 162cb; Rune Hellestad 136bl; Ikon Images 133bl; Images.com 132tl; Imagezoo / Images.com 170cr; JGI / Blend Images 111bl; JLP/ Jose L. Pelaez 132bl; Mike Kemp / Rubberball 103 (Rat); Matthias Kulka 102r; Mehau Kulyk / Science Photo Library 138-139cb; Martin Harvey 114tl; Rob Matheson 132-133t; Dan McCoy—Rainbow/ Science Faction 137cr; MedicalRF.com 97bl; moodboard 125t; Louis Moses 133bc; Nice One Productions 151cr; Roberta Olenick / All Canada Pictures 153cr; ANDREW PARKINSON 113tr; Herbert Pfarrhofer 96ca; PoodlesRock 4bl; Radius Images 151br; Lew Robertson 153crb; Thomas Rodriguez 163tr; Andersen Ross/Blend Images 163cra; Sanford / Agliolo 133br; David Selman 154bl; Athina Strataki / Etsa 155c; Scott Stulberg 154-155c; Sunset Boulavard 143br; Yuji Tanigami / amanaimages 128bl; William Whitehurst 177bl; Harry Williams 160-161c; **Crytek GmbH:** © 2010. All rights reserved. This picture has been created by Sascha Gundlach using CryEngine®3. 119clb; **Dorling Kindersley: Rachael Grady:** 167tr; Tim Ridley / Ted Taylor modelmaker 177cra; **Eyevine Ltd:** 98bl; **Getty Images:** 3D4 Medical.com 97tc; 119br, 161tl; Altrendo 175br; Chad Baker / Thomas Northcut 176bc; Barcroft Media 164-165t; Bettmann 99c; Burazin 172cr; Creative Crop 154tl, 155ftr; Peter Dazeley 118tl; De Agostini 4t, 94tc; Digital Vision 131bc; Edvanderhoek 119bl; Shaun Egan 121cl, 121cr; David Elliott 125cla; Daisy Gilardini 130tr; Hulton 96cl, 97c; Hulton Archive 96c; Imagezoo 155tr; David Job 139c; Mike Kemp 92-93, 94ca, 94-95t; Peter / Stef Lamberti 100c; Catherine Ledner 101cl; Lester Lefkowitz 99tr; Loungepark 154cb; Steve McAlister 124t; Ryan McVay 99br, 150-151; Brian Mullennix 172cl; Gary John Norman 101bl; Carl Pendle 144cl; PM Images 125bc; Reza 151tr; Achim Sass 124br; Venki Talath 138bc, 138cb, 138crb; Alan Thornton 153c; Time & Life Pictures 169br; Eric Van Den Brulle 139tr; **Harlow, John M.:** Recovery from the passage of an iron bar through the head. By John M. Harlow, M.D. Read before the Massachusetts Medical Society, June 3, 1868; Boston, David Clapp & Son, 1869 95cra; **iStockphoto.com:** 4x6 152bl; 100tr; Alexsl 146; Andresr 124c; Andyd 153tr; Cimmerian 165br; Dreamstime 143bc, 143tl, 263b; Dreamstime / Kts 107tl; EcoPic 140cl; Rebecca Ellis 160cl; Julie Felton 160bl, 173tr; Jcdesign 108tc; Sebastian Kaulitzki 172-173t; Jan-Willem Kunnen 175tr; Markus Leiminger 152br; Nancy Louie 4bl, 161cr; Miodrag Nikolic 161b; penfold 94-95ca; TommL 160br; Viorika Prikhodko Photography 100cb; Tomasz Zachariasz 100bl; **David James Killock, (killock@msn.com) http://www.wix.com/dkillock/dkphotography:** 123b; **The Kobal Collection:** 130b; **Nischal Narayanam:** 164b; **NASA:** 118clb; JPL/ Malin Space Science Systems 117tc (Real); The Natural History Museum, London: 98tl, 107br; naturepl.com: Anup Shah 101cr; **Dan Paluska:** 175cr; **PNAS:** 101(105):8174-8179, May 25 2004, Nitin Gogtay et al, Dynamic mapping of human cortical development during childhood through early adulthood © 2004 National Academy of Sciences, USA / image courtesy Paul Thompson, UCLA School of Medicine 150c; **Richard Russell, Assistant Professor of Psychology, Gettysburg College, USA:** Russell, R. (2009) A sex difference in facial pigmentation and its exaggeration by cosmetics. Perception, (122)1211-1219. 122tr; **Aaron Schurger:** 116b; **Professor Philippe Schyns:** Schyns, P. G. & Oliva, A. (1999). Dr. Angry and Mr. Smile: When categorization flexibly modifies the perception of faces in rapid visual presentations. Cognition, 153, 243-265, with permission from Elsevier. 122tl; **Science Museum / Science & Society Picture Library:** Science Museum 176bl; **Science Photo Library:** 99cl; AJ Photo / Hop Americain 169t; John Bavosi 128cl; Gary Carlson 105bl; CNRI 126ca; Equinox Graphics 105cr; Gusto Images 138-139ca; Victor Habbick 177crb; Roger Harris 103br, 148c, 163c; Helene Fournie, ISM 112tl; Jacopin 104b; Mehau Kulyk 150-151t; Laguna Design 105tc, 162-163tc; Lawrence Berkeley National Laboratory 104cr; David Mack 115tl; National Library of Medicine 98cl; National Museum, Denmark 94bl; Omikron 112br; Pasieka 104cl, 177tc; Sovereign, ISM 107bl, 107c, 107ca; Sheila Terry 106c; Geoff Tompkinson 102cl; Jeremy Walker 174tl; Paul Thompson, **UCLA School of Medicine:** 150cr; **University of Leicester:** Adrian White, Analytic Social Psychologist 156bl; **Wellcome Images:** 97cr; **Wikipedia, The Free Encyclopedia:** Bibliothèque nationale de France, département des Estampes et de la Photographie, Paris 174bl; Fibonacci / Permission is granted to copy, distribute and/or modify this document under the terms of the GNU Free Documentation License, Version 1.2 or any later version published by the Free Software Foundation; with no Invariant Sections, no Front-Cover Texts, and no Back-Cover Texts. 120bl; Paul Nasca 122b; Wikimedia Commons / Fred Hsu, March 2005; http://commons.wikimedia.org/wiki/File:Stereogram_Tut_Random_Dot_Shark.png Permission is granted under the terms of the GNU Free Documentation License, Version 1.2 or any later version published by the Free Software Foundation; this License, the copyright notices, and the license notice saying this License applies to the Document. 118br 118br

BODY SCIENCE

Alamy Images: Andy Day 234bl, 234fbl; Everynight Images / Lee Vincent Grubb 234fclb; Extreme Sports Photo 214-215, 234-235; Chris Howes / Wild Places Photography 204cl; James Nesterwitz 233t; Photo Researchers 230tl; Pictorial Press Ltd 203fbr; Trip 239bl; Martyn Vickery 251cr. **Corbis:** 216fcr; Theo Allofs / Zefa 191 (cracked ground); Heide Benser / Zefa 190 (water); David Bergman 228; Bettmann 220clb; Alessandro Bianchi / Reuters 252-253; Tom Brakefield 227crb (gazelle), 227fcrb (cheetah); Gareth Brown / Comet 222bc; China Daily / Reuters 5cla, 200-201; Michael Cole 217br; Pascal Deloche / Godong 216cra; DK Limited / Christopher Cooper 187fbr; Duomo 221c; Randy Faris 230-231; Randy Faris / Flirt 187tr (teeth); Najlah Feanny / Corbis Saba 249fbl; Martin Harvey 232crb; image100 216cl; Dimitri Iundt / TempSport 238br; Jan-Peter Kasper / DPA 253cr; Kulka / Zefa 180-181; Floris Leeuwenberg / The Cover Story 255br; Robert Llewellyn / Zefa 193ftr; Lyon and Amiens hospitals / Handou / Reuters 251cla; Lyon and Amiens hospitals / Handout / Reuters 251fcla; MedicalRF.com 195cr, 224fclb, 226fbr, 235r; Micro Discovery 192cb; Paul Miller / EPA 231bc; Tara Moore / Zefa 223cla; Jim Naughten 217c; David A. Northcott 227crb (lion); Louie Psihoyos 254cr; Louie Psihoyos / Comet 194fbl; Andy Rain / EPA 5bl, 244-245; Jason Reed / Reuters 253br; Reuters 254bl; Lew Robertson / Flame 197cb (nails); Pascal Rossignol / Reuters 251ca; Southern Stock / Brand X 257bc; George Steinmetz 183fcra; Visuals Unlimited 222cra; Nation Wong / Zefa 184tr; Ira Wyman / Sygma 253tr; Bernd G. Schmitz / Zefa 236-237c. **DK Images:** Denoyer - Geppert Intl 195fcla (kidneys); ESPL / Denoyer-Geppert 195fcl (brain), 203clb, 206fcla; Jeremy Hunt - modelmaker 215 (shark); David Peart 237bc. **Fluent Inc.:** Fluent 231tr. **Getty Images:** Francois Nel / Getty Images Sport 252–253(c); 3D4Medical.com 208fcla, 211br, 213cr; 250fclb; Allsport Concepts / Mike Powell 223fcr; Blend Images / JGI 216fclb; Digital Vision 217cr; Digital Vision / Michael Hitoshi 216fcrb, 217cra, 217fcr; Digital Vision / Thomas Northcut 217fcla; DK Stock / Christina Kennedy 222cla; Gallo Images Roots Rf Collection / Clinton Friedman 216fcla; Iconica / Jeffrey Coolidge 217ca, 217cla; Iconica / PM Images 216crb, 217fbr; The Image Bank / Francesco Reginato 221t; Johner Images 222fcl; Jason Kempin / FilmMagic 251clb; Nucleus Medical Art, Inc. 189cl; NucleusMedicalArt.com / Nucleus Medical Art, Inc. 223fbr; OJO Images / Steve Smith 217bl; Photodisc / Thomas Northcut 243crb; Photographer's Choice - Bob Thomas 188-189; Photographer's Choice / Chemistry / Mark Langridge 217bc; Photographer's Choice / Oliver Cleve 203fcla, 208ftr; Photographer's Choice RR / Geri Lavrov 217cb; Photonica / Tommy Flynn 211c; Riser / Andrew Geiger 238bl; Riser / Michael Melford 227br (elephant); Riser / Southern Stock 216clb; Science Faction / Tony Hallas 236t; Stockbyte 216c; Stockbyte / American Images Inc 217tr; Stockbyte / George Doyle 216cb, 217tc; StockFood Creative / Jeff Shaffer / Dawn Smith 217tl; Stone / Dominic DiSaia 227fcra; Stone / Dwight Eschliman 210fcl; Stone / Ed Freeman 223clb; Stone / Erik Dreyer 216bl; Stone / Gandee Vasan 243fcra; Stone / GK Hart / Vikki Hart 217ftr; Stone+ / Lars Borges 223cra; Stringer / AFP 238-239; Taxi / Johannes Kroemer 217fctb, Taxi / Lester Lefkowitz 250c; Taxi / Richard Price 217fclb, 250fcr; Taxi / Shalom Ormsby 217fcl; Taxi / Steve Fitchett 8b, 208-209; Taxi / Tim McGuire 221b. **Gunther von Hagens' BODY WORLDS, Institute for Plastination, Heidelberg, Germany, www.bodyworlds.com:** 225. Olivier Blondeau 212fbr; Leon Bonaventura 186; DSGpro 204tc; Murat $en 187cr (pink measure); Marcus Lindström 205fcra; Kiyoshi Takahase Segundo 205clb; Jacom Stephens 187c (beaker). **The Natural History Museum, London:** 206-207. **Photolibrary:** 192r; Corbis 183tr; Photodisc / PhotoLink PhotoLink 237tl. **Science Photo Library:** 194cr (fat cells), 241tl, 248cla, 264t; David Becker 194cr (nerve cell); Biology Media 241fcr; Dr. Tony Brain 241ftr; BSIP 194cra (eye cell); BSIP Estiot 190cla; BSIP, Duval 255tc; BSIP, Vero / Carlo 209fcra; Andy Crump 256cl, 256fcl; Kevin Curtis 250crb; Colin Cuthbert 257cra; Martin Dohrn 208fcra; Michael Donne, University Of Manchester 247tc; Jim Dowdalls 191fclb; Equinox Graphics 254crb; Eye Of Science 212c, 231cr, 231fcr, 238c; Mauro Fermariello 249fcl; Peter Gardiner 235br; Prof. S.h.e. Kaufmann & Dr J.r Golecki 241fcl; Steve Gschmeissner 190fcr, 193cb, 194bc (skin cells), 222fcrb, 241cl; Gustoimages 5clb, 218-219; Health Protection Agency 197crb (green bottle); Nancy Kedersha / UCLA 194crb (brain cells); Russell Kightley 241cr; James King-Holmes 255cra; Ton Kinsbergen 197crb (walnuts); Ted Kinsman 5tl, 178-179; Chris Knapton 249ftr; Mehau Kulyk 195fclb (stomach); Dr. Najeeb Layyous 250ftr; Dr. P. Marazzi 257 crb; Andrew McClenaghan 254fcl; Peter Menzel 255bc; NIBSC 241tr; Susumu Nishinaga 248fcr, 255fcra; Ria Novosti 196bl; Alfred Pasieka 191cla; Pasieka 193l, 195fcla (lungs); Alain Pol, ISM 191crb, 195fbl (bladder); Cheryl Power 189crb, 194ca (blood cells); Victor De Schwanberg 187tc (brain), 187tc (heart), 187tr (ear), 187tr (lips); Seymour 182tl; Jane Shemilt 255tl; Martin Shields 187tc (skull); Tek Image 247bc; Tim Vernon, LTH NHS Trust 255fcla; Victor Habbick Visions 256-257; Peidong Yang, Lawrence Berkeley National Laboratory 257c. **Shutterstock:** Andraž Cerar 197br.

Page 1 images: Dorling Kindersley: Simon Rawles / Football School Reader at Whittington Park, London cra/ (boy); Dreamstime.com: Erhan Akin / Eakn5409 clb

All other images © Dorling Kindersley
For further information see: www.dkimages.com